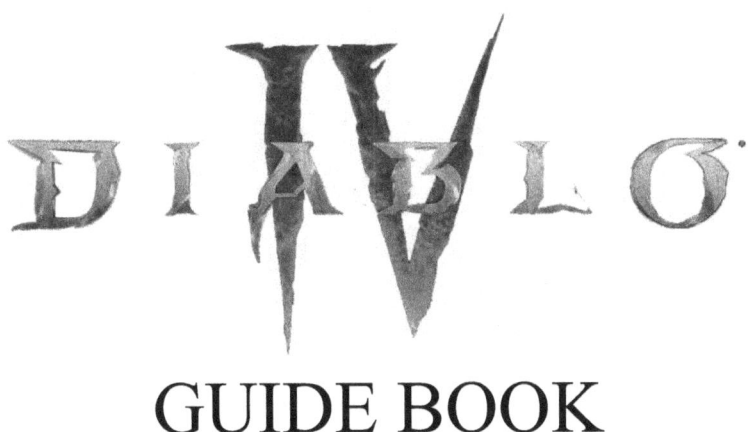

GUIDE BOOK

Eusebio Kshlerin

TABLE OF CONTENTS

Tips & Tricks For Combat --7
   Survey The Scene Before Rushing In -------------------------------7
   Avoid Enemy AOE Indicators --7
   Group Up Enemies ---7
   Know Your Exits & Safe Areas ---------------------------------------7
   Use Corridors To Your Advantage ----------------------------------8
   Engage High-priority Targets First ---------------------------------8
   Maximize Your Potions ---8
   Never Stop Kiting --9
   Isolate Elites --9
   Slow & Steady Wins Every Fight -----------------------------------9

Tips & Tricks For Beginners ---------------------------------------10
   Pick Up Everything --10
   Salvage Instead Of Sell --10
   Don't Spend Your Resources -------------------------------------- 11
   Explore The Cellars And Dungeons ------------------------------ 11
   Use Your Potions Often --- 11
   Upgrade Your Potions -- 12
   Focus On The Main Quests --- 12
   Frequently Check The Map --13
   Positioning Is Paramount In Battle ----------------------------------13
   Survival Should Be Your Goal -------------------------------------- 13

Tips & Tricks For Barbarian --------------------------------------14
   Use Your Arsenal -- 14
   Close The Gap -- 14
   Build Up Fury --- 15
   Whirlwind Is Back Again --15
   Damage Over Time With Bleed ------------------------------------16
   Who Needs Intelli... How Do You Spell It? ---------------------- 16
   Upgrade Your Potions -- 16
   Crowd Control --- 17
   Build Up Thorns --- 17
   Tank It Up --18

Tips & Tricks For Druid -- 18
   Keep Your Distance --- 18
   Specialize Your Skills -- 19
   Don't Fret Over Dying -- 19
   Quest At First -- 20
   Get A Companion Skill --- 20
   Be Careful With Healing Potions ---------------------------------- 20
   Utilize Walls --- 20
   Watch Out For Chests --21

Save Up Your Obols -- 21
Gear Isn't Everything -- 21
Tips & Tricks For Rogue -- **22**
Penetrating Shot Or Twisting Blades ------------------------------ 22
Continually Improve Your Position ---------------------------------- 22
Stick & Move --- 23
Play With A Tank -- 23
Gamble On Weapons -- 23
Hold On To Your Legendaries --24
Complete Dungeons With Rogue Rewards -------------------------- 25
Don't Forget Your Defensive Abilities ---------------------------- 25
Avoid Corners And Crowd-Control -------------------------------- 25
Keep Up Your Imbuements -- 26
Tips & Tricks For Necromancer ------------------------------------ **27**
Use Skeletons To Tank -- 27
How To Build Necro Minions -- 27
Stayin' Alive ---27
Types Of Builds ---28
Exploding Corpses -- 28
Creating Corpses -- 28
Don't Fear The Respec --29
Best Team Ups --29
Avoid Bad Positioning --30
Gear Strategy -- 30
World Boss Timer -- **31**
What Are World Bosses? -- 31
World Boss Timer -- 31
Which Class Should You Pick? ------------------------------------ **32**
The Barbarian -- 32
The Sorcerer -- 32
The Necromancer -- 33
The Druid -- 33
The Rogue -- 34
Which Class Is Best For You? -- 34
HOW_TO GUIDE -- **35**
How To Upgrade Healing Potions And Capacity -------------------- 35
How To Open Silent Chests -- 36
How To Sell Armor & Weapons -- 38
Where To Find Stash & Wardrobe -------------------------------------- 39
How To Refund Skill Points -- 40
How To Transmog Gear -- 42
How To Get Titles -- 44
How To Make & Join A Clan --46

How To Fast Travel -- 47
How To Edit Your Profile ------------------------------------ 49
How To Upgrade Armor --------------------------------------- 51
How To Unlock The Occultist -------------------------------- 53
How To Unlock The Jeweler ---------------------------------- 55
How To Get Baleful Fragments ------------------------------ 58
How To Get Coiling Wards ----------------------------------- 59
How To Switch Weapons As The Barbarian ------------------ 61
How To Get Abstruse Sigil ----------------------------------- 62
How To Beat Astaroth -- 64
How To Get Money, Fast -------------------------------------- 66
Should You Salvage Or Sell Gear --------------------------- 68
How To Reset Dungeons -------------------------------------- 69
How To Craft & Unsocket Gems ---------------------------- 70
Where To Get Demon's Hearts ----------------------------- 73
How To Get Crushed Beast Bones ------------------------- 74
Where To Get Paletongues ---------------------------------- 75
Where To Get Grave Dust ----------------------------------- 76
How To Get Light Bearer Mount --------------------------- 77
How To Clear The Ruins Of Qara-Yisu Stronghold -------- 78
How To Clear The Onyx Watchtower Stronghold --------- 79
How To Clear Temple Of Rot Stronghold ------------------ 80
Where To Find The Entrance To Weeping Cairns --------- 82
How To Beat Airidah --- 83
Where To Get Fiend Rose ------------------------------------ 85
How To Beat Tchort -- 86
How To Gain Experience & Level Up Quickly ------------- 88
How To Make & Use Elixirs --------------------------------- 89
How To Defeat Wandering Death World Boss ------------- 91
How To Get Aspect Of The Alpha Legendary Aspect ----- 95
How To Complete Barbarian: Masters Of Battle --------- 96
How To Get The Aspect Of Bursting Bones --------------- 98
Where To Find Capstone Dungeons ------------------------ 99
How To Farm Murmuring Obols ---------------------------- 100
How To Enchant Items --------------------------------------- 101
How To Beat Vhenard -- 102
How To Defeat Ashava The Pestilent World Boss -------- 103
How To Defeat Avarice The Gold Cursed World Boss ---- 106
Altars Of Lilith Locations -------------------------------- 111
Altars Of Lilith Locations In Fractured Peaks ---------- 111
All Waypoint Locations ----------------------------------- 114
All Waypoint Locations In Fractured Peaks -------------- 114
All Waypoint Locations In Scosglen ----------------------- 118

All Waypoint Locations In Dry Steppes ------------------------------122
All Waypoint Locations In Kehjistan ------------------------------ 125
All Waypoint Locations In Hawezar ------------------------------- 128
All Stronghold Locations --**131**
All Stronghold Locations In Scosglen ----------------------------131
All Stronghold Locations In Fractured Peaks ---------------------- 133
All Stronghold Locations In Dry Steppes ------------------------- 136
All Stronghold Locations In Kehjistan -------------------------- 138
All Stronghold Locations In Hawezar -------------------------- 139
All Side Dungeon Locations -- **141**
All Scosglen Dungeon Locations In Scosglen ----------------------- 141
All Side Dungeon Locations In Dry Steppes ------------------------143
All Side Dungeon Locations In Kehjistan ------------------------- 146
All Side Dungeon Locations In Hawezar ------------------------- 147
Explained -- **150**
World Tiers Explained -- 150
Druidic Spirit Offerings & Boons, Explained ------------------- 151
Renown Explained --154
Lucky Hit Explained --156
Level Scaling Explained ---------------------------------------158
Barrier Generation Explained --------------------------------- 159
Guide --- **160**
Complete Blacksmith Guide ----------------------------------- 160
Keeping The Old Traditions Quest Guide --------------------- 161
Spirits Of The Lost Grove Quest Guide ------------------------162
Treasure Goblin Guide -- 163
Maugan's Works Guide -- 164
Menestad Coffers Quest Guide ------------------------------- 166
Raising Spirits Quest Guide --------------------------------- 167
Champion's Demise Dungeon Walkthrough ---------------------167
Paragon Board Guide --- 169
Reject The Mother Guide -------------------------------------- 171
Cairn Downfall Guide --- 172
The Woodsman Of Nevesk Quest Guide ------------------------173
Traveler's Prayer Quest Guide ------------------------------- 174
The Pilgrim's Footsteps Quest Guide ------------------------- 174
Brought To Heel Quest Guide ---------------------------------175

TIPS & TRICKS FOR COMBAT

SURVEY THE SCENE BEFORE RUSHING IN

Unless you're overpowered by the content, always enter a new area with caution. As you approach a new room or corridor, poke your head in and look around before engaging the enemies inside. Rushing in before surveying the scene is the best way to get overwhelmed and lose your head.

Take note of how many Elites are in the vicinity, the affixes they have, and the layout of the area. These variables will dictate how a fight will unfold as well as how you should respond when the combat begins.

AVOID ENEMY AOE INDICATORS

Elites and bosses telegraph their powerful moves, creating area-of-effect outlines for spells that are about to land. These indicators are a warning that big damage and/or crowd control is about to hit a specific spot.

Once you see an AOE indicator on the ground, there's only a very short delay before that spell will hit. Whenever you see one of these, you need to move immediately. Since much of the damage in Diablo 4 is unavoidable, it's important to dodge spells when you can.

GROUP UP ENEMIES

For each of the classes in Diablo 4, several abilities will hit a designated area pierce through targets, or splash damage to nearby enemies. When enemies are grouped up, they'll take the maximum amount of damage from these spells. To clear areas as efficiently as possible, group up monsters to take advantage of this multi-target damage.

As you engage a group of enemies, run toward the ranged monsters, and the melee attackers will follow you there. Then, use crowd control abilities that help this process along and lay waste to the entire area.

KNOW YOUR EXITS & SAFE AREAS

Controlling the positioning of the battlefield is one of the best ways to win every combat situation. When the enemy has the positional upper hand, be ready to slip out of a sticky situation by knowing the area's exits and safe spaces.

The entrance that you use to enter an area is usually a good exit strategy (aside from arena fights that lock you in). Take note of any spaces that aren't currently under siege, pillars that you can hide behind, or any other environmental objects that let you regain the flow of action.

USE CORRIDORS TO YOUR ADVANTAGE

Unless you're a whirlwind barbarian, being surrounded is the most dangerous position you can be in. When monsters overwhelm your position, they are harder to hit, and they maximize their damage output. This can happen quickly in tight corridors, but these spaces also have their own unique opportunities.

Base your combat strategy on the layout of the area you're fighting in. Monsters can be grouped up and kited much easier in tight spaces, but you can't circle around to avoid damage. Enemy AOE spells can be deadly in these spaces - but so can yours.

ENGAGE HIGH-PRIORITY TARGETS FIRST

Ranged minions are generally high-damage low-health glass cannons that'll melt your HP if left untouched. Summoners have the ability to spawn an inexhaustible army of minions that endlessly assault you no matter how many you kill. Enemies like these need to be irradiated as your top priority in battle.

Whenever you enter a new area, identify all ranged & summoner minions and rush to take them out first. Ignore the high-health low-damage brawlers even if they're Elites, run past them to the high-priority targets, and deal with them later.

MAXIMIZE YOUR POTIONS

When you get caught in crowd-control spells or overwhelmed by a stack of incoming damage, it can be tempting to slam a few potions until you're topped off. If this sounds like you, or if you tend to ignore your potions in combat, work on getting the most value out of this resource.

The early game can create some bad potion use habits, ones that you need to unlearn when pushing challenging content. When you're pushing high-level Nightmare Dungeons or any cutting-edge content, potions become crucial and scarce.

Never Stop Kiting

Whether you play a ranged class or you're on a melee character pushing challenging content, kiting is an important gameplay strategy in Diablo 4. At one point or another, you'll need to kite enemies around to separate monsters or just take a breather. If you're having trouble clearing a room, never stop kiting.

Make sure you're approaching combat differently while in a corridor than in a large open area by using the tight space to your advantage. It's okay to kite in a circle if the area is big enough; otherwise, just kite backward as far as you need to.

Isolate Elites

If you're overpowered for the content, melting several Elites is a walk in the park. But when you take on challenging end-game content, it can be crucial to separate Elites or eliminate them one at a time.

When 2 or more Elites are in a small space, they can quickly cover the area in AOE spells that put your life at risk. Once the affixes start adding up against you, it becomes vital to think about each Elite as its own threat rather than just seeing a group of monsters.

Slow & Steady Wins Every Fight

Old Diablo proverb: you win every fight that you don't lose. As long as you don't die, you'll eventually kill every monster in the game. Focus on staying alive and chipping away at enemy health pools, and you will emerge victorious.

Focusing on damage rather than survivability is a fun way to play, but it's not the most effective. Spend more time thinking about your own health pool than those of the enemies you're fighting, and you'll always be safe. Because it doesn't matter how fast you are if you die.

TIPS & TRICKS FOR BEGINNERS

PICK UP EVERYTHING

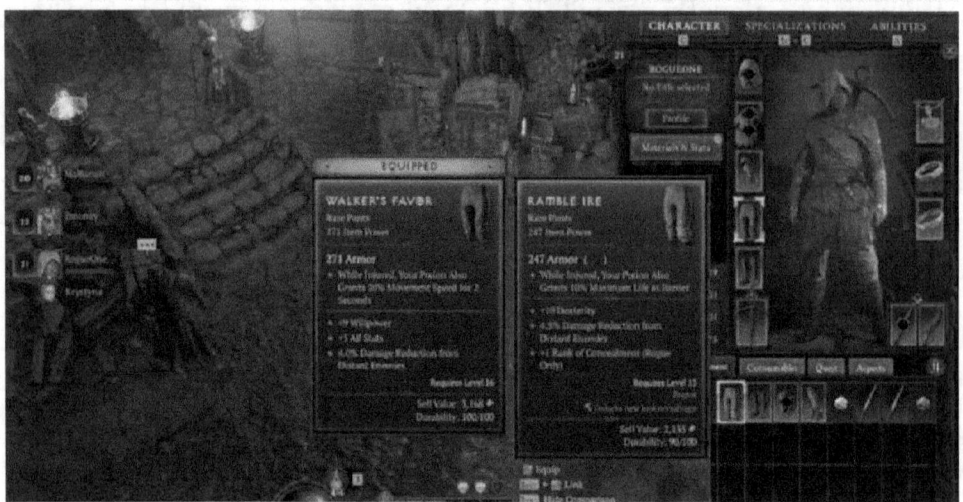

The Diablo franchise is centered around collecting mounds of loot and continually upgrading your gear. Throughout your adventure, you'll encounter items with colored text - white (Normal), blue (Magic), yellow (Rare), tan (Unique), and orange (Legendary). Pick them all up, as they each provide valuable resources.

In the early game, nearly every piece of gear you find can be an upgrade to your current loadout. You should frequently glance at your newly acquired loot to see if equipping anything will gain you an extra advantage in combat. If the gear isn't an upgrade, bring it to town.

SALVAGE INSTEAD OF SELL

When you return to town with an inventory full of junk, don't sell your unused gear to a merchant for gold - salvage everything at the blacksmith. At the first major city, Kyovashad, the blacksmith is located to the southeast of the waypoint.

There are a plethora of resources in Diablo 4. Plants, ore, skins, monster parts, and salvaged materials are just a few of the things you'll collect in Sanctuary. Luckily, most resources will accumulate in your inventory without much hands-on management, but it's important to know they will all come into play at some point.

DON'T SPEND YOUR RESOURCES

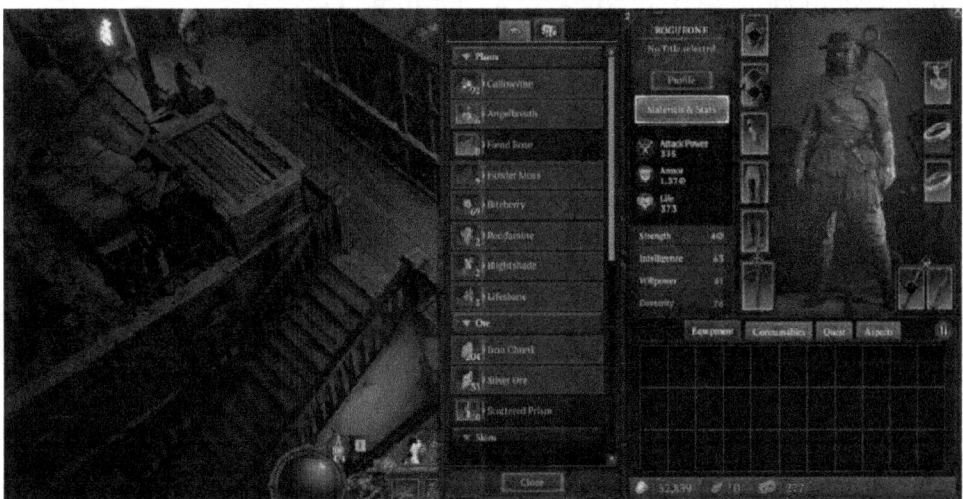

The reason you should salvage everything instead of selling it for gold is that you'll want the salvaged materials in the endgame. Although you can upgrade your gear, craft items, and make elixirs early on in your journey, save all of your materials for later.

Upgrading your early gear is a waste of resources because you'll likely find an upgrade to that piece very quickly. Don't spend materials upgrading a piece of gear until you know it'll stick around for a while. Save all of your materials for upgrading legendary items and make the endgame easier.

EXPLORE THE CELLARS AND DUNGEONS

Along the beaten path, you'll spot the occasional cellar or dungeon. These optional rabbit holes can be well worth your time. Cellars will be small areas with a boss, treasure chest, or another mystery to uncover. Dungeons are much more involved.

The dungeons in Sanctuary are a big part of the gameplay in Diablo 4. These claustrophobic caves are home to the deadliest monsters and the shiniest treasures. As you play through the main story, engage in some optional dungeons to get powerful rewards.

USE YOUR POTIONS OFTEN

For many of the characters battling through the forces of evil, their only source of healing will be to take a drink from their potions. The default potion keybinding is L1 on PlayStation, LB on Xbox, and Q on PC. This button should always be on the top of your mind.

When you're in a pinch, drink your potion quickly and run to safety. Potion refill charges drop on a regular basis, so don't be stingy with your healing. Dying in Diablo 4 can be devastating, especially if you're playing Hardcore. Use those potions early and often.

UPGRADE YOUR POTIONS

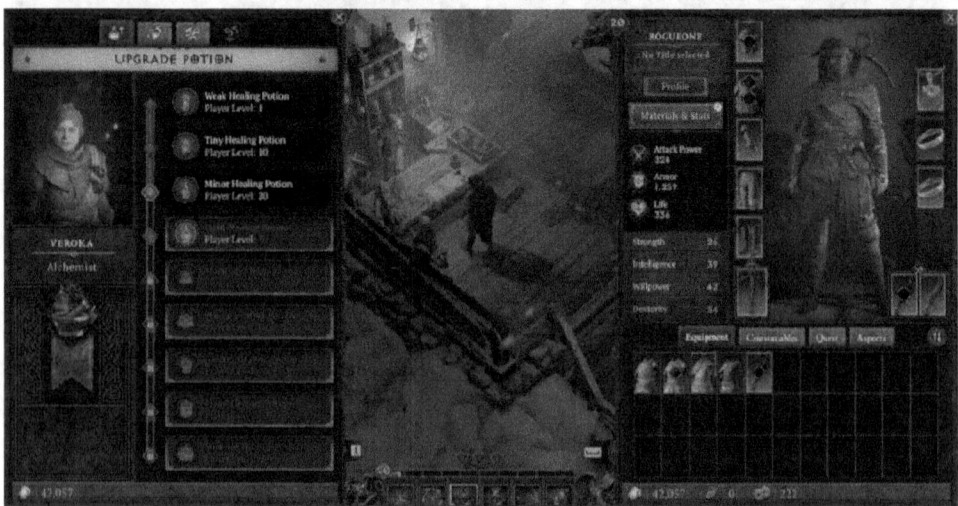

In the city of Kyovashad, Veroka the Alchemist is prepared to upgrade the potency of your potions. As your health pool rises, the amount of HP healed by your potions will become less and less valuable. Upgrading your potions as you level up will help the amount it heals to scale with your needs.

Every 10 or 15 level-ups, make sure to visit the Alchemist. In Kyovashad, Veroka is located in a building directly south of the waypoint. If you're at the proper level and have the required materials, Veroka will enhance your potions.

FOCUS ON THE MAIN QUESTS

If you find yourself lost with all the optional activities in Diablo 4, focus on completing the main story. When you open the map, look at the quest panel to see your active quests. The yellow icon indicates a main story quest, the most important and compelling content that you should tackle first.

Diablo 4 lets you play at your own pace. Quests and zones scale with your character, so you never out-level the content. This means that there's no hurry to play through the content in a certain way. However, if you want to rush to the endgame, follow the yellow indicators and ignore the blue icons.

FREQUENTLY CHECK THE MAP

The zones and dungeons of Diablo 4 are twisting and turning mazes that can send you off in the wrong direction. Smaller dungeons can be linear, but the world of Sanctuary is huge and rich in exploration. When the mini-map isn't enough, consult the map.

The map will be the most valuable companion in Diablo 4. Whether you want to run down the main story or explore the secrets and treasures hiding in the corners of the world, check the map regularly to stay on course.

POSITIONING IS PARAMOUNT IN BATTLE

Once you get past level 15 or 20, the forces of evil will begin to challenge your resolve. Packs of enemies need to be evaluated for the best battle tactics. Rushing straight in isn't always the best move. Ranged attackers and monsters who spawn minions should be eliminated first, while the brawlers can be left for last.

Make sure that you know your enemy's strategy and position yourself accordingly. Flank the low-health, high-threat ranged monsters while avoiding projectiles and melee attackers. Stack up monsters by circling their position or backing into bottlenecks. Then, hit them with area-of-effect spells and end the fight quickly.

SURVIVAL SHOULD BE YOUR GOAL

As you progress through the story and begin to reach higher levels, Diablo 4 will become increasingly more challenging. The boss fights provide unique encounters that'll test your might. Instead of focusing on enemy health pools and doing the most damage, your primary focus should be to survive.

If you survive long enough, you'll win any fight. Avoiding enemy projectiles is more important than landing an additional hit. Whether you're fighting an early-game dungeon boss or Lilith herself, pay more attention to your health pool than theirs.

TIPS & TRICKS FOR BARBARIAN

USE YOUR ARSENAL

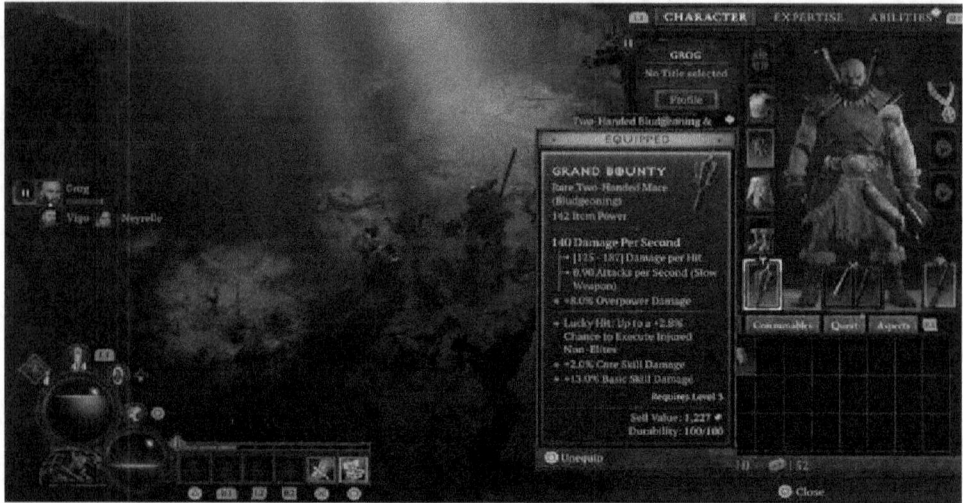

The Barbarian is unique in that they have multiple weapons equipped at once. Each attack is associated with a different weapon, and using different skills will have you switch to different weapons upon activation of the corresponding attack.

While many games will have you finding your favorite weapon type and sticking to it, it's important for Barbarians to utilize all of their available weapons in combat. As you find more unique weapons and have different types for different playstyles, you can quickly switch up your strategy to counter whatever your opponents throw at you. The Barbarian also earns weapon expertise the more he or she uses a specific weapon. This makes them more effective and rewards you for fighting with all of the available weapons.

CLOSE THE GAP

The Barbarian comes with multiple abilities that allow you to jump around the battlefield to get up close and personal with your opponents. Many of these abilities may not excel in damage, but the quick movement is incredibly worthwhile.

While there are other more important skills to work on, finding some armor pieces that give additional movement speed can be quite beneficial. When playing in a party, other classes will be able to attack from a distance, and the additional movement speed will help you get within range at the same time as spell casters.

BUILD UP FURY

Fury is the consumable energy that Barbarians utilize for their more powerful attacks. Some stronger abilities will constantly drain your Fury to deal tons of damage, like the all-too-famous Whirlwind ability. While Barbarians may seem like a tank-focused class, Fury is what helps them deal damage.

Different abilities and passives will help you gain your Fury back quickly, and these should be a priority for any build. Many abilities quickly drain your Fury, you need to get it back just as quickly.

WHIRLWIND IS BACK AGAIN

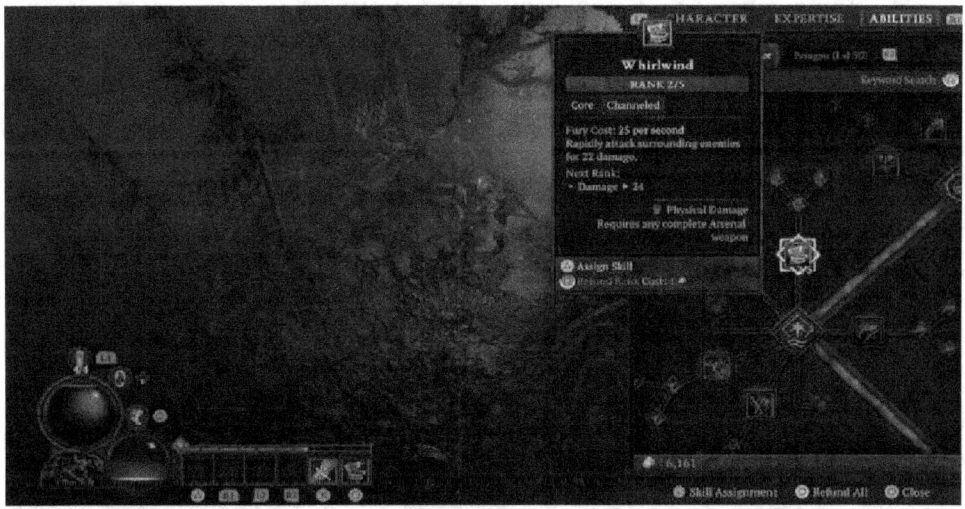

The Whirlwind ability is the cornerstone of the Barbarian class for a very good reason. This ability is easy to use, great in any situation, and deals a level of damage that would make Diablo himself tremble in fear.

Whirlwind is unlocked in the second set of skills for the skill tree, allowing players to get it very early in the game. This skill also has the ability to generate Fury upon hitting enemies, allowing you to use it for longer and wipe out large groups.

DAMAGE OVER TIME WITH BLEED

Bleed is another powerful effect the Barbarian is able to put on his enemies. Through both weapons and skills, you can affect many enemies with Bleed quickly, damaging them further over the next few seconds on top of the initial hit.

You can also scale the damage of Bleed to make it powerful against both bosses and elite enemies. With some abilities you'll barely hit weaker enemies before they drop dead.

WHO NEEDS INTELLI... HOW DO YOU SPELL IT?

Building the perfect character in Diablo 4 requires you to find weapons and armor that increase the right stats for that class. True to form, the most important stat to focus on for your Barbarian is Strength, with Intelligence offering only a boost in resistance.

While finding tons of new items to equip on your character, prioritize gear that increases your strength, and ideally, stay away from an increase in most of the other stats. This helps make building a Barbarian be very simple but has incredibly effective results.

UPGRADE YOUR POTIONS

Being on the front lines means you'll be getting hit from all angles by the demons you're fighting. While the Barbarian is built to take a few hits, it's inevitable that your health will get low, and you'll need to heal up With only four weak starting potions, that may be a problem.

As you achieve more renown in a region; you'll be able to increase the number of potions you hold at a time, allowing you to stock more up for bigger fights. As you level up your character, you'll also be able to increase the efficacy of your potions at the alchemist using different resources, and these potion upgrades are vital.

CROWD CONTROL

The Barbarian has many powerful AOE attacks and abilities, and these should be the base for any strong build. The land of Sanctuary is full of many hordes of weaker enemies, and the Barbarian is made to cleave through them with relative ease.

When playing in a party, your top priority should be thinning the herd and letting the other classes focus on the larger enemies. While the Barbarian does have many abilities that focus on taking down singular strong enemies, your AOE attacks are unmatched, and that is where this class truly shines.

BUILD UP THORNS

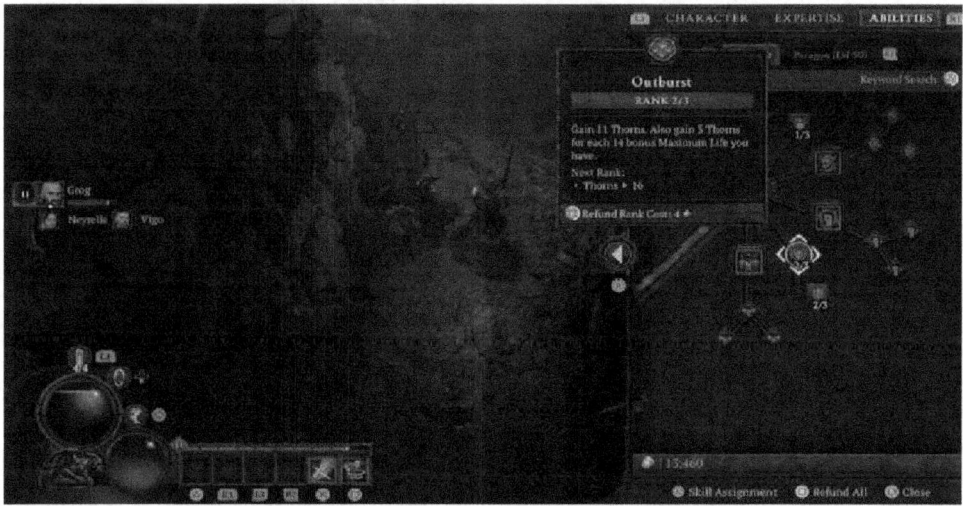

Thorns is a powerful passive ability that can be built up from both skills and bonuses from armor. Thorns deals damage back to enemies that hit you. As a Barbarian that charges straight into large packs of enemies, this couldn't be a better ability.

Through skills and armor pieces, focus on building up thrones as much as possible, They can continue to stack and deal more damage. You'll eventually be dealing more damage back to enemies than they are dealing to you, and that's on top of all of your usual attacks.

TANK IT UP

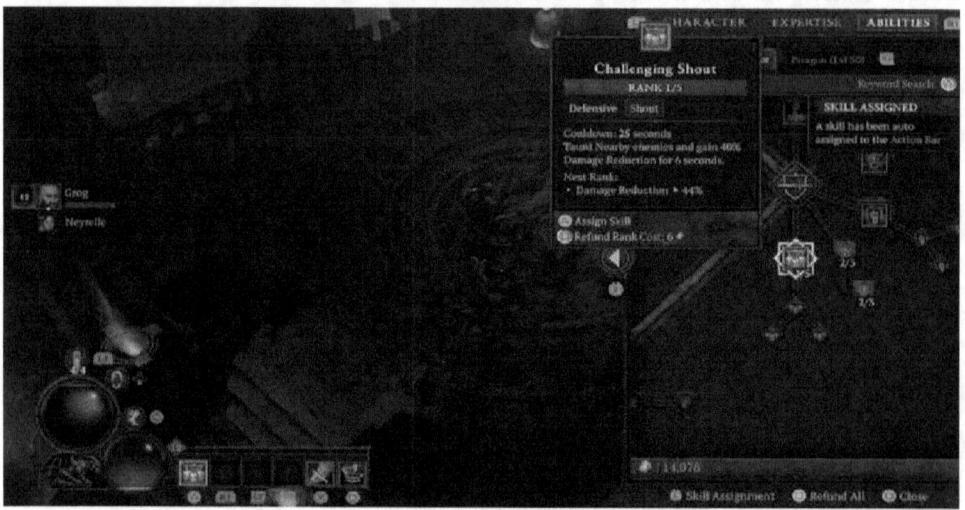

The Barbarian is the closest class to a full tank. While this class does offer a ton of abilities that make you focus on dealing damage, never forget to invest some armor pieces and skills into staying alive and grabbing the attention of your enemies.

When playing multiplayer, you'll be able to draw the attention of nearby enemies with your shout. This will have you receiving more damage, but you can take it, and tacking on bonus thorn damage will have your enemies taking themselves out. With the right armor and abilities, you'll be able to outlast even the worst of attacks.

TIPS & TRICKS FOR DRUID

KEEP YOUR DISTANCE

As you get further into the game and the mobs grow in number, keeping an eye on your surroundings becomes much more important. The only Druid build able to handle being swarmed constantly is the Werebear tank. But, even they can struggle if cornered by heavy-hitting elites.

Use your dodge ability often to create gaps and line enemies up for AOE attacks. Also, don't be afraid to kite tough enemies by running them around in circles just wide enough to avoid their attacks. It might seem cowardly, but it could help you survive a tough fight.

SPECIALIZE YOUR SKILLS

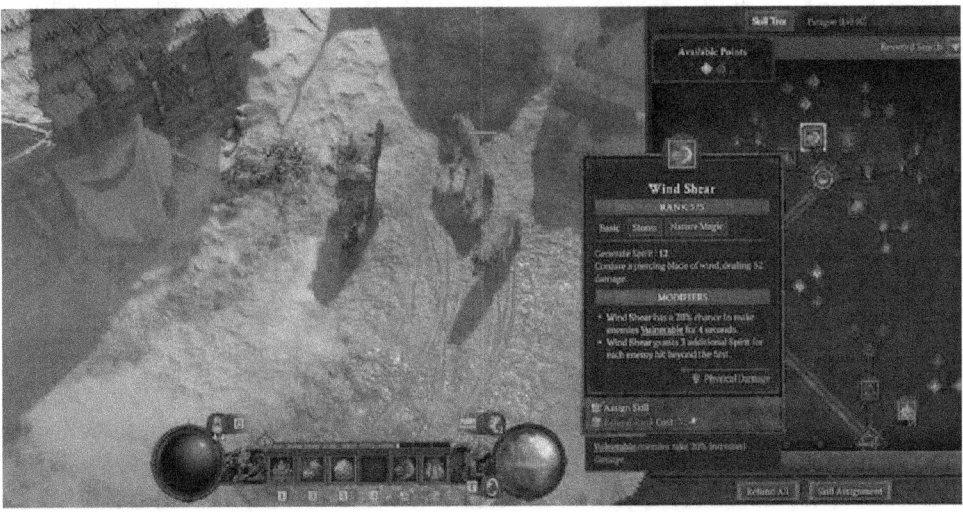

This can mean two different things, and both are equally important. Build up each skill that you choose to the point that you pick specialized effects for them all. Also, choose skills that all align with a specialized build — at least while you're first getting into the game.

Skill specializations give them additional, often very powerful effects that you won't want to miss out on, and choosing a specialized build, for example Werewolf or Nature magic, also has related passive perks that will be extremely useful as you continue to grow in power.

DON'T FRET OVER DYING

It's always frustrating, but unless you're playing on a Hardcore character then death in Diablo 4 isn't the end for you. Unlike the older generations when you had to go back to recover all your stuff, now, your gear just takes a little bit of damage. You even get to respawn at the nearest checkpoint.

Relaxing the consequences for dying has made it much easier to enjoy playing Diablo 4 on a higher difficulty. But, if you keep dying repeatedly during a certain quest or dungeon, it's usually best to find a different way to work on your Druid for a while and then come back later.

QUEST AT FIRST

There's a ridiculous amount of content packed into Diablo 4, from dungeons scattered around the world to PVP battles. But if you want to unlock more content and level up faster, then questing is the way to go. Unlocking services doesn't necessarily require doing quests, but those tutorial quests can teach you how the game works.

Especially when you're in the main towns, always look out for obvious quest icons and other points of interest. Finding special events while you're traveling is always a treat, but don't get too distracted with dungeons early on. They give good XP and loot, but they aren't going anywhere.

GET A COMPANION SKILL

No matter what build you play with, Druid companion skills are awesome. Even Werebear tanks who don't need extra protection can make good use of Poison Creeper's crowd control. Ravens can do more damage than wolves, but they won't distract enemies for you.

Wolves are the best all-around when starting out. They deal decent damage and can keep you from getting swarmed by too many enemies. Their activated attack is extremely useful, allowing you to direct them towards a targeted enemy for high damage.

BE CAREFUL WITH HEALING POTIONS

Similar to Diablo 3, adventurers aren't able to stack up as many potions as their belts can carry. Potions have a hard limit, but unlike Diablo 3, enemies no longer randomly drop health globes. This makes healing potions an extremely precious resource that you should take the time to upgrade.

Boss fights in particular need to be handled with care, since you'll only get healing potions whenever their health drops to certain points. Take some time to gather herbs in the world and visit the herbalist to check out new recipes. You can also craft elixirs there to increase your toughness or power.

UTILIZE WALLS

Although this trick works best in dungeons with lots of little nooks and crannies, you can definitely still take advantage of walls and other hard obstacles in the open world. Even a little bit of cover from ranged attackers can make a huge difference.

There are bound to be many occasions when you're exploring and run right into an overwhelmingly powerful group of enemies. Even a common group of archers can do tons of damage to you out in the open, so there's really no shame in exploiting the natural environment to your advantage.

WATCH OUT FOR CHESTS

Chests are yet again a fantastic source of decent leveling gear, and they're surprisingly common throughout the game. Unlike previous generations, chests in Diablo 4 can be a little tough to spot. Rarer types of chests are usually easy to see, but the basic ones sometimes blend in a little too well.

Just take your time when you're exploring or questing if you don't want to pass up the common chests. In addition to those, there are tons of little hiding spots that you can search for some quick and easy gold.

SAVE UP YOUR OBOLS

It can be super tempting to spend this rare currency on the chance of getting powerful gear from the Curiosity Vendor — especially when you're struggling with certain quests or grinding levels, the thought of getting powerful gear for free can be tantalizing.

But, any gear you get early on is only going to be replaced, and sooner rather than later. Higher-level gear in any Diablo game always puts lower-level gear to shame. It's far better to save up your Obols until you hit max level, then spend them all at once!

GEAR ISN'T EVERYTHING

Once you start to find multiple pieces of Rare gear, inevitably you'll have to start comparing drops. Sometimes, lower quality Magic gear may have way more armor than your Rare gear, but much worse bonus effects. You may find yourself holding onto that gear with less armor but more useful bonuses.

It's important to remember that gear at this point isn't likely to make or break your game. You don't need to use gems on every socketable item you equip, or always have the best weapon possible. Just get out there and have fun, and worry about perfecting your build when you're at max level.

TIPS & TRICKS FOR ROGUE

PENETRATING SHOT OR TWISTING BLADES

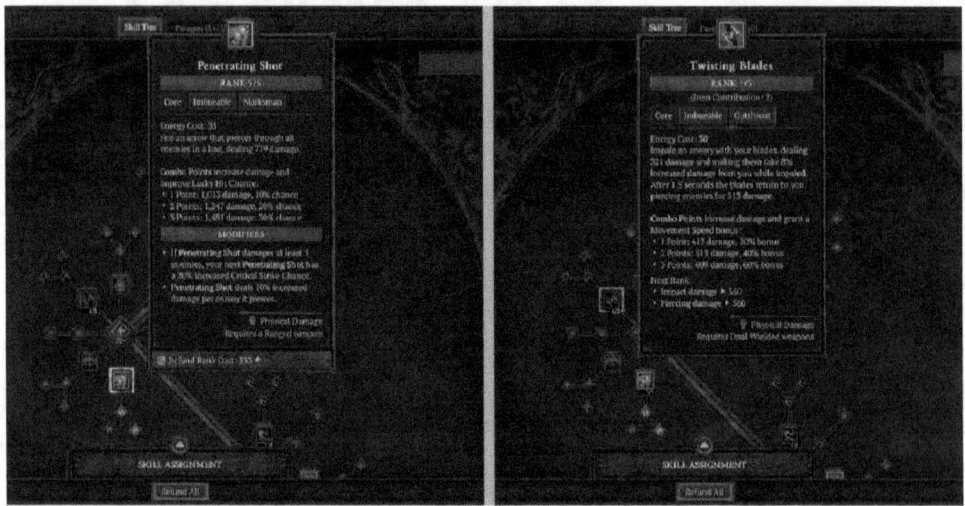

As you're leveling up it's best to focus on building your skills around Penetrating Shot (Marksman) or Twisting Blades (Cutthroat). The Marksman will play safer, but requires you to kite enemies. Twisting Blades will bring Cutthroats closer to the action, but are more at risk of falling in combat.

With Basic and Core skills split between Marksman and Cutthroat abilities, you'll need to decide your preferred playstyle early in the game. There's no wrong choice here, but you'll need to pick one and forsake the other.

CONTINUALLY IMPROVE YOUR POSITION

Playing a Rogue in Diablo 4 requires finesse. When they're rushed by a pack of monsters, Rogues use positioning to regain the advantage. By always working to control the terms of the fight, you can avoid danger and spend more time on the offensive.

Since Rogues have few defensive capabilities, they need to run around the battlefield and use the environment to help their efforts. Look for opportunities to group enemies up, funnel them into bottlenecks, and kite them back when you're overwhelmed.

STICK & MOVE

Barbarians, Bear Druids, and Necromancer summons want to charge into battle and trade blows. Rogues want to land a couple of hits and then dodge incoming attacks. Don't stand in one place launching off attacks. Let a couple of arrows fly or daggers slice and then reposition.

Rogues are an active class. They should always be thinking about their next move. Many spells can be used on the run. When you need to evade an enemy projectile, use that opportunity to refresh an active Imbuement and never waste a second.

PLAY WITH A TANK

If you don't like the idea of continually improving your position or sticking and moving in combat, recruit a friend that plays a tank class. When Rogues are able to sit behind a fortified frontline, they're free to forget about defensive measures.

Adventuring through Sanctuary as a Rogue is a balance between putting out damage and using evasive maneuvers. If you play with a summoner Necro, their minions will soak up incoming attacks, and you can just fire away.

GAMBLE ON WEAPONS

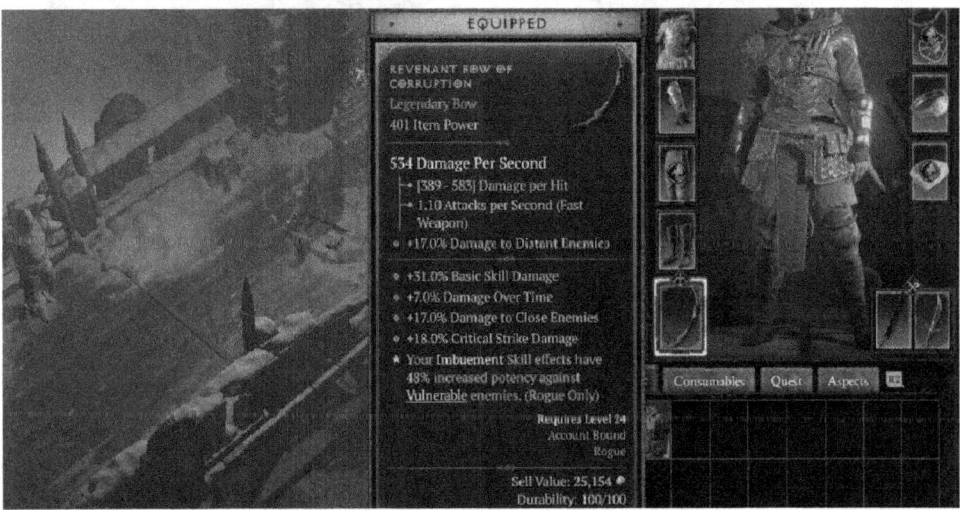

You can only carry 500 Murmuring Obols (the currency that allows you to Gamble) to start, then you'll miss out on any new drops. When you're nearing capacity, visit a Purveyor of Curiosities and see if you're lucky. In the early game, Gamble for weapons and hope to get a big boost.

Purveyors of Curiosities will turn your Murmuring Obols into an equipment type of your choosing with varying rarity. Lucky Gamblers can get Rare or Legendary items that will make combat easier. Use your Murmuring Obols to try for a Legendary weapon, as they will have the most noticeable buffs.

HOLD ON TO YOUR LEGENDARIES

Along your journey through the five regions of Sanctuary, you'll start gathering Legendary items and filling out the Codex of Power. The Legendary Aspects that these collections provide will become the crux of your power in Diablo 4.

As you level up, you'll find early-game Legendaries that will experience the full lifecycle of incredibly powerful to undercooked. Any new Legendaries you find will be in-line with your current level. Ten levels later that same Legendary will look a bit old. Hang on to old Legendary items even after you out-level them - then reuse their Aspect.

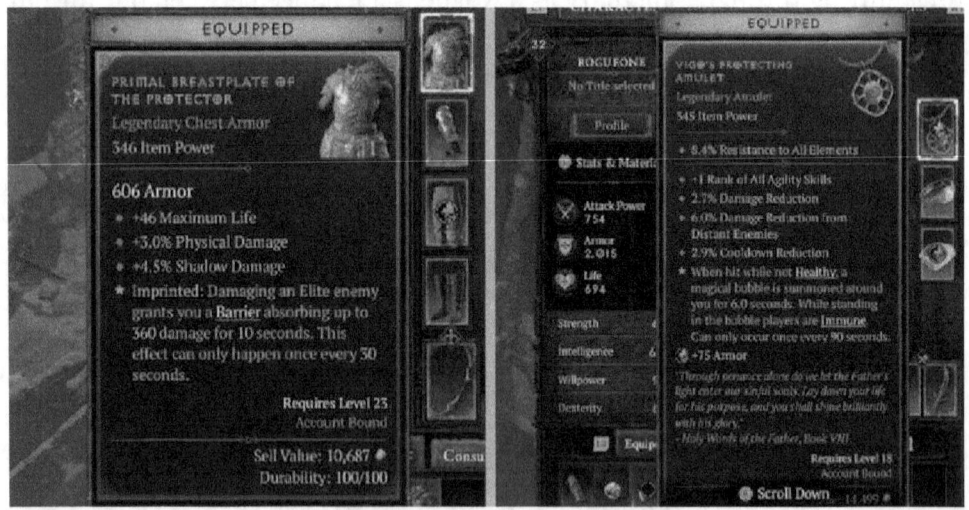

COMPLETE DUNGEONS WITH ROGUE REWARDS

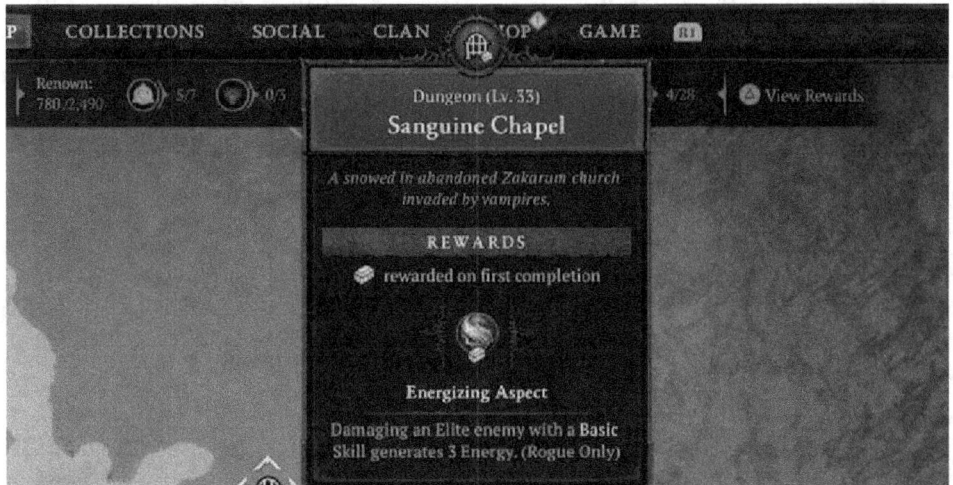

When you discover a new Dungeon throughout your travels, check the rewards that it offers for completing it. If you come across a Dungeon with a Rogue Aspect reward, drop everything and clear it. These Aspects are vital to your journey and will be valuable additions to your Codex of Power.

In certain towns around Sanctuary, a resident Occultist can imbue your Rare and Legendary items with new Legendary Aspects. Any Legendary items you own can have their Aspect taken off of them to improve another item. You can also choose any known Aspects from your Codex.

DON'T FORGET YOUR DEFENSIVE ABILITIES

Remember to use Evade, Caltrops, Subterfuge Skills, and whatever other tricks you have up your sleeve to stay alive. Whether you're playing on Hardcore or not, dying in Diablo 4 is the last thing you want. Keep your health high and your defensive spells at the ready.

In the heat of combat, it can be easy to forget the unsung heroes of Diablo 4 - defensive abilities. Use your defensive spells often and make it a muscle memory to trigger them as your reaction to danger.

AVOID CORNERS AND CROWD-CONTROL

Getting backed into a corner or hit with a crowd-control spell are two of the deadliest situations a Rogue can deal with. Always keep an eye on the floor. Rogues have to dodge area-of-effect spells and avoid trapping themselves in a dead end.

Open space is a Rogue's best friend. When they have plenty of room, Rogues can circle their prey, kite elites, or reset their rhythm when things get out of control. Always know which paths lead to claustrophobic spaces and always break crowd control effects ASAP.

KEEP UP YOUR IMBUEMENTS

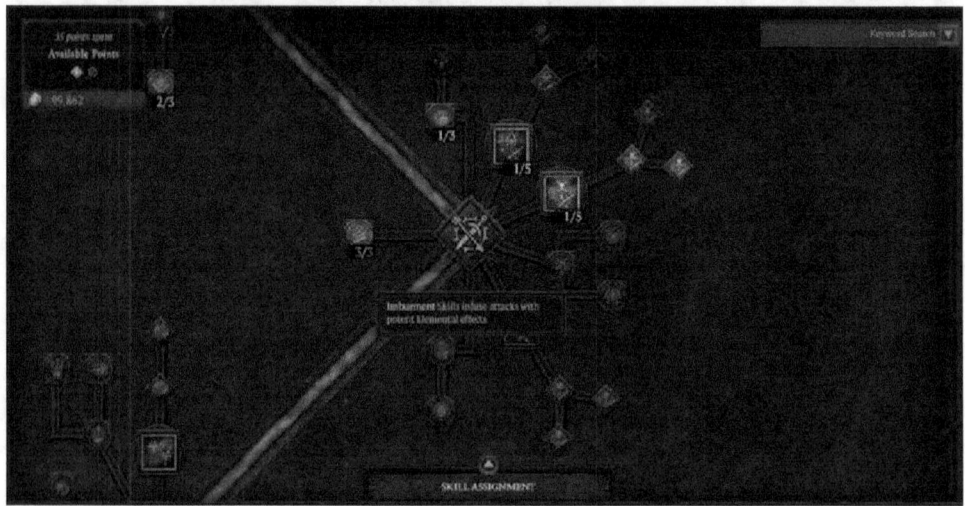

One of the largest boosts to your damage output involves having an active Imbuement up as often as possible. In the fourth tier of the Rogue skill tree, you can learn the Shadow, Poison, and Cold Imbuement skills. These spells empower your next 2 Imbueable Skills with elemental damage and increase potency.

Use these abilities on cooldown. Generally speaking, you should be reactivating these spells every 13 seconds and letting your attacks fly. Just be aware that they don't stack. Make sure to fire off two Imbueable Skills before activating another Imbuement.

TIPS & TRICKS FOR NECROMANCER

USE SKELETONS TO TANK

The Necromancer will need to do some kiting in general, meaning you should avoid standing still and letting enemies melee you to death. However unlike pure casters like the sorcerer, the Necromancer's kit isn't as set up for doing damage while moving. Ideally, the Necromancer should use the skeletons to tank enemies. This allows the Necromancer to set up their bigger spells like Corpse Explosion or Bone Storm. Between the three different types of skeletons, the added abilities in the skill tree, and the golem make for endless combinations for the Necromancer's minions. However, Book of the Dead also supports players' unique customization choices and, if they prefer, they can build the Necromancer for solo-only fighting.

HOW TO BUILD NECRO MINIONS

"The Book of the Dead" gives the Necromancer a free ability in Raise Skeleton and players start with Skirmishers, which are all-around warriors, Defenders that have shields and higher defensive stats, and Reapers which are long-range mage skeletons. You will also have access to The Golem eventually. All minion groups can be built in different ways that compliment the main build of the Necromancer. For example, Defenders and their defensive buffs in the skill tree are great for a Corpse Explosion build, which relies on the Necro staying alive long enough to generate a number of corpses in an area.

STAYIN' ALIVE

One challenging thing for the Necromancer is simply staying alive when things get chaotic. This can be especially true when fighting a tough boss. The Necromancer is well-built to handle endless waves of enemies because they can use the corpses generated by dead enemies to do more damage. However, when fighting a single boss, corpses and large numbers of dead enemies suddenly become scarce, and the Necromancer can struggle to stay alive and do DPS. A couple helpful spells are Hemorrhage and Blood Mist. Hemorrhage will give the Necro direct healing during a fight and can set up strategic Blood Orbs. Blood Mist allows the Necro to avoid all damage and heal up before regaining their corporeal form.

TYPES OF BUILDS

In Diablo 4, there are at lots of main build paths for the Necromancer with endless variation between all of them. The main playstyle revolves around the Necromancer's minions. Whether a huge army, a small crew, or a solo Necro, Book of the Dead sets the baseline for approaches to builds. Bone is the first build type with abilities like Bone Storm and Bone Spirit being great choices. This build focuses on area-of-effect physical damage and is one of the more resilient for the Necromancer. Shadow and Curse builds are next with a more sit-back-and-cast style of play. Both of these types of builds are more caster-friendly, but Shadow is a mix of melee with abilities like Reaper's Pursuit. Blood is another option as the Necro can go more glass-cannon for higher dps and in-battle healing. Corruption is another available option with a focus on Corpse Explosions and generating corpses for free.

EXPLODING CORPSES

The Corruption path in the Necromancer's skill tree is focused around death and dying on the battlefield. One of the earlier skills is called Corpse Explosion. This makes it so that once a single enemy dies and leaves a corpse, the Necro can use their ability to 'blow up' the corpse which does great aoe damage. No matter your intended build, having Corpse Explosion in your pocket is a great way to get through the early levels of the game. Simply let a few enemy bodies stack up in a crowded fight and let loose the dynamite. The beauty of it is that once you kill another enemy with a corpse explosion, you can cast it again and again, making short work of crowds of enemies.

CREATING CORPSES

Between the Raise Skeletons and the corpse-based abilities like Corpse Tendrils, the Necromancer's biggest weakness is fighting against single enemies that don't produce bodies. Soloing a boss as a Necro can become pretty challenging when your abilities and build are based around having corpses for skeletons and damage. So, one way to help offset that weakness is in the Necromancer's skill tree. Abilities like Hewed Flesh, which gives your damage a chance to generate a free corpse, and Necrotic Carapace which buffs your defenses whenever a corpse is used make great combos to help the one-on-one Necromancer fights.

DON'T FEAR THE RESPEC

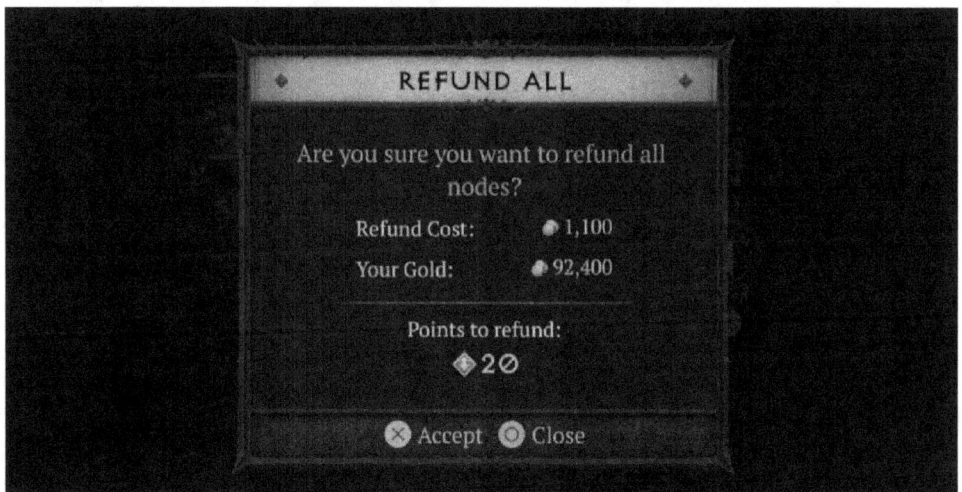

With the ability to save load outs in Diablo 4, the Necromancer is especially one to benefit. Players should have at least 2 to 3 basic builds in their back pocket at all times because circumstances in the game will force you to respec your build. One of the most obvious ones is bosses. The Necromancer is amazing at taking on hordes of demons but a single big boss, like Tchort, will test that aoe build pretty quickly. So, to counter make sure to have a different build that you are comfortable with. Ones focused on Blood, Defender Skellies, or Shadow abilities can help the Necro's survivability, for example.

BEST TEAM UPS

The Necromancer is always going to ideally fit with any character that can tank enemies for the best damage possible. The Necro needs someone in the front to take the main damage that the enemies put out, hence their built-in Raise Skeleton ability. However, the skeletons are more like a temporary barrier and having someone like a Barbarian is a much better choice. A good tank can provide stuns, slows, and bleeds to enemies which helps the Necro pounce on dead bodies and aoe damage. The Necromancer will go great with the DPS classes too, just not as well as if there was a tank in the mix.

AVOID BAD POSITIONING

The Necromancer can build for defense or be a full glass-cannon damage dealer on the battlefield. However, despite your build, positioning in fights is a very important factor for winning. The Necro can get stuck in corners by enemies and, despite the best thorn-based builds, getting pounded my multiple enemies at once with no escape is not going to work out well. So, when crawling through demonic dungeons, always position with an escape route in mind. Although the Necromancer isn't the best at kiting backwards, you'll still need to be able to survive if things go south. Blood Mist is one ability that Necros can use by using the mist to move through enemies and have a chance to regroup.

GEAR STRATEGY

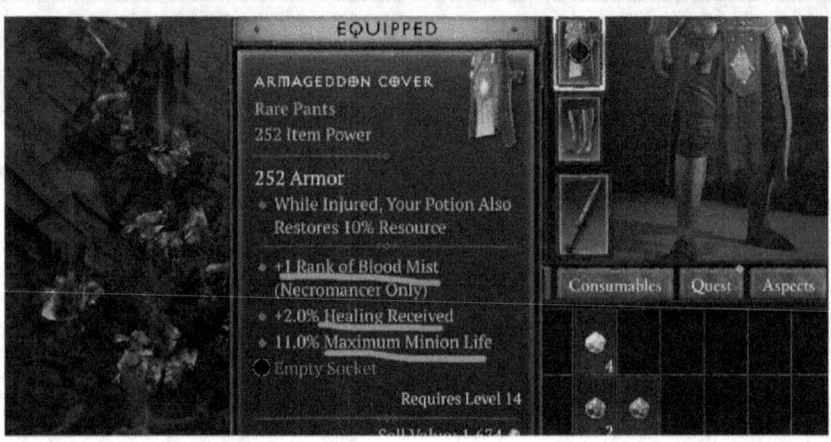

Since the Necromancer is going to be rocking either a small army of minions or completely solo, a player's build should bolster their ability selection whenever possible. In other words, a Bone build with high crit and curses should be looking for gear that will up their defenses with things like buffs to Thorns. Of course, players should be seeking out legendary gear towards the end levels of Diablo 4, but early on it much more about choosing best out of the options you have. Crowd Control and Corpse buffs, for instance, can be great early on to help level up fast. Item power should be considered over most minor stats, and don't get attached to gear. Trying out different combos can make for surprising results and players should strive to have more than one set of gear and builds to choose between. Many Necromancers will end up with at least one main build and one boss build to switch to.

WORLD BOSS TIMER

WHAT ARE WORLD BOSSES?

World Bosses are an advanced boss enemy that spawns in the game world after completing most of the main campaign. Similar to Legion Events, these World Boss events spawn every so often and encourage any and all players to join in the event.

Currently, there are only three World Bosses you can face, with more likely being released alongside larger updates, new Seasons, and DLC. Each of the following World Bosses operates differently from one another and can require a different number of players to complete. Here are all the current World Bosses:

- Ashava the Pestilent
- Avarice, the Gold Cursed
- Wandering Death, Death Given Life

WORLD BOSS TIMER

After reading this, you might want to go find a World Boss to take on immediately. While you may get lucky, chances are you will have to wait a while for them to spawn. Currently, World Bosses are spawning every 6 hours, providing an opportunity for players in all time zones to take one on at some point each day. This timing could get updated eventually in the future, but this is the pattern we are observing currently. As we continue taking on each of the World Bosses, we'll update you here with the exact times they are spawning, so stay tuned!

Whenever a World Boss is spawning, you will get a notification pop-up alerting you the event will start in 15 minutes. When you see that, it is best to quickly wrap up what you are doing and head over to the event area and wait for the battle to start. Happy hunting!

WHICH CLASS SHOULD YOU PICK?

THE BARBARIAN

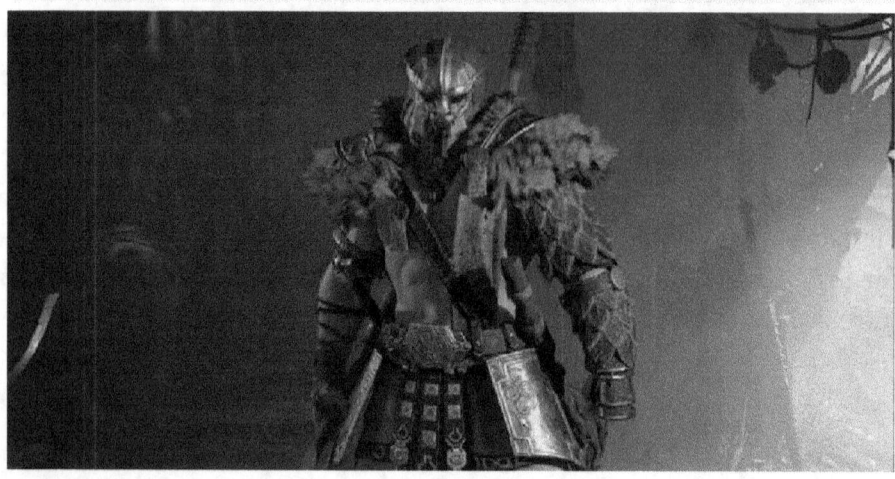

This is the go-to choice if you are all about that melee lifestyle. Charging straight on ahead into the eye of the storm and just unleashing your rage. Their one passive sees them take 10% less damage from enemies, greatly increasing their survivability while staying up close and personal with their targets. Using different weapons will give different benefits, creating a lot of build opportunities for you to try out and explore. This keeps the Barbarian feeling fresh throughout the leveling process. If you like ranged or hybrid-rage classes, avoid this one for one of the others.

THE SORCERER

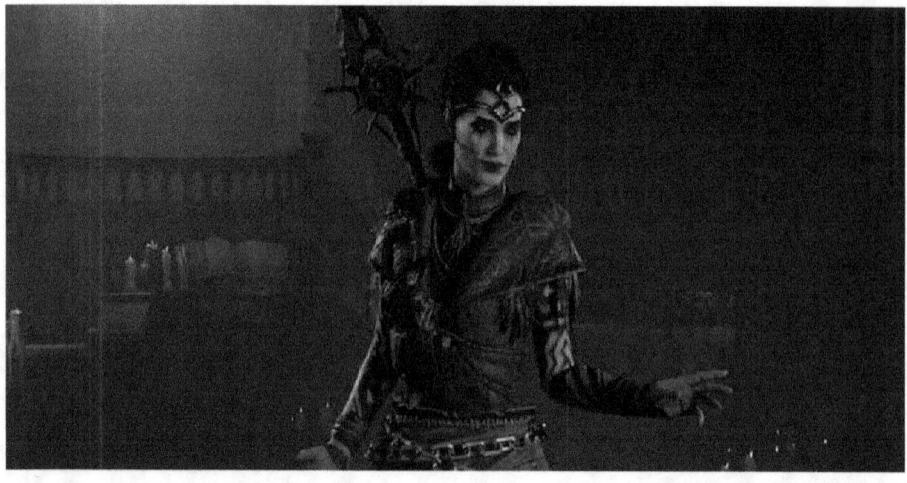

This is the go-to choice for long-range DPS fans. You will have access to a lot of different element types of spells. From unleashing an ice storm to wrapping up enemies in a giant snake of fire. Spells behave very differently from one another, giving you a ton of versatility when deciding what to do in combat. This will keep things very fun throughout the leveling-up process, and very in-depth when making a lot of end-game builds. In order to stay alive, you will need to make use of defensive spells such as teleporting away from incoming threats or creating a barrier. Avoid this class if you hate the feeling of being a glassy character.

THE NECROMANCER

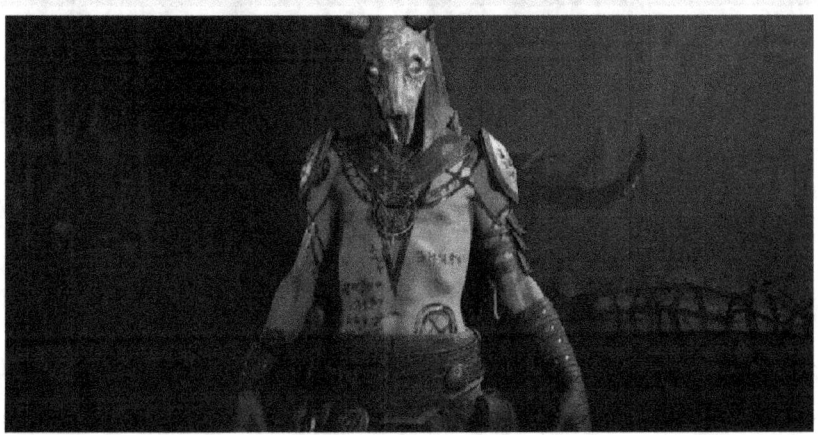

The Necromancer is the best solo class option. It has access to a lot of summons that can tank for you by drawing the attention of enemies. This lets you deal damage from a safe distance. You can use the corpses of your fallen foes in various ways to control the area through features like stunning moving enemies around, summoning minions, or dealing more damage by making them explode. Like the sorcerer, this is a good choice if you prefer range, but with the added benefit of having the summons to fill the role of player allies keeping the aggro focused on themselves.

THE DRUID

The Druid offers a ton of versatility. They can harness the elements in many ways using magic, but what really makes them shine is their ability to shapeshift. The Druid is able to shapeshift into the Werewolf if you favor builds with many attacks and a lot of critical hits. Another option is the Werebear, which would be for players who really prefer being in the melee thick of it. You will be able to still use abilities while in these forms. If neither sounds like your thing, the druid can also have an animal companion that you can synergize with its elemental magic skills. Overall, if there are many different ways you like to play and want to change it up from time to time, then the Druid will be a good pick for you.

THE ROGUE

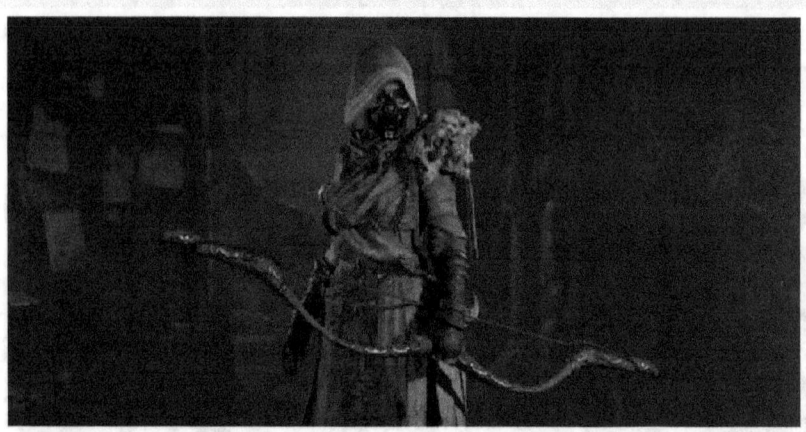

The Rogue has a slew of tricks up its sleeve, and you will be dishing out a ton of damage in bursts. They are not as versatile as a druid, but thanks to their fast movement, they are able to dodge, dip, duck, and dive their way between both melee and ranged damage. You will also have a lot of sneaky little options like dropping damaging caltrops or a smoke bomb to help get you out of danger. This is a great pick for players that want to alternate between both melee and ranged damage in the same build, while also wanting to avoid being hit to be their preferred method of surviving.

WHICH CLASS IS BEST FOR YOU?

As stated before, each class comes with what makes them shine above the others. However, each class has a lot of unique mechanics, making them each feel very different from every other class you can play. Pick the one you feel resonates most with you as your first option, but it cannot be stressed enough to try out each of them. You may discover one you thought was not for you to become one of your favorite options. If you really enjoy melee, start with Barbarian, but also give Druid a chance. If you love fighting from a safe distance and are planning on playing with friends going with melee choices, then the Sorcerer may prove more fun than the Necromancer for you. Experiment and explore the options to find your preferred class.

HOW_TO GUIDE

HOW TO UPGRADE HEALING POTIONS AND CAPACITY

How To Upgrade Your Healing Potions

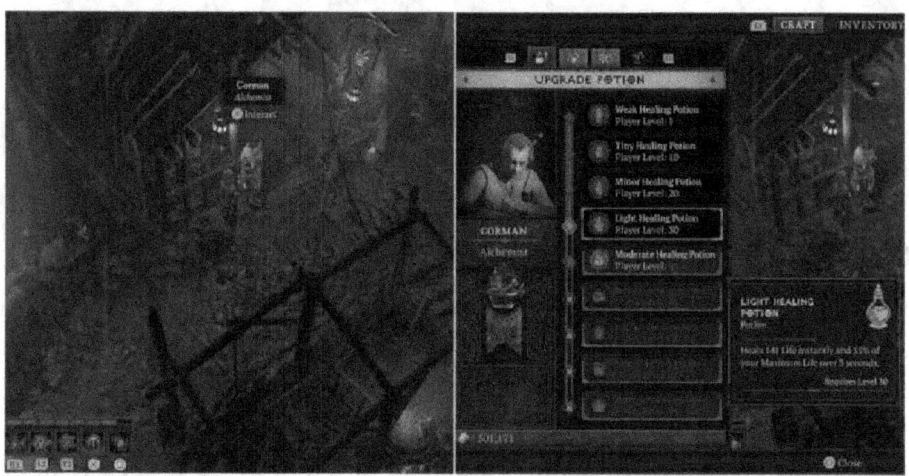

Just like the enemy level scales with your own, so does the availability for you to upgrade your potions. Doing so will not only make them heal more of your health, which is increasingly important as you increase your maximum life stat but will also provide an additional potion for each upgrade.

To begin upgrading your potions, you'll need to visit the Alchemist in any large town. Once you have reached level 10, you'll be able to do your first upgrade, so be sure to pay them a visit no long after you reach that level. Upon doing so, you'll be able to see every level milestone you will need to cross in order to unlock future potion upgrades. You can also use the Alchemist to create single-use potions that buff a variety of stats. These unique potions can be helpful when you find yourself facing off against a tough boss or just want to obliterate your enemies more effectively as you explore the world and dungeons.

How To Increase Potion Capacity

In addition to the capacity increase you'll gain each time you upgrade your potions, you can also increase the capacity by gaining renown in each of the regions across the map. After you have achieved a particular renown level, you will gain access to the additional potion capacity as well as some other perks like increased Murmuring Obols capacity, gold, and skill points.

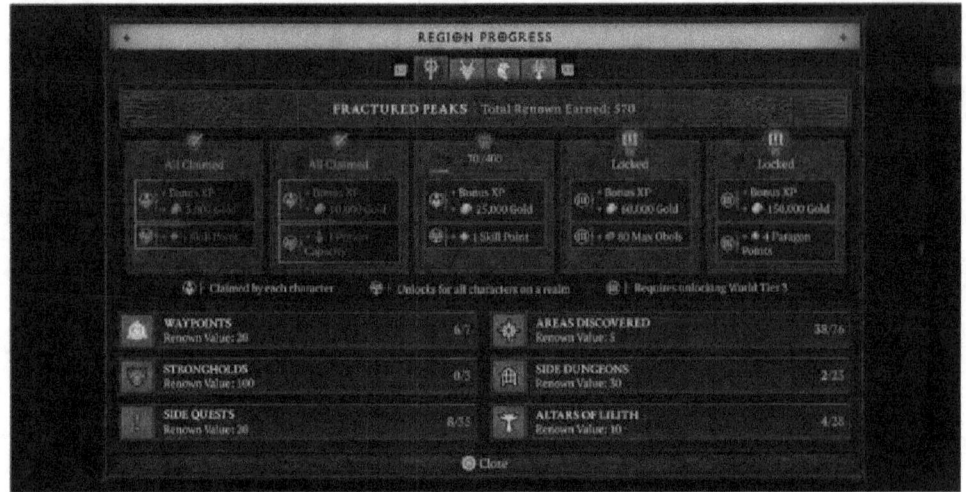

To view your renown level and progress for a particular region, pull up your map and then click the corresponding button to View Rewards. Here, you can cycle between the regions you have discovered, monitor progress toward rewards, and even gain insight into the things you can do to gain renown. You will naturally acquire it as you find new areas in each region or complete dungeons, but be sure to check your renown rewards often, so you don't miss out on these valuable upgrades.

HOW TO OPEN SILENT CHESTS

How To Get Whispering Keys

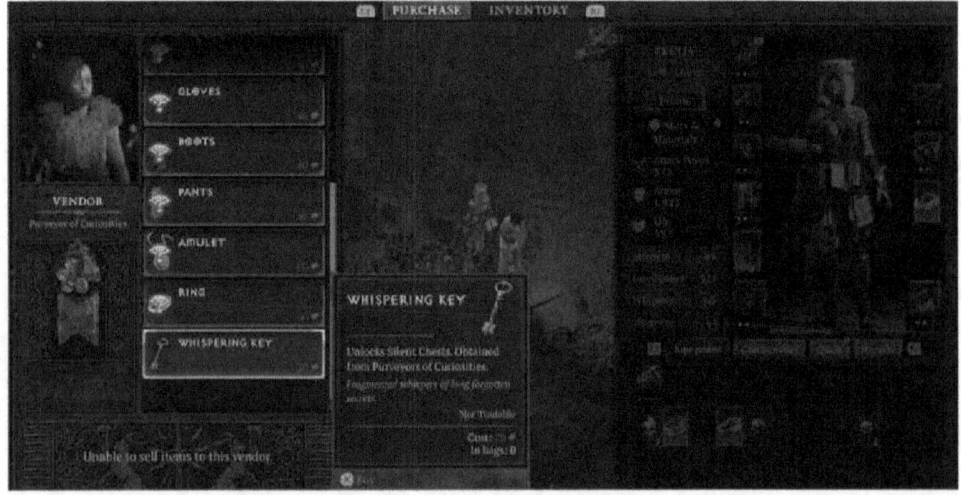

The only way to open a Silent Chest is by using a Whispering Key. These keys cannot be found by killing enemies or opening other treasure chests. Instead, they can only be purchased using a new type of currency, Murmuring Obols.

Once you have scored at least 20 Murmuring Obols, you'll need to visit the Purveyor of Curiosities shop to buy the key. This shop is found in most of the larger towns and is marked on the map by a coin bag icon. Once in the shop menu, scroll all the way down to the bottom to find the key. If you happen to have enough to buy more than one key and aren't planning on gambling your Obols for some gear, then it is a good idea to pick up a few Whispering Keys since you will encounter many Silent Chests on your journey.

Where To Find Silent Chests

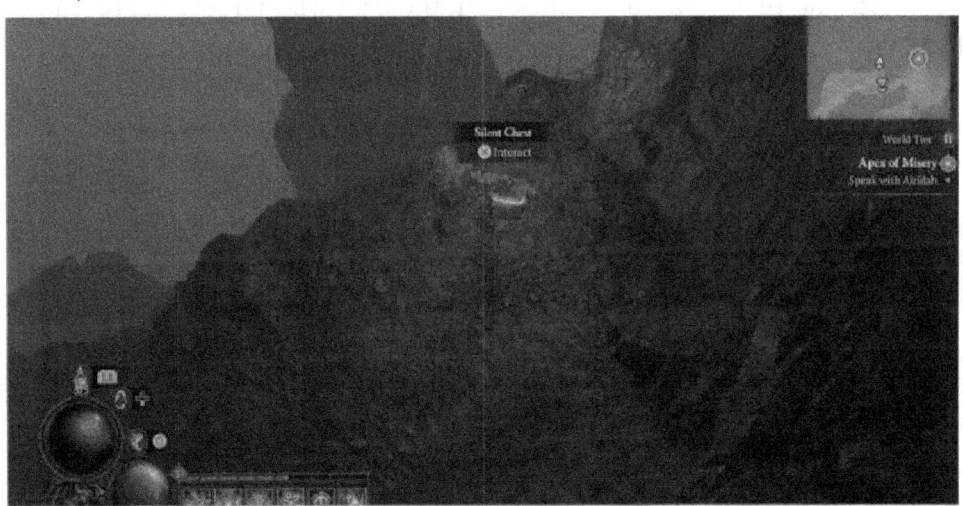

Unlike most of the large treasure chests you'll encounter by completing events or quests, Silent Chests can simply be stumbled upon as you are exploring the world. Usually, they won't be right next to a main road, so it is a good idea to explore all the nooks and crannies on the map if you want to find as many of the chests as possible.

Once you open them, you will get a random drop that usually consists of gold, gems, and some gear. Similar to the gatcha system found at the Purveyor of Curiosities shop, you are sort of gambling your hard-earned Orbols to open each chest. Most often, the Silent Chests won't contain anything of significant value, minus the collection of gems you will acquire. But every once in a while, you will get a great rare or even legendary drop.

How To Sell Armor & Weapons

Where To Sell Your Gear

When you are wanting to sell the gear in your bag, especially those that are lower level, there are a multitude of vendors you can visit to get money in return. If you have a lot of Common and Magic rarity gear items, you can sell them to get a decent amount of money since they won't be of much use to you soon.

You'll be able to start selling your items when you arrive in Kyovashad, the first town you'll find after traversing through the Icehowl Ruins. In here, there will be a multitude of merchants you can visit, including the Blacksmith, Armor Vendor, Weapon Vendor, and Jewelry Vendors to name a few. To find them, they'll be labeled on the map with an icon representing the location of their shop, as shown in the image above. Approach the vendor, and at the bottom you'll notice a 'Buyback' section. You can drag the items you wish to sell from your bag and place them here to get money in return. You'll see the sell value for each item when you hover over it.

What You Can Get For Gear

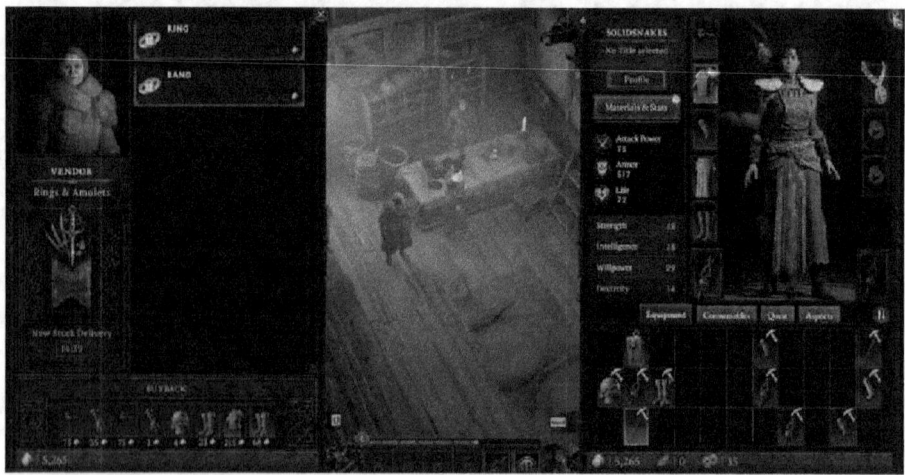

Depending on what items you decide to sell, you'll get a wide variety of money in return. For some Common rarity items, you'll only get about 2 or 4 Gold, but some can get up to 80. When you start selling Magic rarity items some can sell upwards of 200 Gold.

If you have any Rare items in your bag, some can sell for around 500 Gold, and if you decide that you want the item back later, you can buy them back

— 38 —

from the vendor for the labeled price. However, it's better to get rid of your Common and Magic rarity items anyway as these will all start to add up to a large amount of Gold overtime. You'll only need these at the very beginning of the game, since once you start to level up, you'll come across rare items more frequently.

WHERE TO FIND STASH & WARDROBE

Where To Find Stash & Wardrobe

When you first arrive to the village and meet with Vani, she will ask for your help in visiting the ruins and taking out the enemies that lie within. You'll find the Tower Gate towards the north of the Icehowl Taiga map, and inside here will be the Icehowl Ruins.

Explore the ruins to learn more about what is lurking inside, and defeat the boss X'Fal, The Scarred Baron. This boss will be an easy one; all you will need to do is keep using the skills you have learned so far against him and dodge his attacks using dash. You'll now want to return to Nevesk and speak with Vani.

Eventually, you'll need top escape the town with Iosef, and you'll both end up in Kyovashad. On your adventure, make sure to open any treasure chests you find for some gear or break open containers to get items. When you finally arrive in Kyovashad, you and Isoef will part ways, allowing you to explore the town on your own.

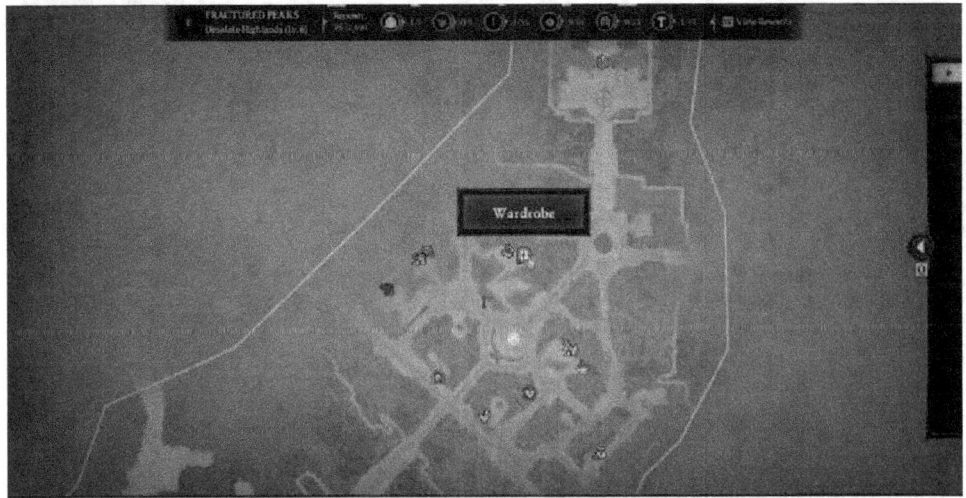

On the map image shown above, you'll see that the Stash and Wardrobe will be found in the northern section of town, east of the three jewelry shops. All you will need to do is head inside the house, and into the bedroom on the right, where the stash can be found between two beds and the wardrobe standing on its own in the back of the room.

How To Use Stash & Wardrobe

Once you access the stash, it will allow you to place up to 50 gear and weapon pieces to save for later. This is a great way to save any rare or legendary items you have picked up and want to upgrade later when you are higher in level. To get more tabs in the stash, you'll want to choose the plus sign next to the chest symbol, and you'll need to offer 100,000 Gold.

Right next to the stash you'll find the wardrobe. Inside here, you'll be able to change the appearance of your gear as much as you want. You will have to unlock transmog options overtime, though, which can be done through salvaging items at the Blacksmith. You can also change the pigment of your gear, so if you're feeling a pink garb one day and a green one the next, you can change it freely.

How To Refund Skill Points

Refunding Skill Points

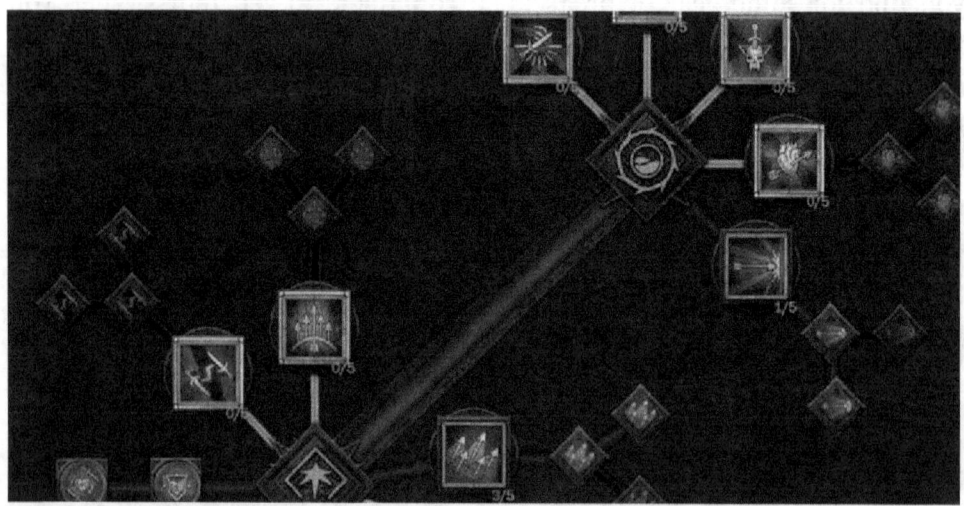

Blizzard simplified the process to refund skill points in Diablo 4. When players open the skill tree, a branching pathway full of unique skills that directly affect playstyle greets the eye. It's a little overwhelming, especially for newcomers of the series. Thankfully, you can respec your character and refund skill points, both individual skills and all skills at once.

❖ *Refunding A Single Skill Point*

Let's say the player accidentally put a skill point into an unwanted ability. Or, even more likely, they don't enjoy the ability they chose. It's commonplace. If either happens, it's entirely possible to refund a single skill in Diablo 4.

- Navigate to the Skill Tree under the Abilities Tab.
- Right-click Skill to refund.

Should players choose to refund a single skill, and it directly affects the next node in the Skill Tree or a child skill associated with the aforementioned ability, the game will require players to refund any affected ability, too.

❖ *Refunding All Skills*

If adventurers would like to completely alter their playstyle by working with a new build altogether, it's possible to refund all skill points on a character. Thankfully, once again, Blizzard made this process as simple as imaginable.

- Navigate to the Skill Tree under the Abilities Tab.
- At the very bottom of the Skill Tree, below all the available nodes, the Refund All button awaits. It's bright and hard to miss.
- Once selected, the Refund All option will bring up a prompt confirming a total reset of all skills. The popup will also list the associated cost to respec the character.

By refunding all skills, players are taking the nuclear option. It's important to note this fact. While the total cost associated with refunding skills isn't enough to break the bank, it can have an impact. Players should choose wisely before a total respec. At the very least, have a plan in mind and consider exploring a build guide for a favorite class beforehand.

Cost Of Refunding Skill Points

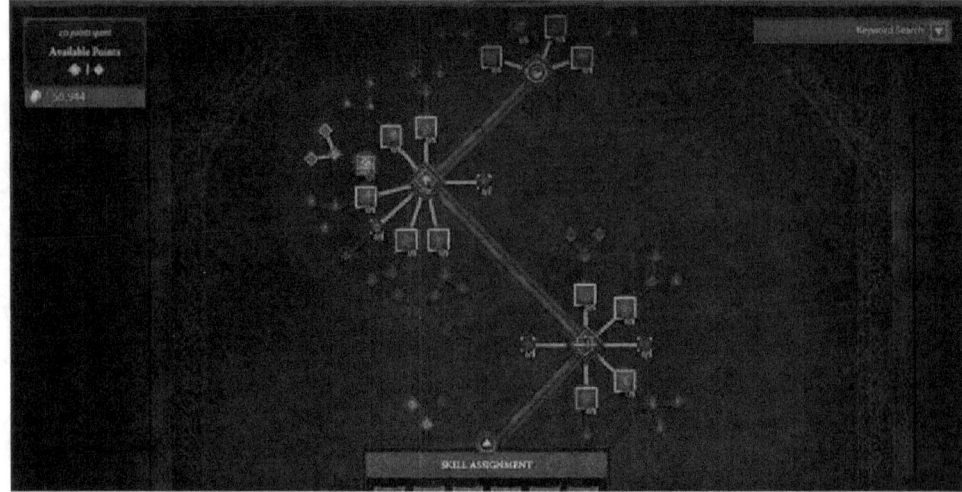

Speaking of costs, when refunding skill points in Diablo 4, it will cost gold for every skill point refunded. And unfortunately, it's not a single base price. As the player levels up, the gold cost to respec skills will increase with every level. Once players hit the end game, as shown off in a preview build from Blizzard, it can cost upwards of 100,000 gold to refund all skills. It's important to note that the gold price to refund each skill may change as time goes on. Blizzard is sure to release balance patches and alter how the in-game economy functions, including the cost to respec a character fully.

As players begin their journey, the cost to respec skills is completely free. At least, that's the case until around level 7. At that point, it will cost approximately one gold per skill point. Upon reaching level 10, the cost rises and continues to do so with each level gained. For example, at level 25, it will cost players about 110 gold per skill point refunded. As players progress, so does the cost. It's unclear how much it will cost to refund all skills at level 100, the max level, though it's surely an eye-opener.

HOW TO TRANSMOG GEAR

How To Transmog Gear

To be able to transmog the gear you've acquired in Diablo 4, you'll need to find the wardrobe. The location of the wardrobe is within the first town of Kyovashad, which you will arrive in after exploring the Icehowl Ruins.

You can find the wardrobe at the location shown above. When you arrive at the house, open up the wardrobe to be able to change your armor. There are a multitude of options available to you, such as your headgear, top, bottom, bracers, shoes, and even weapons. When you choose which piece you'd like to change, you'll be able to select a variant based on what you have acquired already. For example, if you want to wear a crown but have a helmet equipped, you'll be able to change the look of the helmet to match a crown you've received.

You'll also be able to change the colors of your items, with a few different colorways available. All you will need to do is go under the Select a Pigment section and choose from the options available to you.

How To Hide Gear

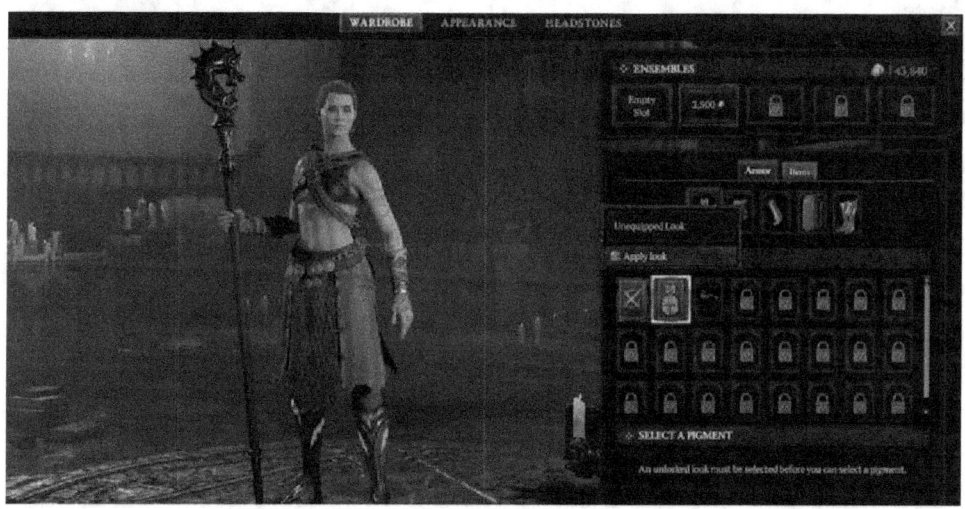

There might be some pieces on your character that you wish to hide completely, like your helmet or bracers. To do this, open up the wardrobe again and go to the armor piece you want to keep hidden.

Underneath the 'Select a Variant' section, you'll find all the variants that you have unlocked, as well as two options at the start that say 'Default Look' and 'Unequipped Look'. Default Look will be whatever piece you currently have on your character in its original form, and Unequipped Look will completely remove the item from your character. So, if you're wanting to show off your character customization without a helmet on, choose Unequipped Look.

How To Get More Transmog Options

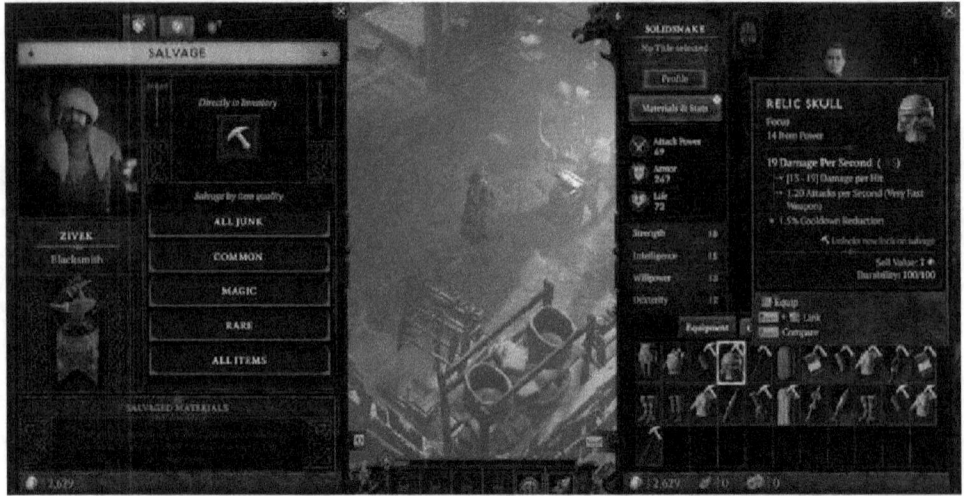

Getting new Transmog options for your character is a relatively simple task. All you will need to do is salvage items you have in your equipment bag at the Blacksmith. You can visit Zivek in Kyovashad to do this.

You'll only get new Transmog looks on items that have an axe symbol above them, meaning that they are not currently in your Transmog catalog. Remember not to salvage any items that you plan on equipping to your character later.

You can also visit the shops in new towns and purchase the items they have for sale. This includes Armor Vendors, Weapon Vendors, Jewelry Vendors, and more. Often times the items you find from vendors will be particularly expensive, though, so it's better to explore and find new pieces on your own.

HOW TO GET TITLES

What Is A Title?

A title is just a word or phrase that will show up under your character's name in the overworld and on their profile. It is not something that you have to have, but there are some pretty interesting ones if you want to spice up your profile a little.

How To Change Titles

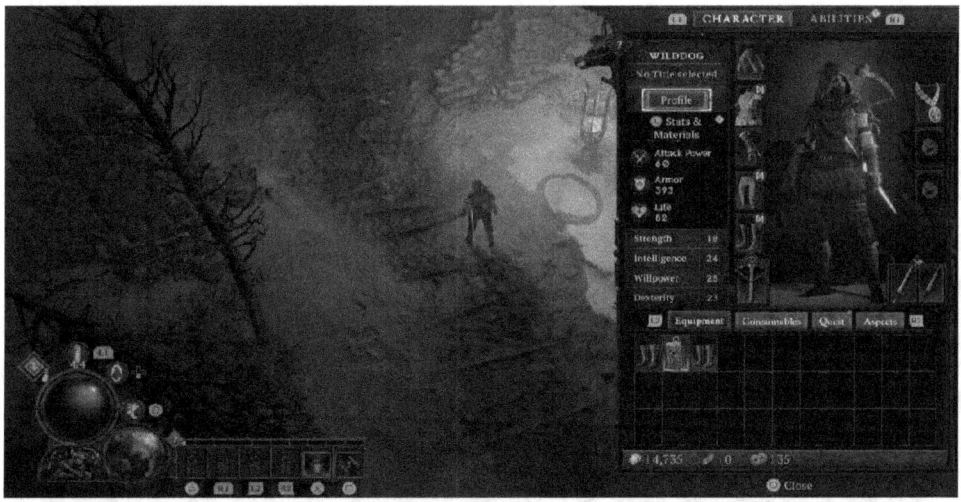

Changing your title is pretty easy. First, you will want to go to your inventory. Then, you will want to navigate to where it says Profile (the upper left-hand side of the inventory).

This will bring up your character's profile. You will then be able to see if you have an Emblem or Title selected or if you are a member of a Clan. From here, you just need to edit your profile. You will see the prompt to pick what you want to edit.

Selecting the title option will bring you to the screen that displays all your titles. The grey titles are ones you can pick from. If they are black, then you have not unlocked them yet. You're able to pick a prefix and a suffix for your title.

How To Unlock Titles

Some titles will be extremely easy to unlock, others may take a long time. You'll need to complete Challenges in order to obtain new titles. The Challenges can be found on your menu. These can be as simple as reaching a certain level with a specific class to as difficult as beating the game on Hardcore mode. If you want to browse the Challenges, you can find some that reward titles and won't be too difficult for you.

How To Join Clans

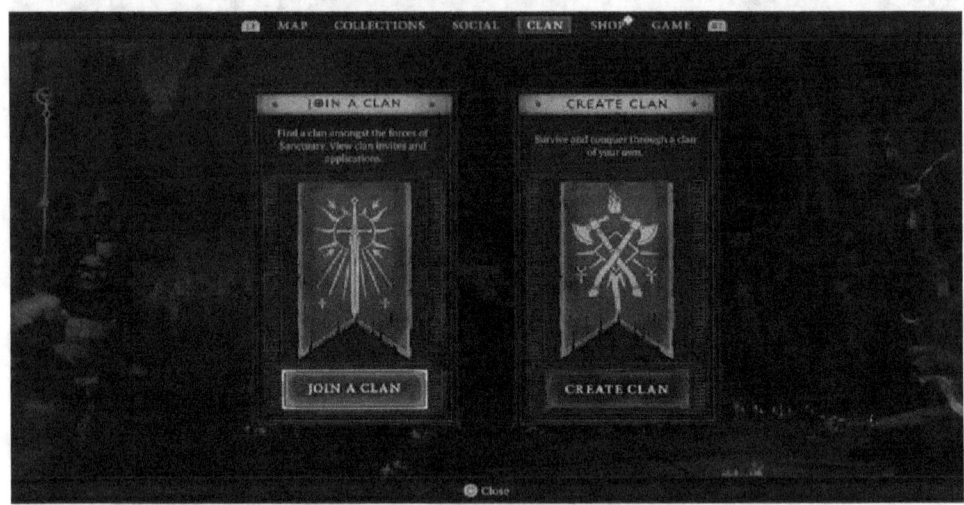

If you want to join a clan, you need to go to your menu. Then move over to the Clan section. From there, you will be greeted with 2 options. Either you can join a Clan or create a Clan.

❖ *Join A Clan*

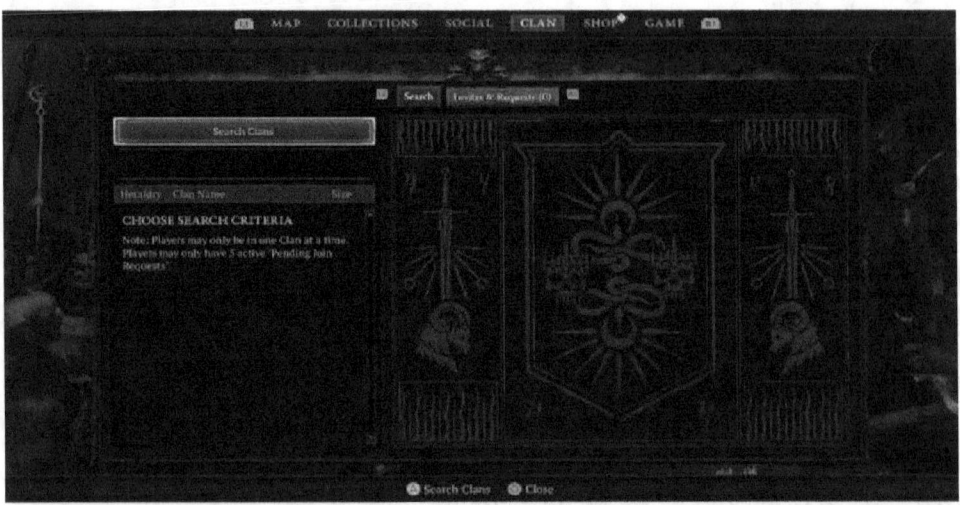

Selecting "Join A Clan" will bring you to this screen. This is the screen that will show you Clans once you put in the search criteria you are looking for. You will also see that there's a notice telling players you can only join a single Clan at a time.

❖ *Search For A Clan*

Hit the button shown at the bottom of your screen for searching Clans. You will then get a search bar to pop up. From here, you can search by the Clan's name, what language they speak, and what labels the Clan uses. Clans can use five labels including Casual, Hardcore, PvP, PvE, Leveling, and Social.

If you want a clan that is for a casual gamer, select casual. The Hardcore label is for veteran players who want to play in the Hardcore mode. PvP and PvE focus on player vs player and player vs everything respectively. Finally, leveling is for anyone wanting help with leveling. Social is for those wanting to make friends.

How To Create A Clan

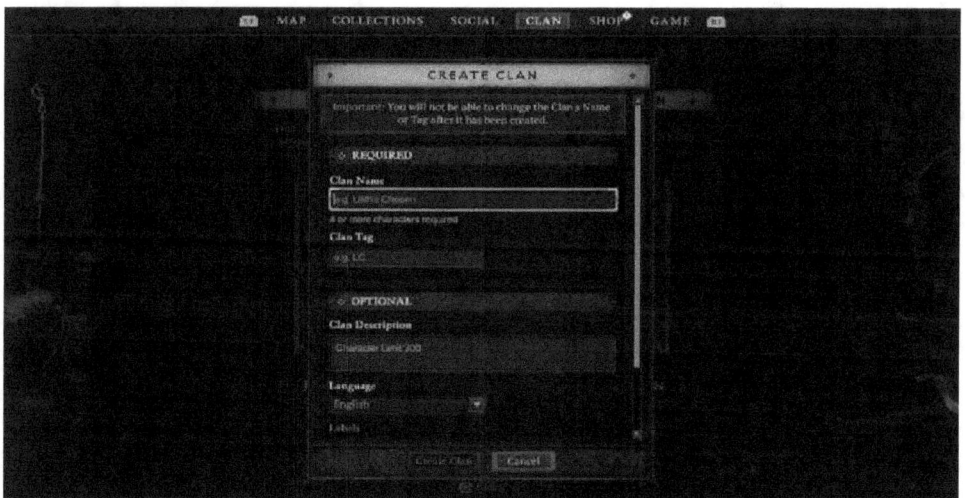

Creating a Clan gives you the control. You will need to come up with a Clan name that hasn't been taken. You'll also need a Clan Tag. This is almost like a nickname for the Clan. It will be what other players can see without expanding someone's profile. You'll then have the option to fill out a Clan description, language, and the labels from earlier. Once you fill this out, you will be taken to a screen where you can design your Clan's banner or leave it as the default one the game gives you.

HOW TO FAST TRAVEL

How To Fast Travel

There are two major ways to fast travel in Diablo 4. One involves your map and the other just involves pressing a specific button. Whether you're trying to get to a specific town or just the closest place, you can easily reach your destination.

❖ Waypoints

Diablo 4 Waypoint

The first type of fast travel you will come across is known as Waypoints. These are points found in major cities, settlements, or important locations, that will allow you to activate them and return at a later date. Once the Waypoint is glowing blue, you will know you have activated it. You will also get a prompt on your screen.

❖ Use Your Map

All you need to do is pull up your menu and select the map. You will then see activated Waypoints. They have a specific icon and will glow bright blue. This indicates that they are there for you to use. If they are grey, that means you will need to approach the Waypoint and activate it.

You can also see these on your mini-map if you're close enough. The more Waypoints you activate, the more locations you can fast travel to. In addition, you also earn Renown when you activate all Waypoints in a specific area.

❖ Teleport To The Nearest Major Town

There is another way to fast travel if you don't want to pull up your map. This can be done by hitting down on the D-Pad if you're playing consoles, or by tapping T on your keyboard while playing on the PC.

If you are ever in a dungeon and run out of inventory space, use this. You can teleport to town to sell or salvage items and then go through the portal to return to where you were. This is the best way to ensure you never miss out on loot.

This will start a teleporting animation. If you move before the bar fills, the teleportation will cancel. You can also see which town you are teleporting to by looking at the name above your character's head. You can also use the same portal to fast travel back to the location you were in when you originally teleported.

Teleporting To Party Members

Another way you can teleport is by teleporting to your party members. You can do this one of two ways. Depending on what your party members are doing, the game will ask you to teleport to them. Otherwise, you can find a portal to teleport to them.

❖ Being Prompted To Teleport

If your party is about to enter a dungeon, is doing a specific quest, or is in another World Tier than you, the game will prompt you to teleport to them. You'll need to press a button and then either accept or reject the offer to teleport. Depending on the circumstance, you may get automatically removed from the party for rejecting.

❖ Using Portals To Teleport To Party Members

If your party members are just out exploring, you can use a portal to teleport to them. To do this, find a Waypoint in the closest major city. The teleportation portal should be beside the Waypoint. It will say "Teleport to (Party Member's Name)." This will lead you right to them.

HOW TO EDIT YOUR PROFILE

What Is A Profile?

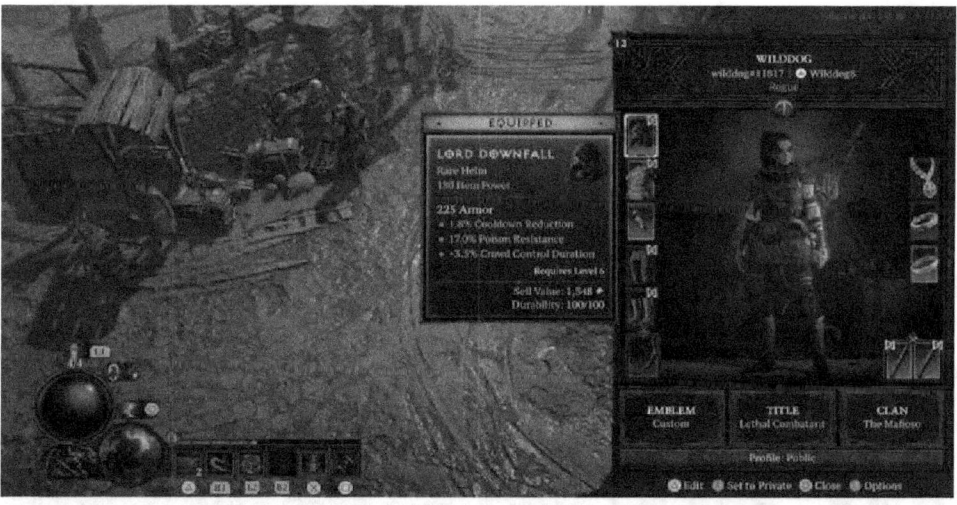

Profiles are just pages with information about your character on them. For instance, it will show your armor, name, level, Class, Battle Tag, Emblems, Titles, and Clan. These are all items that can be edited. You can also set your profile to private. The buttons at the bottom of the profile menu will show you how to do this.

How To Access Your Profile

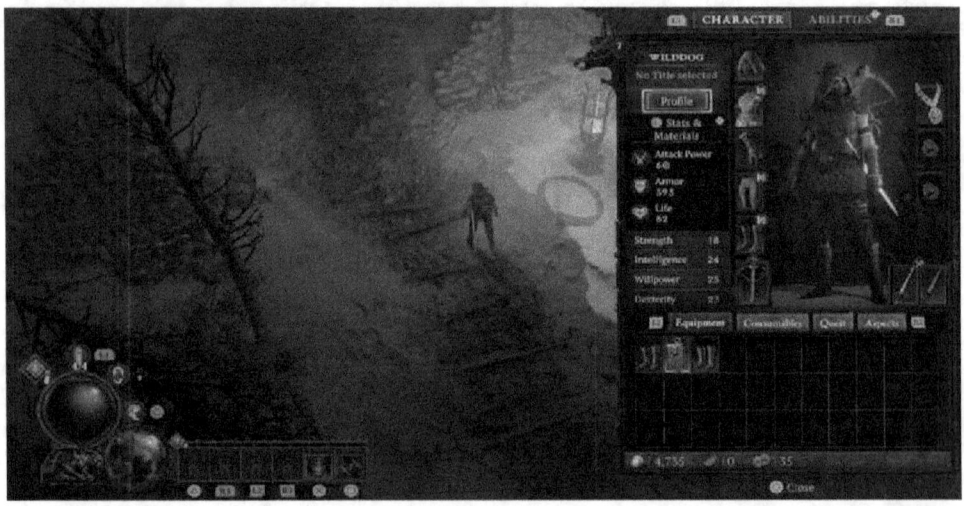

Accessing your profile is fairly simple. First, you will want to access your inventory. From there, you will want to navigate to the profile option shown in the top left of your inventory screen.

Your profile will then show up. This is where you can decide to change the privacy settings or edit the profile.

What Can You Edit?

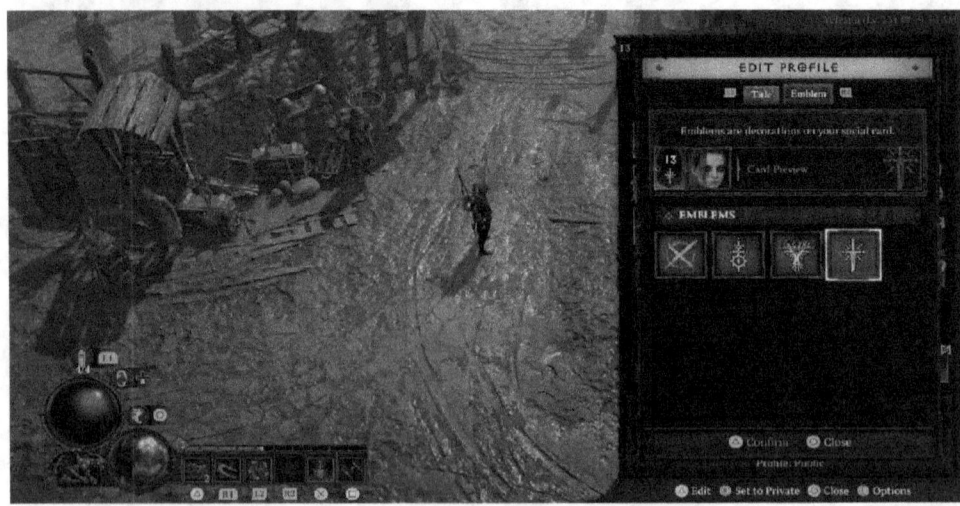

The first option at the bottom of the profile screen is the ability to edit your

Emblem. This is just the design on your Social Card. It is what shows your Class, level, and name. Once you select it, you can change it to whichever design you prefer.

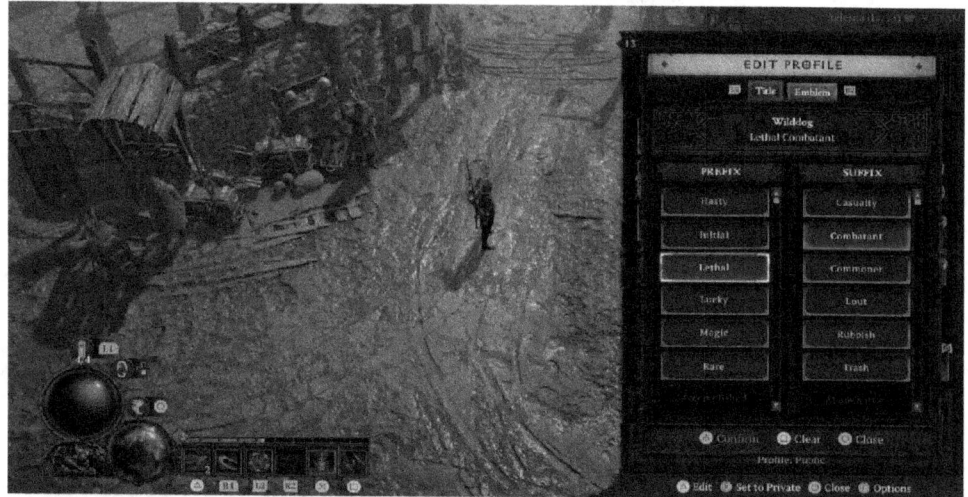

The next option involves editing your Title. This is the word or phrase that will appear by your name in the overworld. You can select a Prefix or a Suffix (or both) for your Title. Once you have decided on that, you just need to close out of the screen.

The final option shows your Clan's name. If you want to join or start a Clan, you can go to the menu and navigate to the Clan section. From there, you will be able to do whichever you prefer.

HOW TO UPGRADE ARMOR

Where To Upgrade Armor

Upgrading armor is done with the Blacksmith NPC. Most settlements will have a Blacksmith, which you can find by looking out for the anvil icon on your map. This NPC is very useful, performing many functions.

❖ How To Unlock Armor Upgrades

Upgrading isn't something you'll be able to do immediately. To unlock the ability to upgrade your gear, you will need to complete a quest. This is a priority quest from the NPC Zivek in Kyovashad. It unlocks when your character reaches level 10.

The quest itself is extremely simple - speak to the Blacksmith about upgrading gear, and then upgrade something. The upgrade window is the third tab in the Blacksmith's menu.

| Why Upgrade Armor

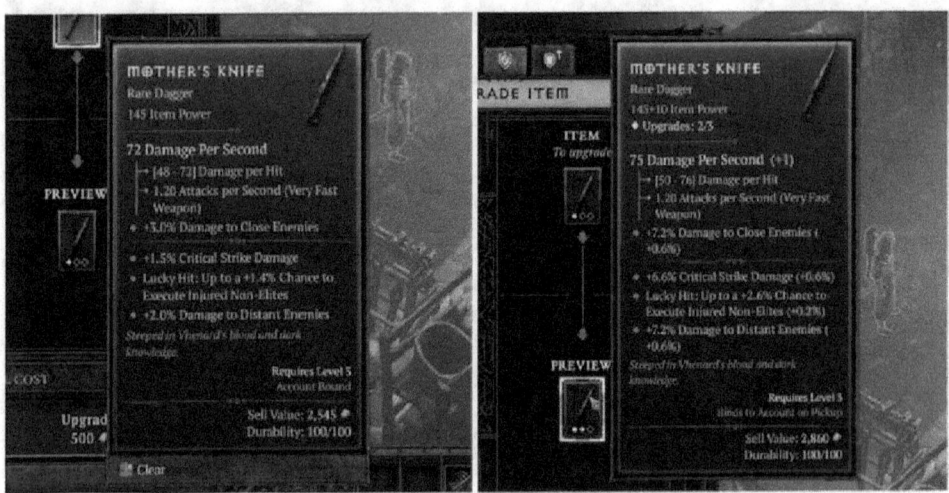

Upgrading armor and weapons in Diablo 4 can help a piece of gear you like stay relevant longer. It can also round out a piece of gear that has a superb stat, but other unimpressive characteristics.

A piece of gear that is fully upgraded will have 1-2 additional damage or armor as well as a percentage point increase in its other properties.

❖ When To Upgrade Armor

Upgrading gear is best pursued later on in the game, especially during endgame activities. Upgrading right at level 10 isn't advised/ It is expensive, and you will be replacing that gear quickly anyway.

Later on, once you've reached the later stages of the game (Act 4 onwards is a good estimate), you might consider upgrading your favorite items. Legendary items with a class-specific perk are always good candidates.

❖ How Much Does Upgrading Armor Really Matter?

As with the coveted armor sets in Diablo 3, it's unlikely that players will see a need for upgrading gear until they are playing at higher-world difficulties. This will come as part of endgame content and subsequent replays of the game.

When enjoying the game for the first time, and/or playing on one of the first difficulties, upgrading doesn't matter.

The Cost Of Upgrading Armor

Despite how early the mechanic is introduced, upgrading isn't cheap. Players can expect to spend the following to fully upgrade a piece:

- Around 2000 gold
- Scattered Prisms
- Silver Ore
- Iron Chunks

These resources are obtained via salvaging other gear and interacting with ore deposits in the Overworld. You'll likely have some lying around, but not enough to fully upgrade every piece of gear you use in the first playthrough.

HOW TO UNLOCK THE OCCULTIST

Where To Find The Occultist

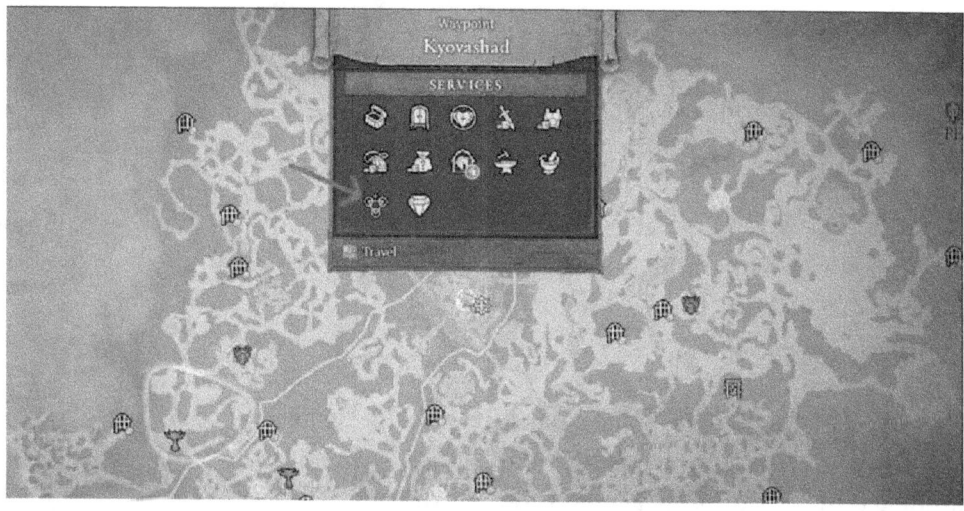

Many (but not all) towns will have an Occultist for players to visit. The first location is in Kyovashad in the building just below the Jeweler. To locate the Occultist, look for a symbol on your map of a triangle with circles at each point.

You can see if a settlement has an Occultist by selecting it on your map. A drop-down menu will then appear listing the services offered in that town.

How To Unlock The Occultist

The Occultist will initially be locked. In order to unlock this vendor, players need to reach level 25 or have unlocked the Codex of Power (usually acquired by completing side dungeons for aspect rewards).

After you've met the requirements for unlocking the Occultist, a priority quest will become available. In this priority quest, players will speak with the Occultist vendor in Kyovashad and be instructed on what services he offers.

To see your current priority quests, open the journal, then select the tab showing a white ornate cross (to the left of the main story tab). Additionally, you can track a priority quest by checking the box next to the name in the Journal.

How To Use The Occultist

The Occultist has several functions in Diablo 4, most of which will be key for endgame content. For veteran players, one can consider him to be the replacement for Kanai's Cube from Diablo 3. This vendor is where players will:

- Extract and Imprint Aspects
- Craft and Salvage Nightmare Sigils
- Enchant Items

Most of these will be useful in end-game content but are too expensive to justify while playing through the main story.

❖ Aspects

Aspects are the powers that make Legendary gear special. They can be extracted from Legendary gear found in the world for a single-use Aspect, or unlocked in the Codex of Power and used multiple times.

These Aspects can then be Imprinted on any gear of Rare or higher quality. This gear then becomes an Imprinted Legendary item.

❖ Nightmare Sigils

Nightmare Sigils are a resource used to increase Dungeon difficulty. These Sigils will be used similarly to rifts in Diablo 3. Players run them at the end of the game as a challenge and to get rare loot drops.

❖ *Enchanting*

Enchanting is a returning mechanic from previous Diablo titles. The player can pay a small fee to reroll a property on a piece of gear. For example, you might reroll a property that increases your poison resistance to one that gives you additional movement speed. This is useful for Legendary items with qualities you want to make even better.

HOW TO UNLOCK THE JEWELER

Where To Find The Jeweler

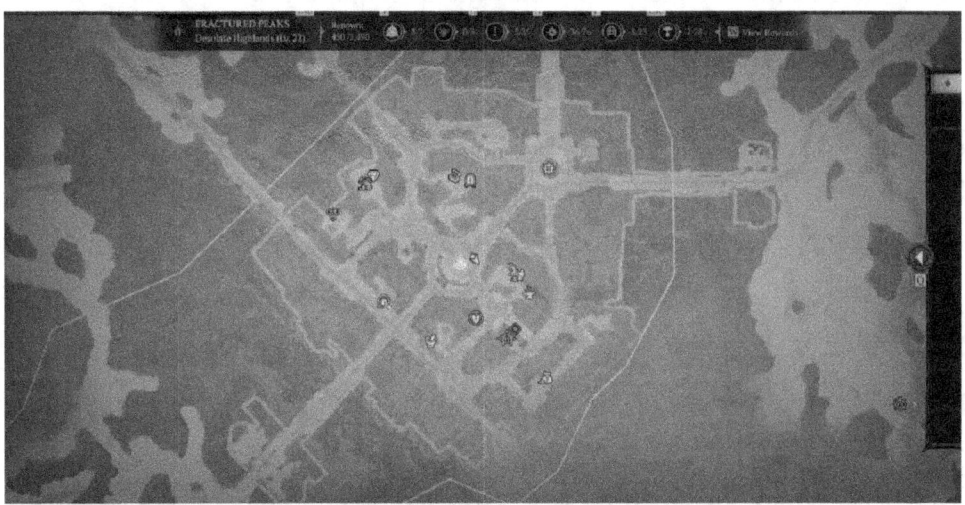

A Jeweler will be available in multiple towns, although not every Waypoint will have one. To see if a place has a certain vendor, you can select it on your map, and peruse the icons under Available Services. The Jeweler's icon is, unsurprisingly, a gem cut into the stereotypical diamond shape. The first Jeweler in the game can be found in Kyovashad inside a small two-story building.

How To Unlock The Jeweler

To unlock the Jeweler, you must first reach level 20 and have completed the Prologue. The end of the prologue occurs when you hand Lorath his amulet. Once you've met these prerequisites, a priority quest will appear in your Journal.

❖ Tracking The Quest

To track the quest, open the journal and navigate to the third tab (just after the yellow main story tab). Then, select the quest to unlock the Jeweler.

❖ Completing The Quest

To complete this quest, you'll need to speak with the Jeweler in Kyovashad (Kratia). She will give you a speech about her abilities and then suggest you craft a Crude Ruby. As part of this quest, you will receive the components to craft a gem of the correct type. However, you will need to supply the gold yourself. Crafting the gem completes the quest, unlocking Jewelers all over Sanctuary.

Services Of The Jeweler

Once you've unlocked the Jeweler, several services will become available. These include:

- Crafting gems
- Unsocketing gems
- Adding Sockets to gear
- Upgrading rings and amulets

❖ Crafting Gems

The Jeweler will allow you to craft gems using gold and a gem resource of the matching type. In Diablo 3, three of an inferior gem type were used to craft higher-level gems, a mechanic that Blizzard has said is returning to Diablo 4. In Diablo 4, the following qualities of gems will be available:

- Crude
- Chipped
- Standard
- Flawless
- Royal

Higher-level gems will grant larger buffs when socketed into gear, so be sure to keep upgrading them when you can.

❖ How to Unsocket Gems

Unsocketing gems can be done at the Jeweler by navigating to the relevant tab (it has a pair of pliers holding a gemstone on it) and dragging the gear with the socketed gem into the box. Then, you'll spend a small amount of gold to remove the gem.

If you sell or salvage a piece of gear with a gem still inside, the gem will be lost forever. This is a big deal later on when gems are rare. They're also one of the best ways to improve late-game gear.

❖ *How To Add Sockets*

Adding sockets to gear that doesn't have them is a great way to improve your gear. To add a socket, you'll need a Scattered Prism, which is dropped by World Bosses and Treasure Goblins.

Each gear type has an associated maximum number of sockets.

- Helm - 1 Socket
- Chest - 2 Sockets
- Pants - 2 Sockets
- Amulet - 1 Socket
- Ring - 1 Socket
- 1-Handed Weapon - 1 Socket
- 2-Handed Weapon - 2 Socket
- Bow - 2 Socket
- Focus - 1 Socket

Once a socket has been added to a piece of gear, the materials used cannot be recovered.

❖ *Upgrading Rings and Amulets*

Similar to the upgrading function of the Blacksmith, the Jeweler can upgrade jewelry such as rings and amulets. To do so, you'll need the following resources:

- Gold
- Veiled Crystals
- Silver Ore
- Iron Chunks
- Abstruse Sigils

These resources can be collected from Ore deposits in the Overworld, or through salvaging unneeded gear.

HOW TO GET BALEFUL FRAGMENTS

Where To Find Baleful Fragments

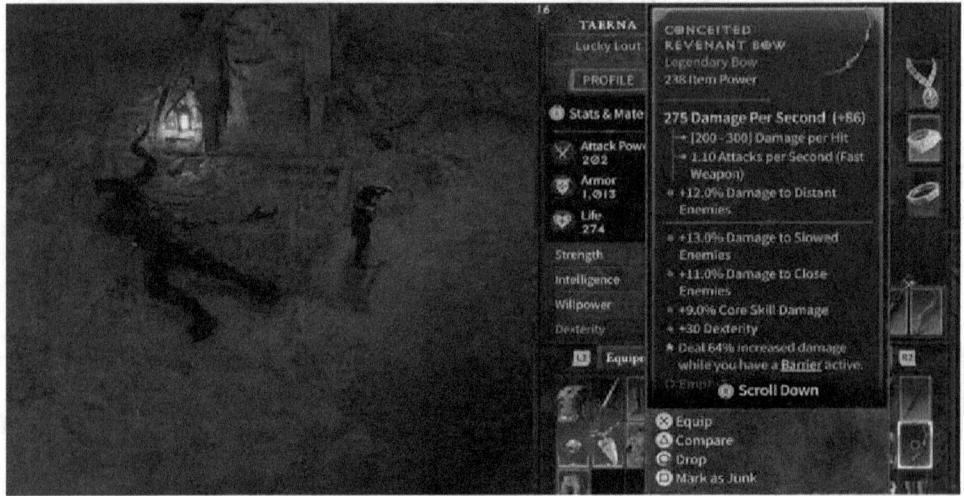

Baleful Fragments are only obtained by breaking down legendary weapons at the blacksmith. After finally finding a legendary weapon, it may not seem like a great idea to destroy it. However, this is necessary if you want to upgrade future legendary weapons. It is usually best to hold onto legendary weapons until they are much lower than your current level, or until you find another legendary weapon you want to upgrade.

Legendary weapons are incredibly rare drops that won't often be found defeating basic enemies in the world. Fighting powerful bosses, elite enemies, and world bosses give you the best chances at farming legendary weapons. World bosses will spawn all over the map, making it best to find as many waypoints as possible to reach these bosses when they spawn. World bosses also cannot be fought until after completing the main campaign. Unfortunately, there is no set way to get legendary weapons to drop, but upping your world tier when fighting these bosses will help increase your chances.

How To Use Baleful Fragments

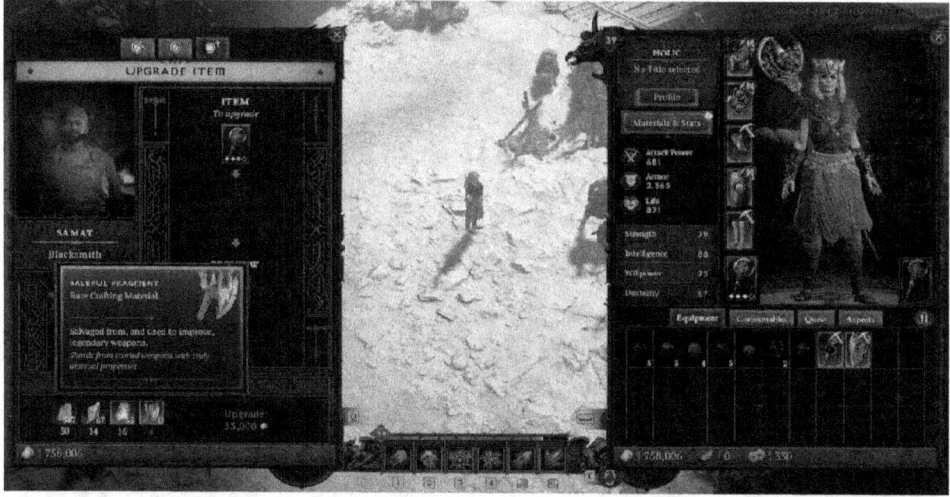

Baleful Fragments are used by the blacksmith to further upgrade legendary weapons. This allows you to get further use out of other legendary weapons that may fall behind or are inefficient for your playstyle. Getting the right bonus stats on a weapon is also important, and breaking down legendary weapons with bad stats will give you the resources to upgrade the right weapon.

Like all upgrades with the blacksmith, you'll need materials of equal rarity to upgrade a weapon. Baleful Fragments only upgrade legendary weapons, not armor pieces. Breaking down a legendary weapon will only provide Baleful Fragments, making players find legendary armor to break down when wanting to upgrade other legendary armor pieces.

HOW TO GET COILING WARDS

How To Get Coiling Wards

Coiling Wards are obtained by breaking down legendary armor at the blacksmith. These items can only be obtained from legendary armor pieces and only be used to upgrade armor pieces. Blacksmiths can be found in just about every major town in Sanctuary and are able to break things down in their Salvage menu.

Legendary drops are incredibly rare, and there is no sure way to make them happen. To greatly increase your chances of legendary drops, play on the highest world tier you have available, and unlock the higher-end tiers after you complete the main campaign. Later bosses in the campaign will also have a better chance of dropping legendary items. After completing the main campaign, you'll gain access to fighting world bosses, which have a better chance of dropping legendary weapons. Legendary weapons will almost never drop in broken containers or off ofbasic enemies. So, focus on elite enemies and strong bosses found later in the game.

How To Use Coiling Wards

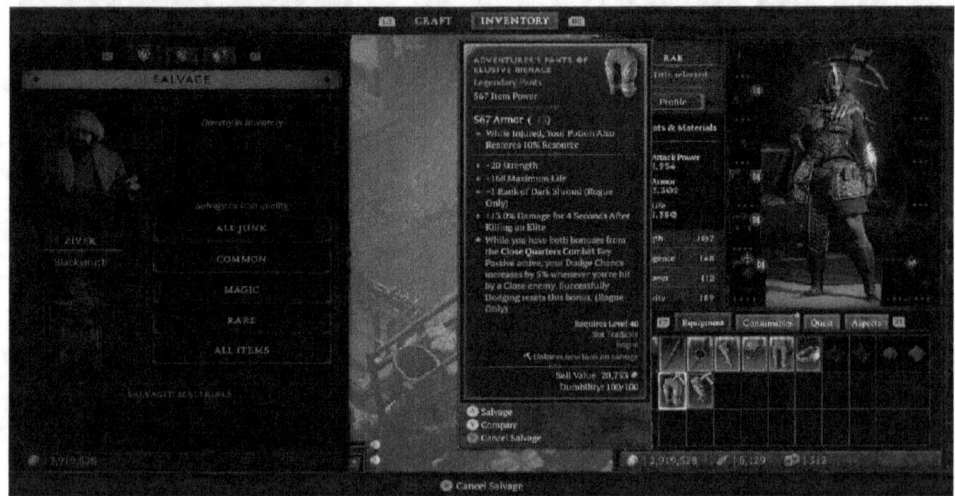

Coiling Wards can be used by a blacksmith to further upgrade legendary armor pieces. This system will have you destroying your less desirable legendary armor pieces to strengthen the ones you like. Make sure you've compared them closely before breaking one down. The Coiling Ward is also only a rare crafting material and is one of the few times the rarities don't match up.

Coiling Wards can only be used on armor pieces, as a different legendary material is used to upgrade legendary weapons. Until later in the game, when you're finalizing your build, it's best to hold onto legendary gear and materials as you may change which stats you're looking for over time. For those wanting to experiment, you can find an infinite number of legendary items over time; you'll just need to grind for them.

How To Switch Weapons As The Barbarian

How To Switch Weapons

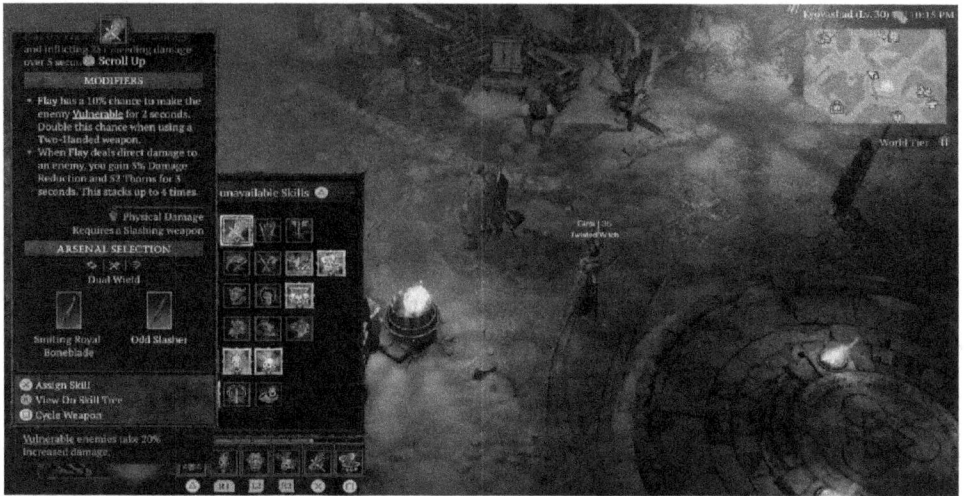

There is no direct way to switch between each weapon at any time that you want. Your weapon selection is assigned to a skill when selecting the skill, meaning the selected weapon will be used when you use its assigned skill in combat. Different skills are associated with the different weapon types in your arsenal. You have two one-handed weapons that count as Dual-Wield, Bludgeoning, and Slashing (depending on your weapon selection), a two-handed weapon that's Slashing, and the other two-handed weapon that is Bludgeoning. Each skill has one of these words under its name, letting you know which weapon can be used when you utilize that particular skill.

While selecting your skills, you're able to decide which weapon will be used with which skill. That weapon is then tied to that skill selection but can be changed at any time when you go back to the Skill Selection Menu. When selecting a skill and reading its description, scroll down to find the Arsenal Selection menu. This will let you decide which weapon to assign.

Flay Skill Description In Menu

When regularly selecting your skills, the game will automatically decide which weapon to assign to that skill based on the total DPS for each weapon when using that skill. While this will often select the better option, there are many bonus abilities on higher-rarity weapons that you may deem more important. Any bonuses to the weapon will only be applied when it is equipped, making it difficult for the game to properly decide what's best for your build with legendary gear and higher. Luckily, it is easy to switch your assigned weapons out of combat, allowing you to test out many different options between battles.

How To Get Abstruse Sigil

What Are Abstruse Sigils?

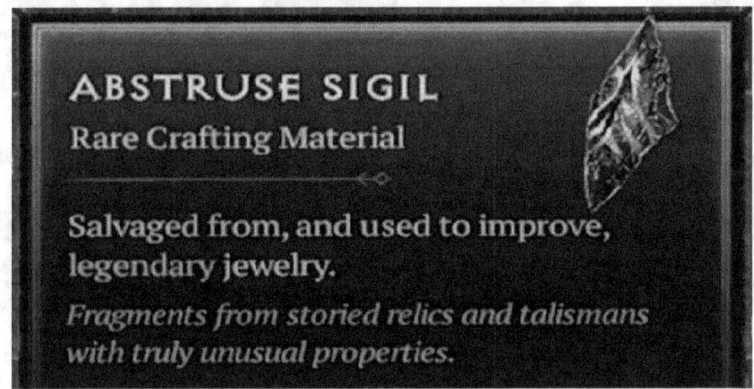

Abstruse Sigils are one of the salvageable materials you will be able to get in Diablo 4. You will not want to spend them needlessly. Instead, it is better to save them up for when you have something you know you will be making use of for a long time. Endgame pieces of gear are perfect candidates for upgrades.

What Do They Do?

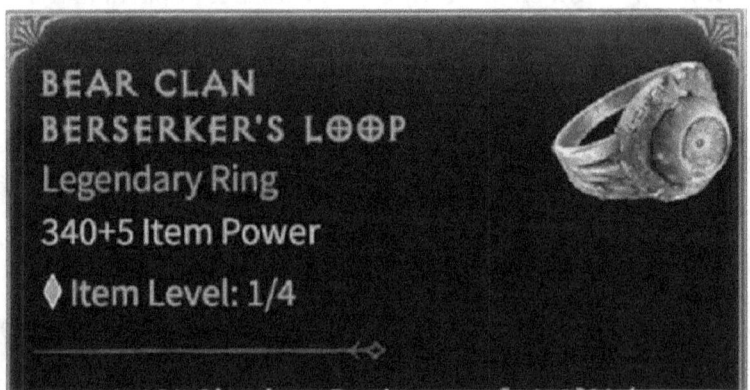

Abstruse Sigils can be used to upgrade your legendary jewelry item up to level 4.

How Do You Use Abstruse Sigils?

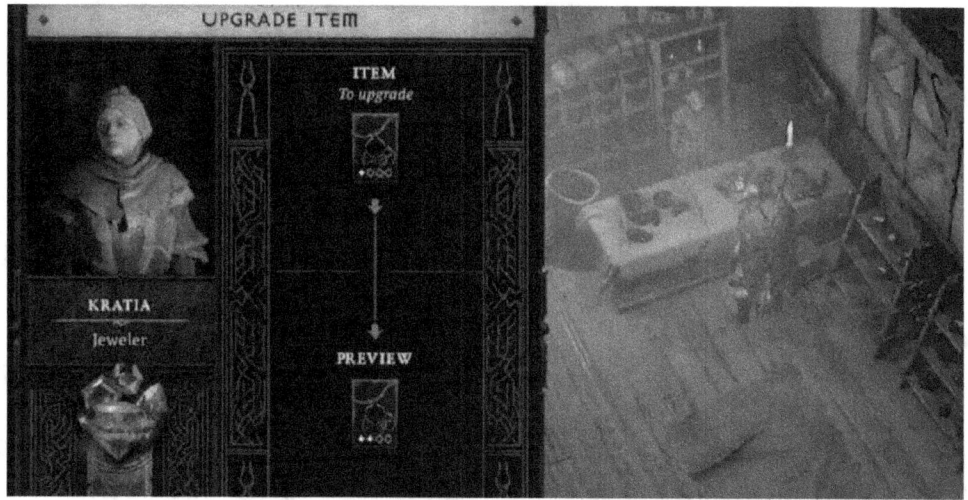

To use these materials, you will start by interacting with a blacksmith. Select the "Upgrade Jewelry" choice. The Jewelry item must be of Legendary Rarity.

Where Can You Find It?

You can acquire this material by taking Legendary Jewelry in your inventory to one of the game's many blacksmiths and salvaging it. You will also get additional materials when salvaging Legendary Jewelry, each with its own purpose. This means there are no specific farm locations for this material. You will need to play the game in order to get enemies to drop legendary jewelry. You will then be able to salvage it for Abstruse Sigils.

Can You Increase The Rate You Acquire Abstruse Sigils?

Yes, the game features the option to increase the difficulty of the game. The higher the difficulty, the better the loot. It is recommended you always play on the highest difficulty you can handle. Do this to get the best drop rates you can achieve, as this will dramatically speed up your progression through the game.

Astaroth Explained

Astaroth is the demonic boss at the end of Act 2. This takes place in an instanced version of Cerrigar. During the cut scenes leading up to the fight, you'll see him in all his terrifying glory atop his mount - The Amalgam of Hatred.

❖ Abilities Of The Enemy

Astaroth has an attack pattern similar to what you'd expect from a hulking, mounted combatant. His attacks are powerful but slow. Most of the demon's damage is done in a cone in front of him, although he is able to call down AoE attacks occasionally.

The main threats in the fight are:

- His staff swing
- The flaming breath attack of his mount
- The fireballs (his AoE)

He will also sometimes call Lycans into the fight with a howl, but these shrimp minions mostly provide fodder for players whose builds require enemy kills.

❖ Phases Of The Fight

Astaroth's health bar is divided into three sections to reflect the three phases of the fight. However, unlike other bosses, Astaroth does not gain new abilities in each phase. Instead, his attack rotation speeds up, and he runs to a new section of the arena.

To help players sustain themselves through the fight, health potions will spawn whenever Astaroth enters a new phase. This seems to be 2–3 health potions per phase, but it is currently unknown whether the amount of potions goes down at higher difficulties.

Tips To Prepare For Astaroth

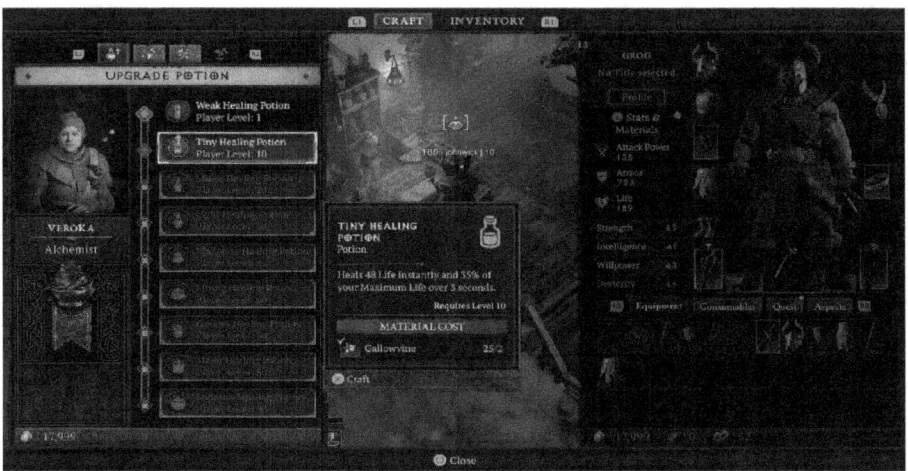

When you are approaching this boss, it is very well-telegraphed. You even fought a weaker version of Astaroth's mount in a previous boss battle. Due to its telegraphed nature, players should be able to prepare to their heart's content.

While there are many small things you can do to give yourself an edge, your priority should be your gear and acquiring a specific consumable.

❖ *Preparing Your Gear*

Gear in Diablo 4 is responsible for your character's power level more than anything else. As a result, wearing subpar or damaged gear into a big fight is a major disadvantage. Just before entering the boss arena (encountered while running through ruined Cerrigar) it is wise to teleport back to town to put on your latest and best gear. While you're there, repair all your gear, and maybe even upgrade a couple of pieces.

❖ *Acquiring Consumables*

A mechanic that is new in Diablo 4, and thus commonly overlooked by veteran players, are elixirs. The Alchemist sells them in the second tab of their menu for cheap. They only cost a couple of the herbs you've been finding all over Sanctuary.

There are a plethora of elixirs with differing effects available, but one of the best when fighting Astaroth is The Elixir of Fire Resistance. Depending on what stage of the game you are playing through, the quality of these elixirs will be different (much like upgrading healing potions).

Strategy When Fighting Astaroth

Once you've begun the fight, there are a few strategies that will help you stay healthy while doing damage.

- Dash forward underneath Astaroth when he winds up for a staff swing or fire cone to avoid the damage. These attacks are very wide and hard to dodge otherwise.

- Take advantage of Astaroth's frequent pauses and slow reaction time to stay behind or to the side of him whenever possible (this essentially eliminates 2/3 of his damage output).

- Dash away from him when the mount bends low to the ground. He will then jump and daze nearby characters.

- Watch for the fireball outlines on the floor, which appear about 1 second before the damage triggers. Walk out of these but try not to dash (you're saving that for other attacks). These circles will linger on the ground for a while after triggering, dealing high burn damage Avoid them at all costs.

With the combination of a Fire Resistance Elixir and staying behind Astaroth, this fight gets much easier. You should be able to dodge most of his other damage and heal through what you cannot dodge. Good luck and happy demon slaying!

How To Get Money, Fast

What Activities In Diablo 4 Give You The Most Gold?

The things that give you the biggest influx of gold in Diablo 4 include:

- Activating a Gold Shrine
- Killing a Treasure Goblin
- Fighting Elite Enemies

However, the things on this list are random spawns, meaning the player won't be able to plan for them. For a more reliable method, look elsewhere.

The Best Way To Farm Gold In Diablo 4

There are a couple of ways to farm gold, but the ones with the highest return tend to involve selling gear and killing mobs in some specific locations. Selling gear or going to enemy-dense areas may not give you as much gold as a gold shrine, but you will be able to do them whenever you like.

❖ *Selling Gear*

Selling gear, the number one choice for gold farming, is easy and straightforward to do. Players receive far more gear than they could ever hope to use in Diablo 4, making it a no-brainer. Additionally, almost every settlement has a vendor ready to buy gear for sizable amounts at the press of a button.

Vendor NPCs decide the price of a gear item based on the rarity (common, magic, rare, or legendary) and then the item level. You can increase your World Tier and play as a high-level character to increase the value of the gear dropped.

The time investment when farming gold by selling gear is heavily dependent on whether you already have the gear, or are collecting it (more on that below). However, considering the hoarding tendencies of the average player you might already have a stash full of shiny junk ripe for selling.

The only downside when using this method is that you'll sacrifice the crafting materials you would have gotten from salvaging, which means that ideally, you'll want to alternate how you dispose of extra gear.

❖ *Overworld Regions With Many Fragile Mobs*

A player fighting mobs in diablo 4

If you want another way to farm gold, then going to a location with many fragile mobs is a good way to go. Not only do monsters drop gold on death, but you can also do any events, shrines, or goblins that spawn while you're there. This method gets more lucrative on higher world tiers, so it scales well into the endgame. Possible locations could include:

- The Shrouded Moors
- The Desolate Highlands
- The Westering Lowlands

Any region with an enemy that summons or turns into many more enemies is a fantastic choice for this method, such as places where Fallen Shamans and Spider Hosts reside. You can also use events that spawn continuous enemies until completed, such as Legion Events or Cull The Wicked.

The Best Ways To Get Equipment Drops

If you want to sell gear for gold but don't have any extra lying around, then you'll want to prioritize running dungeons. Strongholds and Side Dungeons are the best choices since they are numerous and can be run repeatedly (or one after another).

The most efficient dungeons to farm are those with few dead ends and many enemies. An example might be Dead Man's Dredge in The Gale Valley, which players during the beta clocked as a great dungeon to farm. Anica's Claim in the Malnok region is another good candidate.

In early access versions of Diablo 4, a dungeon could be reset by leaving it and re-entering. However, this no longer works in the full release of the game. Instead, the dungeon will reset when the player has killed the boss at the end.

The Honorable Mention: Trading

While trading gear with other players can be lucrative, it is not the best method. This is because it requires more luck and obsessive in-game knowledge to be successful. NPCs buy gear based on item level for a reliable price, while other players buy gear based on rolled stats at ever-changing prices.

If you'd like to dip your toes into the world of gear trading, prioritize rare gear with aspects that have rolled as close to the maximum as possible. Legendary gear cannot be traded.

SHOULD YOU SALVAGE OR SELL GEAR

Salvaging Items

Salvaging items can be extremely helpful for you. When you salvage your armor, you can gain some valuable resources. These resources can help you upgrade your armor or craft items later on. However, it isn't recommended that you upgrade armor until you are later in the game. Early on, you will constantly find better gear. You want to use these resources on armor that you will use for a good amount of time. If you need these resources, you should start salvaging them to collect them.

In addition to those resources, you can obtain Veiled Crystals. These items are given to you when you salvage rare items. They can be used when you imprint Aspects onto your items. You will need certain amounts depending on the Aspect and item. These Aspects are pretty important and can be a huge help if you use them correctly. If you are going to imprint Aspects, start salvaging the rare items you don't need.

You can also salvage items in order to transmog them later at the wardrobe. If there is a hammer on the item when looking at it in your inventory, that means you can salvage it and obtain the cosmetic to transmog later. If you want to be able to have these transmogs for later, make sure you salvage the items rather than sell them.

Selling Items

Selling items can be as helpful as salvaging them. When you sell items, you will only obtain gold. However, this is the main currency in the game, and you will need a good amount while playing. Anytime you are upgrading items, you'll need gold. You can also use this currency to buy items from merchants. If you don't need to collect resources, Veiled Crystals, or transmogs, you may want to just consider selling the items and saving up your money.

How To Reset Dungeons

What Types Of Dungeons Can Reset?

Before diving into the process of resetting dungeons, it's essential to understand the types of dungeons you can reset in Diablo 4. The game features a variety of dungeons, but not all of them can be reset using the methods described in this guide. You can only reset the Normal Dungeons and Nightmare Dungeons in Diablo 4.

Resetting Dungeons

In Diablo 4 beta, resetting the dungeons used to be a feature that players could rely on. However, since then, this feature has been removed. Previously, players were able to reset the dungeon with ease by simply opening up the journal while inside. But with this feature no longer in play, players are now forced to leave the dungeon in order to reset it. There are two ways to leave the dungeon. The first option is to make your way to the entry point and leave from there. Alternatively, you can use the Leave Dungeon option found in the emote wheel. Once you've successfully left the dungeon, wait for around 60 seconds before attempting to re-enter it.

If you happen to be playing online with a friend or in a group, there is a simple and effective way to reset a particular dungeon – by leaving and rejoining the party. Simply navigate to the Social menu and have the lead player in the party select "Leave Party". This will automatically exit the dungeon and reset it to its original state. Once the dungeon has been reset, the lead player can re-enter. Other players can then rejoin the same leader's party, placing them in the new instance of the dungeon that has been fully reset. Following this method ensures a quick and seamless resetting of the dungeon, allowing you to continue your online adventures hassle-free.

How To Craft & Unsocket Gems

The Jeweler

Whereas vendors like the Blacksmith tend to turn into glorified trashcans in the late game, NPCs like the Occultist and the Jeweler will continue to be relevant long past your first playthrough. The Jeweler is where you will:

- Craft gems
- Unsocket gems
- Add sockets to items
- Upgrade jewelry

The number of sockets on a piece of gear, as well as the quality of the gem inside, can make a huge difference to the power of that item - these mechanics shouldn't be ignored.

How To Craft Gems

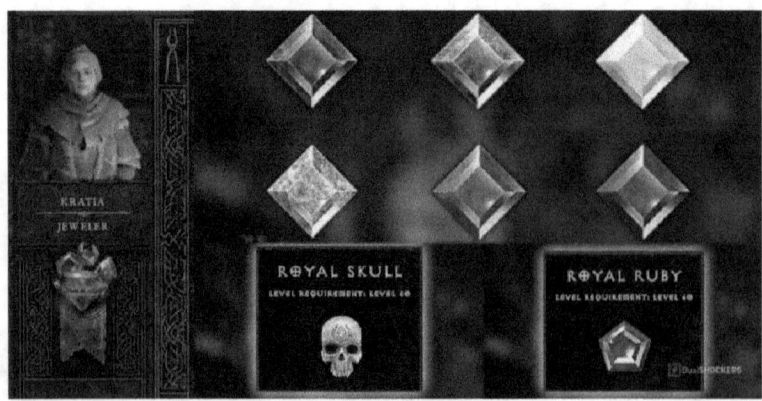

Crafting gems at the Jeweler is a key method of upping your power level in the early stages of the game. Gems are crafted using a handful of resources and can be made into different tiers.

❖ Required Materials

In order to craft gems, players will need a modest amount of gold and three of the previous tier gems of the same type. Gems will drop similarly to gear from enemies and from chests, so you can slowly build up a cache of them to craft into higher-quality versions.

❖ Gem Tiers

There are a total of five gem tiers currently in Diablo 4. These are:

- Crude
- Chipped
- Standard
- Flawless
- Royal

The tier of gems that drops from chests and enemies is dependent on your character level. However, gems that you craft will usually be a higher tier than those you encounter in the wild.

Everything About Gem Sockets

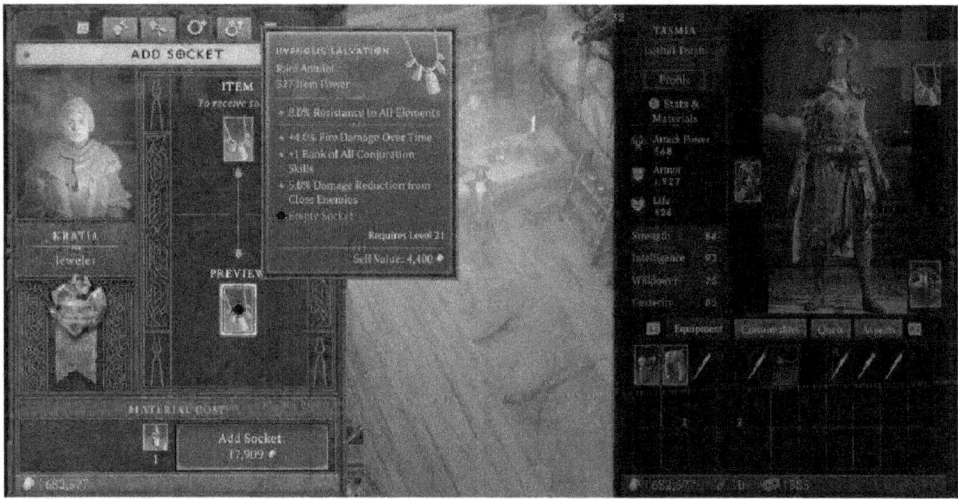

Gem sockets allow you to affix gems to your gear. Some gear will drop with sockets already on it, but you can also add sockets to your favorite gear pieces. In Diablo 3, some gear could not have gem sockets (such as gear sets), but it is currently unknown if this mechanic will make a return.

The bonus granted by your gem is dependent on the type of gear it has been attached to, so be sure to read before dropping things in. You can see what bonus a gem is currently giving to an item by hovering over the gear.

❖ Socketing A Gem

Socketing a gem is very easy in Diablo 4. If you have an item with an empty socket and a gem, simply drag the gem onto the gear piece. This will cause the gem to stop taking up its own inventory slot and instead display inside the gear piece. However, once a gem has been socketed, it cannot be unsocketed so easily.

❖ Unsocketing A Gem

To remove a gem from a piece of gear, you'll need to use the relevant menu at the Jeweler. This will look like a pair of pliers and is the second tab for this vendor. Despite it being mildly inconvenient that you must use a Jeweler NPC to retrieve gems from equipment, it does not cost anything.

Always unsocket gems before selling gear. Selling a piece of equipment with a gem inside will cause the gem to disappear, and you will not be able to retrieve it. If you attempt to buy the gear back, the socket will be empty.

❖ Adding Sockets To Gear

Adding a socket to your favorite gear, it's going to cost you a pretty penny. For this reason, it is recommended to wait to add sockets until you have your late-game gear. Adding a socket to an amulet can cost around 18,000 gold and a Shattered Prism (these are difficult to farm).

If you have equipment whose aspects you really love, then adding sockets can be a great way to keep the gear relevant. The number of sockets any one piece of gear can hold depend on its type:

- Helm - 1 Socket
- Chest - 2 Sockets
- Pants - 2 Sockets
- Amulet - 1 Socket
- Ring - 1 Socket
- 1-Handed Weapon - 1 Socket

- 2-Handed Weapon - 2 Socket
- Bow - 2 Socket
- Focus - 1 Socket

Once a gear item has a socket, there does not appear to be any way to remove it or otherwise recover the materials.

WHERE TO GET DEMON'S HEARTS

Where Do You Get Demon's Hearts From?

You will be able to get Demon's Hearts from slaying enemies in the game. You will need to slay specifically demon enemies in order for them to drop, though. Having a higher world tier can help with the drop rate.

Where Can You Farm Demon's Heart's From?

Luckily for players, there is an enemy that players can farm for these Demon's Hearts. The enemy in question is Almunn. Move to the Area indicated on the map; this location is part of the Dry Steppes and is along The Scarred Coast. After you have slain Almunn, you can log out and log back in for a chance to make him respawn. Which is actually faster than if you needed to fast travel away and back again. Thankfully he is not a Super Unique Monster, which does not respawn when you try this.

What Are Demon's Hearts Used For?

These Monster Parts have two options for upgrading your potions. They can be used to upgrade your healing potion to a Moderate Healing Potion. These potions will heal you for 255 Life instantly and also restore 35 percent of your maximum Life over the course of the next 3 seconds. You will need 5 Demon's Hearts, along with 20 Gallowvine, 12 Howlers Moss and 900 gold. The second upgrade provided using this material is the Superior Healing Potion. This is a lot more resource costly, having you require 20 Demon's Hearts, along with 20 Angelbreath, 36 Blightshade, 10 Forgotten Souls, 10 Fiend Rose, 20 Grave Dust, 36 Howler Moss, and 12500 gold. This will be worth spending, as it will instantly heal you 1,274 Life and an additional 35 Percent of your total Life over the next 3 seconds. You will need to accrue quite a lot of gold for this upgrade.

How To Get Crushed Beast Bones

Crushed Beast Bones are rare items used to enhance your health potions in Diablo 4. However, acquiring these rare items is not an easy task. To obtain them, players must take down beast-type enemies, such as bears, werewolves, and spiders. Since these bones are not commonly dropped, players must defeat a significant number of these monsters to collect a meaningful amount of Crushed Beast Bones.

Crushed Beast Bones Farming Locations

When it comes to farming Crushed Beast Bones, the best locations to focus on are Scosglen and the Dry Steppes. These regions have a higher likelihood of beast-type enemies dropping Crushed Beast Bones compared to other areas, such as the Fractured Peaks.

❖ *Scosglen*

Scosglen is an area known for its abundance of beast-type enemies. The Eastern part of Scosglen, specifically the Highland Wilds, is an excellent spot to farm Crushed Beast Bones. In this area, you will find the Whispering Pines dungeon, which houses numerous beast-type enemies, making it an optimal location for farming.

❖ *Dry Steppes*

The Dry Steppes is another region with a high concentration of beast-type enemies. As you progress through the game and explore this area, focus on defeating all beasts you encounter. Doing so will increase your chances of finding Crushed Beast Bones.

Tips & Tricks For Farming Crushed Beast Bones

Here are some tips & tricks for farming Crushed Beast Bones in Diablo 4:

- Focus on farming Crushed Beast Bones in Scosglen and Dry Steppes, as the drop rate is higher in these locations.
- Target giant monsters like Werebeasts, Lycans, and bears for a higher chance of obtaining Crushed Beast Bones.
- Make use of cellar chests in the Frosty Mine, Flooded Mine, and Disturbed Grave as additional sources of Crushed Beast Bones.

- Be patient when farming Crushed Beast Bones, as the drop rate can be low.

Uses Of Crushed Beast Bones

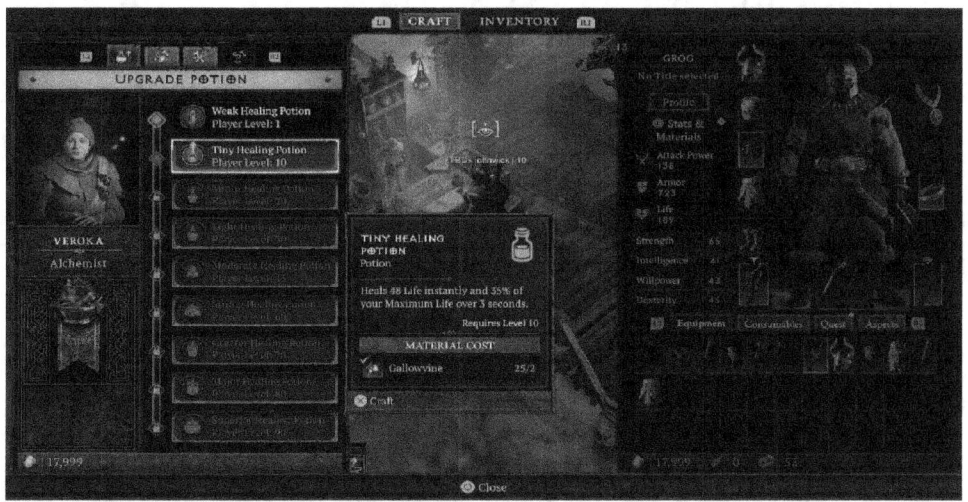

As mentioned earlier, Crushed Beast Bones are used for upgrading the healing potions in Diablo 4. Starting with the basic Weak Healing Potion available at the game's outset, the potions increase in potency as you gain levels. At level 10, you'll unlock the Tiny Healing Potion, followed by the Minor Healing Potion at level 20, and so on. Finally, at level 30, players can upgrade their Minor Healing Potion to the Light Healing Potion. To achieve this, you will need five Crushed Beast Bones, along with 20 Gallowvine, 10 Biteberry, and 470 gold.

WHERE TO GET PALETONGUES

Where Do You Get Paletongues From

Paletongues are said to be inside the mouths of evil humans, this means you won't find it in the more beast-like abominations in the game and can expect it to drop from the more wicked humanoid ones. You can increase your odds by cranking up the world tier difficulty for a higher drop rate.

Where Can You Farm Paletongues

Super Unique Enemies do not respawn, meaning after fighting one that does drop Paletongues, you won't be able to come back for more. However, there is an elite from whom you can farm Paletongues. As luck should have it, they are also the same enemy that you can farm other monster parts from as well. This enemy is named Almunn, and they can be found at the Dry Steppes Location along The Scarred Coast.

What Are Paletongues Used For

Paletongues can be brought to the Alchemist to upgrade your potions. Using them, you will be able to acquire the following options. Strong Healing Potion, for instantly healing yourself 378 Life, as well as 35 percent of your total Life over the next 3 seconds. Chorus Of War, for increasing all of your stats by 40 and giving you a 5 percent increase to your crit and overpower.

Soothing Spices will grant you a 10 percent increase to all of your resistances and grant you 150 armor for every player ally near you. Spirit Dance will increase your dodge chance by 5 percent for each player ally that is near you. Lastly, Paletongues can be used for Blessed Guide. Blessed Guide will increase your Willpower by 25 for each player ally that is near you. Chorus Of War, Soothing Spices, Spirit Dance and Blessed Guide each have a duration that will last 20 minutes once applied.

WHERE TO GET GRAVE DUST

How To Get Grave Dust

This Monster Part's description reads as follows in the game: "Long exposure to the walking dead imbues this dust with their inverse vitality, used in necromantic alchemies." So you can expect to be rewarded with this drop from vanquishing undead enemies. The higher you set the game's world tier, the more frequently you will get rarer drops.

Grave Dust Farming Location

Like with all Monster Parts, there is a single "Go-to" farming option. This is Almunn. What makes farming Almunn so great is that while you are farming the Monster Part you want, you will also be getting other Monster Parts for useful upgrades as well. This means you will have to farm those materials less when the need for them arises.

Grave Dust Uses

This Monster Part has several uses, starting with upgrading your healing potion game. The Greater Healing Potion will instantly heal you for 559 Life as well as 35 Percent of your Life total over the course of the next 3 seconds.

It will also be able to upgrade to the even more impressive Superior Healing Potion. This will instead instantly heal you by 1274 Life with the 35 Percent healing of your Life total over the course of the next 3 seconds.

Grave Dust can also be used for Chorus Of War to increase all your stats by 40, as well as give you a 5 percent increase to your overpower and crit damage for each nearby player ally. Reddamine Buzz will increase your total Life by 500 for each nearby player ally. Lastly, Sage's Whisper will increase your intelligence by 25 for each player ally that is near you. Chorus Of War, Reddamine Buzz, and Sage's Whisper each will last 20 minutes once used.

How To Get Light Bearer Mount

How To Get Light Bearer Mount

In order to obtain the highly coveted Light Bearer mount, it is required that you pre-order Diablo 4. This incredible reward is available for all editions of the game, including the Standard Edition, and can be obtained by pre-purchasing the game through the official Blizzard store or any authorized retailer. Not only will you secure the Light Bearer mount, but you will also gain access to a plethora of exclusive rewards and benefits.

How To Claim Light Bearer Mount

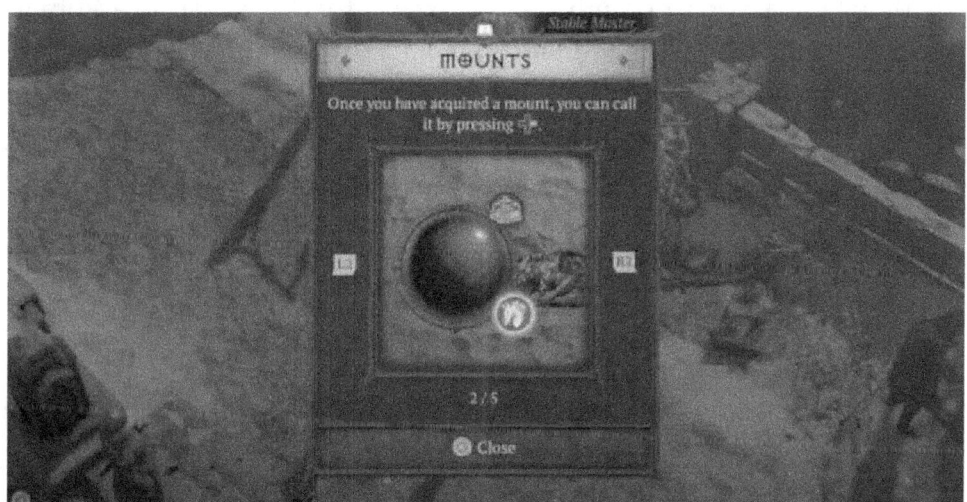

After the game's official release, you can claim your Light Bearer Mount by following these steps:

- Ensure that your Diablo 4 account is linked to the same account used for pre-ordering the game.

- Progress through the main story and complete the side quest "Mount: Donan's Favor" to unlock the mount.

- Once unlocked, the Light Bearer Mount will be available for use throughout your Diablo 4 adventure.

Importance Of Mounts In Diablo 4

Mounts are an indispensable addition to the highly anticipated game Diablo 4, as they significantly impact gameplay in a positive way. The vast open world of the sanctuary can be daunting to explore, but having a reliable mount to traverse it quickly and efficiently is essential. Not only do mounts provide increased mobility, allowing players to travel between locations faster, but they also provide a safe escape in dangerous situations.

Diablo 4 Editions & Pre-Order Rewards

Diablo 4 is available in three different editions, each offering various rewards and bonuses. These editions include:

- Standard Edition: This edition comes with the base game, the Light Bearer Mount, and the Caparison of Faith Mount Armor as a pre-order reward.

- Digital Deluxe Edition: Along with the base game, the Light Bearer Mount, Caparison of Faith Mount Armor, the Digital Deluxe Edition includes the Temptation Mount, Hellborn Carapace Mount Armor, and additional digital content.

- Ultimate Edition: This edition offers the most extensive collection of rewards, including everything from Standard and Digital Edition, along with additional in-game rewards.

HOW TO CLEAR THE RUINS OF QARA-YISU STRONGHOLD

Find And Destroy The Infernal Spires

There are three Infernal Spires spread around the ruins, and the fight to destroy each Spire is the same every time. Once you approach a Spire, you'll be attacked by a group of demons led by two Elites. All these Elites make the Ruins of Qara-Yisu perfect for some fast XP. Focus on the non-Elite caster demons first because their magic attacks can stack up against you very quickly.

One of the two Elite demons that spawn each time will have a name, and one will be called "Cursed Yasuni." Target the Cursed Yasuni next. They have an additional magical buff and can actually deal more damage than the named demons. The Infernal Spires themselves are rather helpless. If they aren't destroyed by AOE damage at some point, they can be taken care of very easily at this point.

This Stronghold is arranged more or less in a circular pattern, with many alternate routes between. After clearing your first Infernal Spire, circle around in either direction to find the next one. You can also check the world map and zoom in on your location to see their icons.

How To Defeat Utulku, The Voice Below

All throughout your conquest of the Ruins of Yara-Qisu, you'll notice the sounds of a disembodied voice growing angry at your success. That voice belongs to Utulku, a masterfully powerful demon warlock. You'll fight him and his legion after you destroy all three Infernal Spires. This is the kind of fight you'll want to upgrade potions for in Diablo 4.

Legion is an adequate word for the vast number of demons that Utulku spawns at the start of the encounter. Clear out these mobs as quickly as possible so that you can start to deal with the boss itself. Periodically, Utulku will summon more demons that you should dispatch with similar haste.

But once the first vast army is cleared, the demon wizard actually doesn't seem to spawn very often. Utulku's main move is actually a series of lightning bolts. Watch out for the red rings, which show where the lightning bolts are going to strike. At first, it'll only cast two bolts at a time, rising to five lightning bolts as you start to get closer to victory. Keep dodging or finding other ways to evade those bolts, and you'll conquer this Stronghold in no time.

How To Clear The Onyx Watchtower Stronghold

Slay The Captain's Lieutenants

The first objective for this Stronghold actually involves destroying objects and defeating the general groups of bandits. But that's easily done while pursuing the Lieutenants. Just be sure to destroy any supply carts, tents, or support beams that you come across.

Once you enter the Onyx Watchtower, you should go over to the western side to fight Crocus the Greedy. He'll drop the Storeroom Key that will unlock the gate over on the eastern side, which leads to another Lieutenant and a group of bandits. None of these Elites are particularly dangerous. After clearing the Storeroom, go back west to climb the watchtower.

Thidrek, the Beast-Master, is one of the tougher enemies in the Onyx Watchtower. He has a devastating knockdown ability in addition to poison. But the real threat is that he keeps Elite beasts in cages around him. If you can help it, do not break the cages while fighting Thidrek. Use any Crowd Control moves you have to get the Beast-Master away from his captives.

The final Lieutenant to fight is Talida. She's quite deadly with her Multishot move and paired with her Mortar ability, she has excellent attacks for both long and close range. Fortunately for us, she's just not very tough. Evade her attacks until you can unleash all of your own most powerful moves.

Slay Captain Ezmin

After defeating the last of the Lieutenants, the gate at the center of the Onyx Watchtower will open automatically. In the alcove beyond, you'll find Captain Ezmin waiting for you. She has some pretty strong mortar attacks, but her true power is repeatedly summoning hordes of bandits.

This is actually a really easy boss fight compared to the others in Diablo 4. Ignore the endlessly spawning bandits and keep attacking Captain Ezmin. Avoid the burning rings that she summons on the ground at all costs. If you do feel like taking out some of the additional bandits during the fight, then at least focus on the Firebrands. That will give you the most free time to take down the boss herself. Then turn in the conquest and unlock a well-earned Renown increase.

How To Clear Temple Of Rot Stronghold

Slay The Cannibal Champions

The quickest way to reach the Temple of Rot is by traveling directly north from Jirandai, on the border with Kehjistan. After gaining entrance to the main Temple grounds, you'll face Bostar, the Breaker. This Elite has an annoying Terrify ability that can send you running in Fear. Just be sure to wait until you're back inside the bubble created by its Suppressor enchantment, which blocks outside ranged attacks.

The door behind Bostar remains locked, so you'll have to follow the pathway around to the left. Reach the main Temple building itself and enter to face Corpse Spawn, Child of the Devourer. This Champion has Terrify and Poison Enchanted attacks. Worst of all are the poison pools created by its Plaguebearer effect. Avoid these at all costs.

Razorface, the Carrion Zealout, waits further inside the Temple of Rot. He can create both Frozen and Explosive bubbles, sometimes over the same spot. On top of those, his Waller enchantment can block off your escape routes. Watch your environment, and avoid staying too close to existing walls so that you can always escape.

The last and most distant of Molqarth's Champions is Arden, the Ravenous. You can find him way down south of the Temple. Arden's Lightning Enchanted attacks are further enhanced by his rare Shock Lance ability. He's also a Teleporter, so wait until after he jumps before you use your most powerful attacks.

Locate Molqarth's Lair

Once you finally defeat the last of his champions, it's time to hunt down Molqarth himself. He's located at the ritual circle all the way to the far north side of the Temple of Rot. But as you approach the final path, you'll be greeted by one last mini-boss challenge.

The three Molqarth's Chosen will magically appear to stop you just before the final path. All three are Vampiric and have an additional powerful effect to boot. Bonecruncher has Chilling Wind, which creates an icy pillar to slow you and your projectiles. Fleshtearer summons Electrified Obelisks that send bolts between each other. And Blooddrinker has Hellbound, which chains you in place.

Having all three of these monstrosities pounce on top of you with no warning can be a little overwhelming. With the rest of the Temple already cleared, you have plenty of space to fall back. Then either slay one Chosen at a time or all at once, but whatever you do, don't let up. The Vampiric buff lets them heal too quickly.

Slay Molqarth

Once you reach Molqarth, The Hungerer, at the Temple of Rot's ritual circle, you may notice the egg that sits on a pedestal before him. Molqarth will seek out identical eggs all around and eat them to restore some Life during the fight. Going around the room and destroying the eggs first can save you some trouble. It's highly recommended that you upgrade your healing potion capacity before fighting Molqarth as well.

The Hungerer can dish out some pretty heavy damage, but as long as you avoid his signature slamming move, slaying him isn't too difficult. At certain times, he'll lift his hammer to prepare an earth-shattering slam that sends out waves in a cone shape. Hide behind a pillar if you must, but it's better to get behind him instead so that you can keep hitting him. Molqarth doesn't have much health compared to other Stronghold bosses for an interesting reason.

Slay The Spawn Of Molqarth

As soon as you succeed in slaying Molqarth, the final and toughest stage of the Temple of Rot will begin immediately. The Spawn of Molqarth can deal unbelievably high melee damage, as well as create a Poison pool on the ground and fire Poison projectiles at you. It can also leap right to your location to continue the melee assault.

Fortunately, this thing has even less health than Molqarth. Just keep moving to avoid constant melee attacks as well as the various Poison moves, and never stay in the same spot for more than a few seconds. After slaying the Spawn of Molqarth, you'll be free to reclaim this Stronghold for the people of Sanctuary and the associated Renown boost that goes with it.

WHERE TO FIND THE ENTRANCE TO WEEPING CAIRNS

Finding The Entrance

The Weeping Cairns is a dungeon located in the Scosglen region of Diablo 4. It is associated with the Encroaching Shadows quest, which is an essential part of the game's main campaign. To gain access to this mystical dungeon, you must make your way to the Bronagh Expanse. Here, you will encounter a host of enemies, including Wargs, Thorn Beasts, and Blood Clan Marauders. Overcoming these hurdles will not only clear your path to the Weeping Cairns, but it will also yield you valuable rewards.

After doing so, a footprint will be visible on the ground near a cliff. Make your way up the cliff, and continue straight ahead until you come to a gap that you must leap across to gain entry into the Valley of Passing. Follow the path, and to the end of it, you will find a menacing stone wall. This serves as the entrance to the Weeping Cairns.

Although the entrance is sealed, there is a message to be found there. As Yorin diligently attempts to open the gate, you may find yourselves under attack from a slew of malicious spirits. You must defend your ally from the evil spirits that appears. Once the final foe, Ruhana the Anguished, has been vanquished, the entrance to the Weeping Cairns will be opened.

HOW TO BEAT AIRIDAH

Airidah Explained

Airidah is a boss with a fast attacking ranged caster who survives by virtue of being mobile or invulnerable for a good portion of the fight. She will frequently become mist, teleporting away from the player while raining down lightning strikes and throwing out whirlwinds.

Twice during the fight, she will surround herself in the wind and summon Wraiths. The first time there will be two, while on the second, there will be four. You will need to burst these wraiths down in order to continue attacking her.

Due to her lightning attack's speed, it's very difficult to dodge all of Airidah's damage. However, this is usually okay - her lightning strikes don't hit very hard. The whirlwinds hurt, however, so it is more important to dodge them (tips on that later).

Tips To Prepare For Airidah

Fighting Airidah is the last big boss encounter before Astaroth, the final boss of Act 2. At this point, you'll likely have stumbled your way into eligibility for some power-level upgrades. Before heading into The Apex of Misery, take a visit to the Alchemist, Jeweler, and Blacksmith to see what you can add to your arsenal.

❖ *Gear*

Taking a quick trip to the Jeweler and Blacksmith prior to any boss fight is a good idea. You can use these NPCs to go through a quick power level checklist and empty your inventory to make ready for that sweet, sweet loot. Before starting the fight with Airidah:

- Repair your gear
- Salvage unwanted gear
- Fill any empty sockets
- Upgrade key gear

And, of course, it goes without saying that you should be wearing the best gear you have. Unless the item has an aspect you love, the best gear will be that which has the highest item level (visible just under the name of the item).

If you don't have a particularly good item for a certain slot, consider equipping one that gives you resistance to Lightning damage. This is always a good start when fighting Airidah. Jewelry with elemental resistance, in particular, is very common.

❖ Healing Potions

Depending on your World Tier, you should have access to a potion upgrade such as Tiny Healing Potions (level 10), Minor Healing Potions (level 20), and maybe even Light Healing Potions (level 30). It can be tempting to forget to purchase this upgrade or to forgo it if you don't have the required Crushed Beast Bones but don't. It's very difficult to avoid taking any damage while fighting Airidah, and potion upgrades massively increase your sustain.

❖ Elixirs

Airidah is a boss who overwhelmingly does Lightning damage. Her attacks will not do massive damage, but they'll slowly and surely chip away at you. If you're struggling to sustain even after upgrading your potions, you can purchase an Elixir of Lightning Resistance to give you an edge. Elixirs are found at the Alchemist, and the resistance ones are dirt cheap to make.

Strategy When Fighting Airidah

While fighting Airidah, mobility is key. The Lightning strikes will spawn under your feet but have a slight delay. The best way to avoid them is to never stop moving. You will also need to be quick on your toes to damage her while she teleports around the arena. This fight tends to be a struggle for melee characters.

The most important attack to avoid in this fight are the Whirlwinds, as they hit hard and knock down your character. This usually results in getting hit by enough lightning to kill you (or at least make it close). As an added challenge, the whirlwinds will follow the player for several seconds. You don't want to be too close to Airidah when these spawn, and the cue for when she makes this attack isn't very clear. The only warning is that she'll raise her arms a little right before they spawn.

To dodge them, you can dash through them while using an ability that makes you invulnerable (several classes have this, notably, the Necromancer's Blood Mist can be used to great effect here). This will trigger the explosion without dealing any damage to you. If you don't have the option to do this, running away until they despawn is your only option.

WHERE TO GET FIEND ROSE

Where To Find Fiend Roses

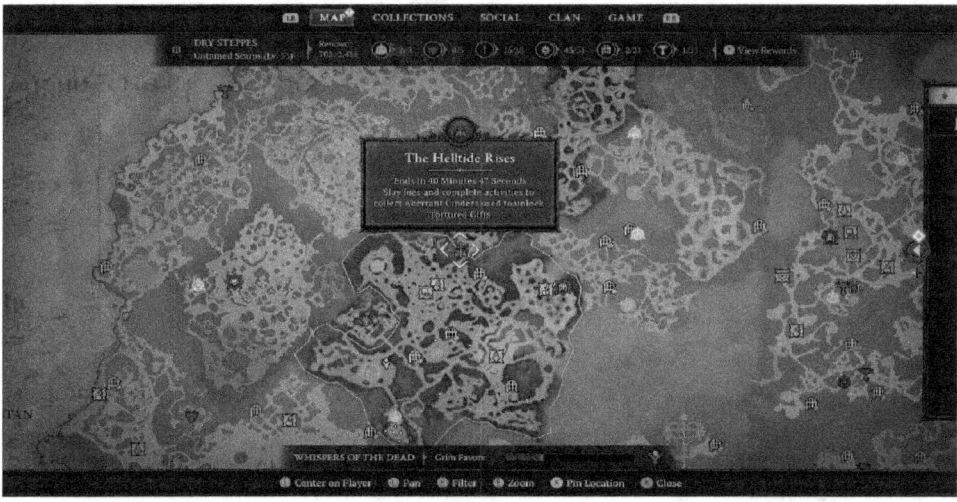

Fiend Roses are found only in the end-game content, as you'll first have to beat the campaign and complete the Cathedral Of Light Capstone dungeon to unlock World Tier 3. While playing in World Tier 3 or higher, there will be a new random event known as Helltides. Helltides infect an area of the map for a one-hour event, greatly strengthening the monsters of that area but giving you more loot to find. Much like World Bosses, Helltide events run off of the real-world clock, meaning you should prioritize these events the minute they spawn. Enemies in the Helltide will also be slightly higher level than your character, making sure they are always a challenge to survive through.

In these Helltide-affected areas will be a demonic flower that blooms, which players can pluck to obtain Fiend Roses. After seeing a Helltide event begin, simply run around in the infected areas, and you'll occasionally find the demonic-looking flowers. Fiend Roses can also be found in the special chests that spawn during Helltide events, but they don't have a high or reliable drop rate, making it best to continue exploring the whole infected area looking for them. These chests are opened using the special cinders currency only dropped during the Helltide event for those wanting to open the chests.

How To Use Fiend Roses

After obtaining a Fiend Rose, you'll need to head to the occultist. Select which legendary gear piece you wish to tinker with, and by using the Fiend Rose, select which attribute you wish to replace and the new attribute to take its place. Fiend Roses are rare to come by but are well worth the effort to help you create the perfect legendary gear piece to round out your build. Given Fiend Roses rarity, it's best to be careful with which weapons you want to respec.

HOW TO BEAT TCHORT

Tchort, Herald Of Lilith

Tchort is a boss found in the later half of Act 1. Her arena, called the Desecrated Archives, is a large circular room with a book at the center. The major threats in this fight are the many attacks of Tchort and the cyclone surrounding the book.

❖ *The Book*

The book is an environmental hazard in this fight. The cyclone surrounding the book at the center will slow you down and deal damage over time. While you may occasionally get pushed into this area or need to use it to dodge something else, you should try to avoid it as much as possible.

Preparing To Fight Tchort

You won't get too much lead-up to the Fight with Tchort, as it occurs just after your encounter with Vhenard. However, it's always useful to make sure that your gear is repaired and your potions upgraded. You can create a portal back to town to do this just before triggering the boss fight (the last room where you can leave is the one with the blue portal on the left side).

Your gear gets damaged each time you die, causing the statistics to become lower. This means that you'll want to repair it if you fail the fight against Tchort and need to try again.

You could also bring an elixir into this fight with you, such as an Elixir of Acrobatics. This will reduce the cooldown on your evade and allow you to dodge attacks more easily.

Strategies For Fighting Tchort

Tchort has a number of attacks to keep the player on their toes, as well as a built-in environmental hazard in her arena. However, these should be fairly easy to avoid, as they do not hone onto the player.

❖ Basic Attacks

Tchort has two basic attacks that are used when the player is semi-close to her. These are a swipe with claws and three balls of red lightning shot in a cone. She will swipe if you are in melee range and shoot if you move away. These attacks can be dodged by moving to the side.

❖ Lightning Jump

If the player ever moves too far away from Tchort, she will close the distance by teleporting. Upon landing next to you, a lightning shockwave goes off. To dodge this, try not to stand still (especially if you are on the other side of the arena from her).

❖ Summoning

Occasionally, Tchort will pause her onslaught to summon fireballs across the area. A pentagram appears under her feet during the channel, making this attack very telegraphed. Once the channel is complete, balls of fire will appear on the floor and, after a short duration, explode. You can hide in the book Cyclone during this attack if you cannot get anywhere else safe.

❖ Lightning Push

During the final phase of the fight, Tchort will begin to try pushing you around the arena with a wave of lightning. This will often shove you into the cyclone at the center and is probably the most difficult to avoid. Ideally, you'll want to avoid positioning yourself between Tchort and the cyclone so that she doesn't push you into it.

How To Gain Experience & Level Up Quickly

How To Earn Experience

The most basic way of earning experience is by killing demons found in the world. With a setting full of foes, simply running around and killing everything you find will consistently earn you experience. You will also find stronger enemies with much higher stats and special abilities that make them more challenging. These enemies give you more experience than their weaker counterparts.

Players will also be rewarded with large sums of experience for finishing quests. Side quests will offer a decent amount of bonus experience as a reward. Completing main quests will offer higher amounts of experience. Completing quests will reward you with experience and sometimes loot upon completion. Quests also bring you face-to-face with many demons to kill for more experience along the way.

Fighting Together

Diablo 4 has made many steps to being a multiplayer experience where you can play with friends or random people you come across in Sanctuary. For those engaging in the game's multiplayer aspects, you'll also get XP faster. Those playing in a party of two or more people will receive a bonus of 10% XP across the board. For those playing solo but still running into players in the world, you'll gain an additional 5% XP simply by fighting the same enemies. This is especially helpful in World Events, where you're more likely to come across other players and will be fighting many powerful enemies.

World Tiers And Challenging Areas

When you first start the game, players will be given access to the first two World Tiers. World Tier 1 is the easiest and offers no bonuses for playing on it. Those who play on Veteran or any of the higher tiers will gain increased XP with each tier. To maximize your XP gain, play on the highest World Tier you can, and quickly unlock the later two after completing the main story. There are also areas of the game that scale enemies to be stronger than the player, such as Strongholds and Helltide events. These areas are great places to farm for XP as the higher-leveled enemies naturally drop more XP than what you'll usually find.

Using Elixirs

Elixirs are unique potions that give more benefits than your usual healing potions. Elixirs often have specific buffs to help you in fights but also give a small boost in XP for a short period of time. While this bonus is only small, it's worthwhile to stack onto other XP boosts to maximize play sessions and level up quickly. The main use of Elixirs may not be the additional XP, but it is worth using them for grinding.

HOW TO MAKE & USE ELIXIRS

What Are Elixirs?

Elixirs are an essential part of Diablo 4 as they grant temporary stat boosts and other benefits to your character. These consumables offer a plethora of improvements to all aspects of gameplay, including increasing damage output, enhancing elemental resistances, and providing experience boosts. Most Elixirs remain active for around 30 minutes, so they are ideal for undertaking challenging content like Strongholds or World Bosses.

How To Make Elixir In Diablo 4

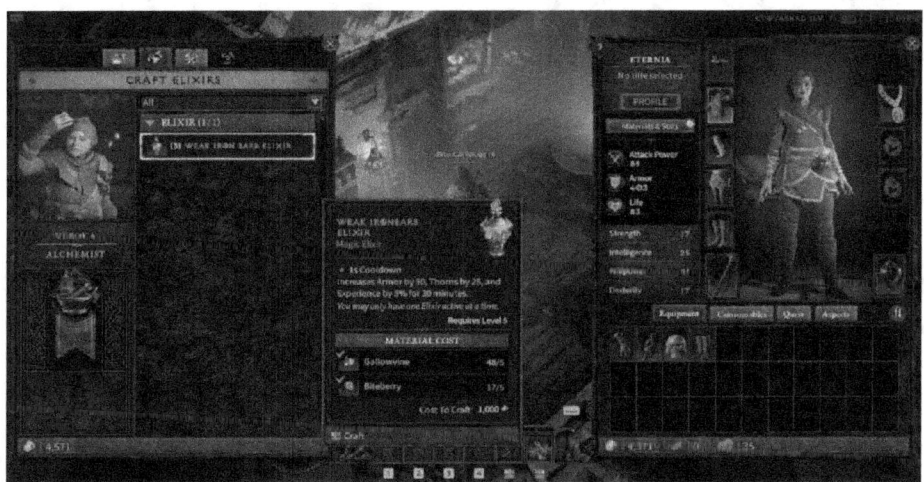

In order to craft Elixirs, you will first need to gather the necessary reagents. These include Herbs and Monster Parts. The herbs can be found in the glowing plants scattered throughout the game world, while the monster parts can be obtained by defeating enemies. Keep your eyes peeled for nodes in the wilds, as these can be harvested for valuable crafting materials.

Once you've gathered a sufficient amount of reagents, locate one of the Alchemists in major towns across the region. These Alchemists are marked on the map with a mortar and pestle icon. Once you find one, interact with them and navigate to the Elixir menu on the right. From there, browse the available Elixirs, which will vary in strength and cost. Select the desired Elixir and confirm the crafting process.

The Alchemist provides a wide range of 24 different types of Elixirs that can be crafted. The Elixirs range from basic resistances to more powerful concoctions, each with its own unique capabilities and rarity. The price for each of the Elixirs is dependent on various factors, such as the strength and rarity of the potion being brewed. The weaker mixtures, for instance, require only herbs and a small amount of gold, whereas the more potent ones demand rarer ingredients and large sums of currency.

All Elixirs provide a 30-minute buff, making them ideal for grinding levels, farming Paragon Points, or tackling challenges, such as bosses, dungeons, and events.

How To Use Elixirs In Diablo 4

There are two ways to use Elixirs in Diablo 4:

❖ *Consumables Menu*

- Open your inventory and navigate to the Consumables tab.
- Browse your collection of crafted Elixirs.
- Choose your desired Elixir and consume it to activate its effects.

❖ *Emote Wheel*

- Press 'E' on your keyboard or up on your d-pad to open the emote wheel.
- Navigate to the Consumables menu.
- Choose your desired Elixir and consume it to activate its effects.

It's important to note that you can only have one active Elixir at a time, and consuming a second Elixir will replace the effects of the first.

Adding Elixirs To Your Emote Wheel

To optimize your Elixir usage and access them more efficiently, you can add them to your action wheel. To do this, follow these steps:

- Press the 'E' or up arrow on your d-pad to open the emote wheel.
- Click the 'Customize' button to modify your emote wheel.
- Navigate to the Consumables menu.
- Select the desired Elixir and drag it to the appropriate spot on the wheel.
- Click Save Changes to update the Emote Wheel.

With your Elixirs added to the action wheel, you can quickly access and consume them mid-battle or on the go.

Optimizing Elixir Use

Elixirs can be a valuable asset in high World Tiers and challenging areas, so it's essential to maintain a stockpile and use them strategically. Consider the following tips to optimize your Elixir usage:

- Plan ahead and craft Elixirs suited to specific challenges, such as elemental resistance potions for bosses with powerful elemental attacks.
- Rotate your Elixirs based on the situation, using damage-boosting potions for mob-clearing and defensive ones for boss encounters.
- Keep a variety of Elixirs on hand to adapt to changing circumstances and maximize their utility.

Elixirs are potent tools in Diablo 4, offering a variety of enhancements and benefits to help you overcome the challenges of Sanctuary. By gathering ingredients, locating Alchemists, and crafting a diverse selection of potions, you'll be well-equipped to face the demonic hordes and emerge victorious. Now that you know how to make and use Elixirs in Diablo 4, it's time to venture forth and conquer the darkness.

HOW TO DEFEAT WANDERING DEATH WORLD BOSS

Preparing For The Wandering Death

Fighting the Wandering Death shouldn't be taken lightly; if you plan to fight him, consider taking a portal back to town for a quick elixir and examination of your gear. When looking over your layout, consider how well-suited it is to deal with The Wandering Death's attacks.

❖ *Damage Type*

The first step in taking on a World Boss is knowing what their primary damage type is. In the case of Wandering Death, this will be Shadow damage and physical damage. Additionally, most of the boss' attacks are AoE based and can be dodged.

This means that a good way to prepare has Elixirs and gear with the following:

- Shadow resistance
- Movement speed
- Armor

Obviously, you won't want to change out gear that gives you levels in your main skill or provides key aspects of your build, but Elixirs are dirt cheap and easy to throw on before the fight. Remember, you can only have one active at a time.

❖ *How To Tell When The Wandering Death Is Spawning*

The Wandering Death is thought to spawn every 4–6 hours. You will see an icon over the boss arena on your map shortly before Wandering Death spawns if you are:

- Playing a character who has beaten the main campaign
- Are in at least World Tier 3

Once you see that icon, gather your stuff and book it to the location, as the arena will lock out late arrivals shortly after the battle begins.

❖ *Number Of Players Required*

World Bosses are meant to be big, multiplayer experiences. While it's impossible to rule out that someone will eventually solo the Wandering Death, this is ridiculously difficult. Instead, plan on having at least 15 - 20 players for a successful takedown.

How To Fight The Wandering Death

Once you have everything you need, your next task will be finding and fighting the boss.

❖ *Spawn Locations*

The Wandering Death can spawn in any of the five World Boss Arenas currently included in Diablo 4. For best results, keep an eye on your map page and explore each region, so you can get there fast after the marker pops up.

❖ *Health Bar*

World Bosses have a much larger version of a standard Health bar. It will be broken up into three sections to signify the boss' phases, as well as dropping potions at each marker. It is unknown exactly what the health pool looks like on World Bosses, but it usually takes almost the entire 15-minute timer to defeat them.

❖ *Stagger Bar*

World Bosses cannot be affected by regular crowd control abilities, unlike regular enemies. Instead, The Wandering Death has a stagger bar. When players use crowd control abilities, this stagger bar will slowly fill. When the bar is full, the boss will pause its onslaught and take additional damage.

In addition, the Wandering Death has a unique mechanic tied to the stagger bar. When staggered, the boss spawns two soul cages, which he will consume after the stagger is over. The boss heals a small amount and becomes enraged when consuming trapped souls, but players can destroy the cages to deal massive damage to The Wandering Death and prevent this healing.

Abilities of The Wandering Death

In addition to the more generic mechanics of the fight, The Wandering Death has several powerful attacks. Keep reading to learn the effects of each and how to avoid them, starting with the most dangerous.

❖ *Beam*

The boss' Laser Beams are the biggest threat in this fight. These do massive damage and will slowly rotate while being channeled. During the different stages of the boss fight, the number of beams starts at two and will gradually increase to four beams. During the final stages of the fight, the boss may also pair its beam attack with a grasping attack.

To avoid damage from this ability, move in the same direction at the same speed as the beams. Resist the temptation to use dash abilities during this period, as you are more likely to kill yourself than accomplish anything useful. If you need to move out of the grasp, move diagonally backward.

❖ *Crater*

The next most dangerous attack when fighting The Wandering Death is its

Crater of Bones. This ability will have a five-second windup followed by a large AoE attack. Initially, there will be only one crater spawning at a time, but this number will go up.

During this phase, use your Evade or Dash to exit the AoE before detonation The crater has a clear indicator with plenty of time, which is lucky since this ability can easily one-shot squishier characters.

❖ Grasp

This attack uses multiple hooked claws to drag the player toward The Wandering Death. The ability packs a punch, and there will be more and more hooks spawning as the boss' health gets lower. To dodge this attack, watch for comb marks to appear on the ground -- this will tell you where the claws will travel.

❖ Pound

The final high-damage ability in this boss' kit is a Pound attack. The boss will slam his hands down on the ground, causing initial damage as well as a secondary wave of spikes to pass over the area. At the beginning of the fight, most of the damage is backloaded into the spikes, while in later stages, the pound portion of the attack is more devastating.

When dealing with this attack, watch the position of the Wandering Death's arms (the first phase has two while the later phases have four). This will tell you where the pound is likely to hit. Additionally, keep in might which portion of the attack deals the most damage, and prioritize dodging that half

❖ Shout

This ability is a knockback doing moderate damage. While annoying for melee characters, this ability is unlikely to kill you if you're dodging everything else. The distance you are thrown will increase as the boss' health depletes, and its radial nature means it is almost impossible to dodge.

❖ Tornadoes

Finally, the boss will occasionally spawn three tornados. A number of bosses have a similar mechanic, such as the druid Airidah in Act 2. The tornados will follow the player and deal great damage, but they move very slowly and will dissipate after a set amount of time.

Trigger these tornadoes to explode by moving through them while invulnerable (such as with the Necromancer's Blood Mist) or run from them until they despawn to avoid damage and crowd control.

Rewards For Beating The Wandering Death

World Bosses drop a host of valuable loot, including:

- Level-synced experience points and gold
- Scattered Prisms
- A guaranteed Legendary Item
- A Legendary Grand Cache

If you experience connection problems during the fight and are not able to receive your loot for participating, don't worry. The game places it automatically in your stash to be claimed later.

HOW TO GET ASPECT OF THE ALPHA LEGENDARY ASPECT

Aspect Of The Alpha Legendary Aspect Uses

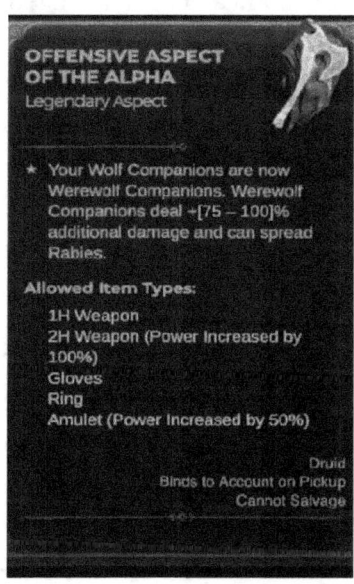

The Aspect Of The Alpha Legendary Aspect is an aspect that you can use to turn your wolf companions into werewolves, giving them not only a boost in size and intimidation but also in damage. With the Aspect Of The Alpha, your now-werewolf companions can deal 75-100% additional damage on top of their base damage, as well as spread Rabies to any enemies they hit.

Find The Aspect Of The Alpha

Finding the Aspect Of The Alpha requires a bit of luck, as the only way to find it is to extract it from a Legendary item. This means you have to find a Legendary item to extract it from. In order to do this, you will have to sacrifice the item that it is in, but being able to take the aspect and use it to upgrade your companions is well worth the sacrifice.

The Aspect Of The Alpha can appear on any of the following types of items:

- Amulets
- Gloves
- Offhand Item
- Rings
- One-Handed Weapons
- Two-Handed Weapons

The recommended way to farm some Legendary items that could carry this aspect is to farm Dungeons, World Events, and World Bosses. All of these activities give you the best chance to get a Legendary item, and none of them are entirely too time-consuming.

You can also trade with the Purveyor of Curiousities for Obols, and the best item to trade for are Offhand items, as these are the cheapest ones, running you only 40 Obols. They also will only come with an Offensive aspect that you can use.

How To Complete Barbarian: Masters Of Battle

Complete Barbarian: Masters Of Battle Quest

Upon arriving at Ked Baru and reaching level 15 as a Barbarian, you'll get a marker on the blacksmith indicating that they have a quest for you. The Blacksmith will tell you of another nearby Barbarian who would be willing to let you into their clan as long as you pass the test. Go out of the town to find Katra, who will mark the hunting grounds on your map.

To complete this quest, you'll need to first kill 30 bandits and 30 beasts within the hunting grounds. This is a fairly simple task, as enemies will scale to your level. Bandits are found more around the edges of the hunting grounds, with beasts being found towards the middle. There is no specification on what kind of beasts or bandits need to be defeated, letting you ignore tougher ones should you wish. There is also a shrine near the center of the hunting ground that can be used to help you eliminate the required enemies. Katra will also be fighting with you, giving you a bit of help when needed.

Upon finishing off the enemies, you'll be led to a cave where a much larger beast must be faced in a small cave. This beast will charge around the cave, making dodging out of the way important. It also comes with the bonus Shadowed ability, summoning a second shadow beast to attack your current location. Once the shadow beast is spawned, reposition on the other side of the main beast and out of range of the shadow beast, as it won't be able to follow you around. Defeat this beast and return its head to Katra, then turn in at the blacksmith to complete this quest.

Using Weapon Expertise

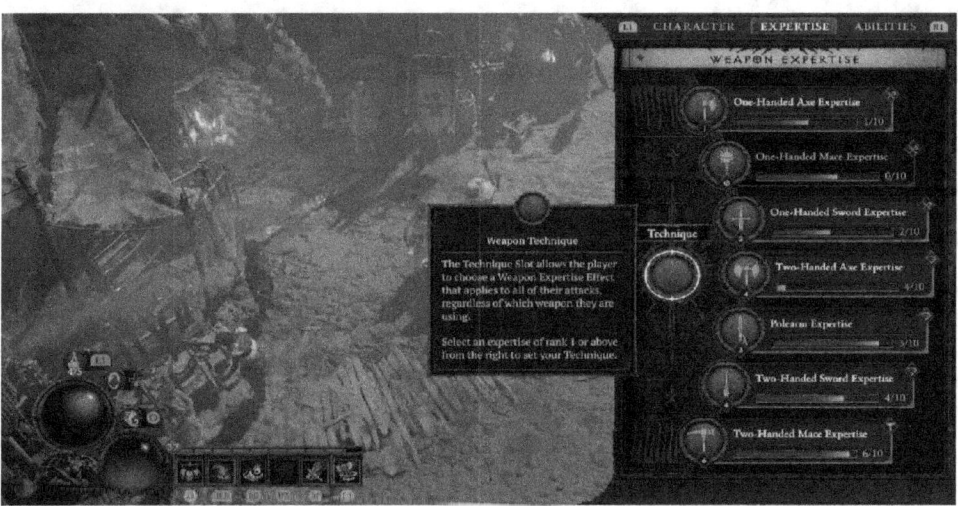

Weapon Expertise is a unique Barbarian mechanic that rewards players for using a specific weapon more often. In the expertise menu, you can see your progression for each weapon type, along with all the available weapon types you can level up. You can gain expertise on a weapon simply by fighting with it. After reaching specific levels of expertise with a weapon type, you'll gain a bonus with that weapon type. While a weapon, its corresponding weapon expertise will be in effect. After completing the Barbarian: Masters Of Battle quest, you'll be able to equip a second expertise that will always be in effect, no matter what weapon you are using.

Get The Aspect Of Bursting Bones

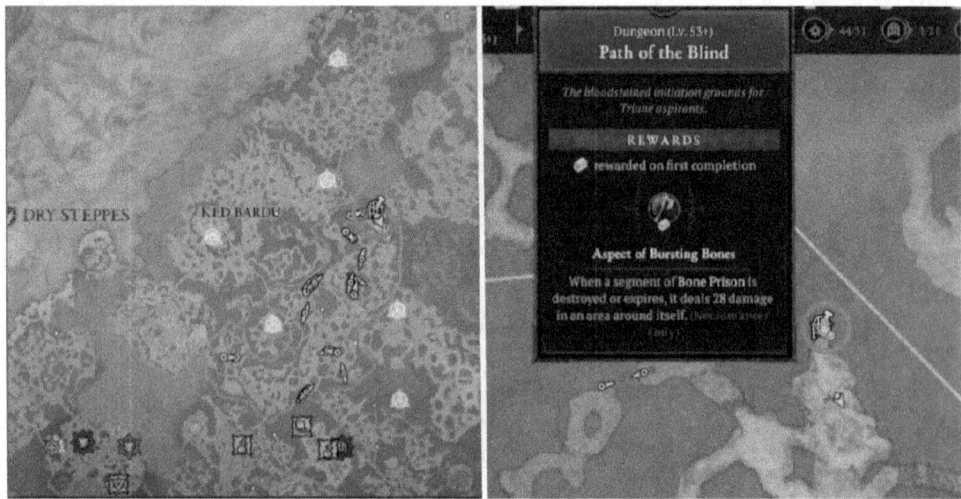

You can get the Aspect of Bursting Bones by completing the Path of the Blind Dungeon. The dungeon is located in Dry Steppes near Farobru Waypoint. To make things easier for you, we have shared the exact location on the above-mentioned map.

Once you have successfully made your way into this intricate Dungeon, your primary objective is to find the three Bloodstones. These Bloodstones can be obtained by engaging in combat with the Mother's Herald enemies that can be found throughout the area. Once you have obtained these precious Bloodstones, your next step is to place them on the Altar in order to summon the ultimate boss of the Dungeon. The boss is not that tough, and you can defeat him quite easily. Succeeding in defeating the final boss will reward you with the Aspect of Bursting Bones.

Other Ways To Get The Aspect Of Bursting Bones

You have a slight chance of obtaining the Aspect of Bursting Bones randomly from the Legendary item drops. To increase your chances, you can focus on farming Dungeons, participating in World Events, or taking down the World Bosses. This way, you'll have a better shot at obtaining this Aspect.

Usable Equipment Types

The Aspect of Bursting Bones is usable on the following Equipment Types for the Necromancer class only:

- Rings
- Amulets
- Gloves
- Offhand
- One-handed Weapons
- Two-handed Weapons

WHERE TO FIND CAPSTONE DUNGEONS

Where To Find The Capstone Dungeons In Diablo 4

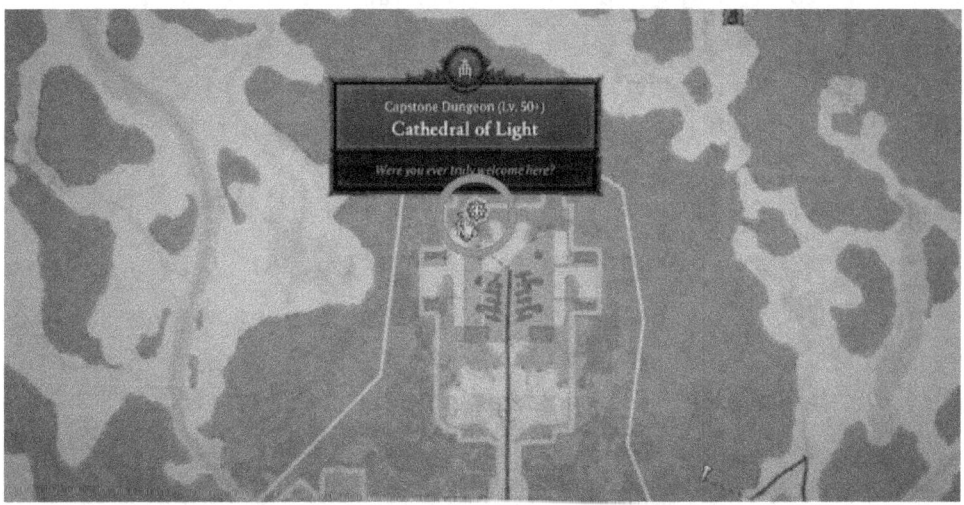

There are currently two Capstone Dungeons available in the game: the Cathedral of Light and the Fallen Temple.

❖ *Cathedral of Light*

The Cathedral of Light, the first Capstone Dungeon players will discover, can be found in the northwest corner of the building above the World Tier Statue in Kyovashad. This dungeon presents itself as a challenging starting point for players venturing into the world of Capstone Dungeons, with its level cap of 50. In order to conquer this dungeon, players must complete their objectives and defeat the final boss, Curator. Upon defeating the final boss, you will be rewarded with loot and unlock a new level of difficulty, World Tier 3: Nightmare.

❖ *Fallen Temple*

The Fallen Temple is a challenging dungeon located in the eastern reaches of the Dry Steppes. It presents an even greater obstacle than the Cathedral of Light and is specifically targeted toward players with greater experience and skill. The level cap for this dungeon is 70, making it an ideal challenge for those who have already triumphed in the first Capstone Dungeon.

How To Unlock Capstone Dungeons

Before you can access a Capstone Dungeon, you must first fulfill certain prerequisites:

- Complete the main campaign.
- Set the difficulty to World Tier 2: Veteran, which can be adjusted by interacting with the World Tier statues found in the major cities.

Once these requirements are met, you will be able to enter the Cathedral of Light and begin your journey through the Capstone Dungeons.

HOW TO FARM MURMURING OBOLS

What Are Murmuring Obols

As mentioned before, Murmuring Obols is a new form of currency that you will gain access to in the game. Unlike the core currency, gold, Murmuring Obols can only be used to purchase specific items in the game.

To use your Murmuring Obols, you'll need to visit the Purveyor of Curiosities shop found in most towns. Here, you can spend anywhere from 20-80 Murmuring Obols to get a random weapon gear item. This shop functions essentially as a gatcha system, giving you a chance to score anything from a common to a legendary item.

How To Farm Murmuring Obols

Since you will basically be gambling your Obols to get quality gear, you are going to need a steady supply of them if you want to score some legendary items. You can earn Murmuring Obols by completing events throughout the world.

Events will randomly pop up on the map and are marked by a golden outline surrounding the event area. While they are random, there are always plenty of them available if you are willing to make the trip. You can even jump from event to event as you make your way across the map. Upon completing each event, a loot chest will drop containing gold, weapons, gear items, and those precious Murmuring Obols.

Best Farming Path

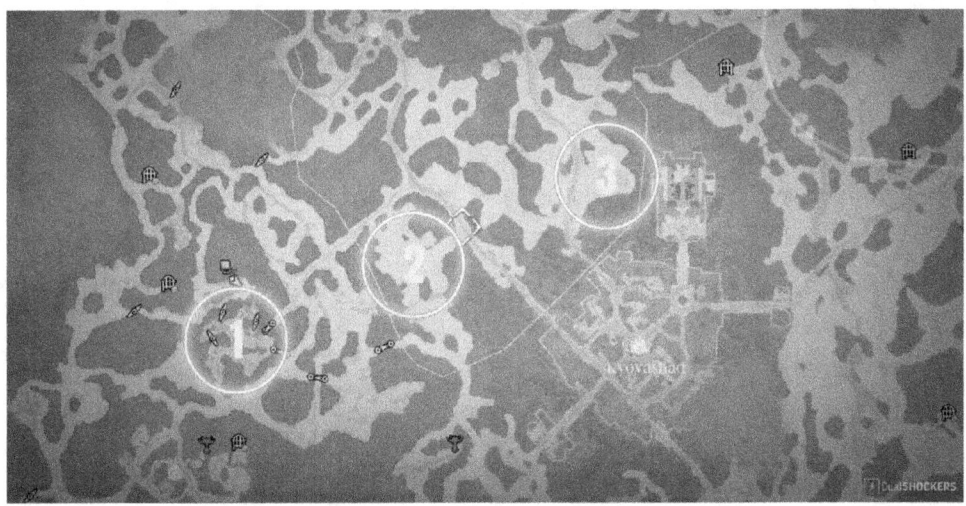

Since events randomly pop up all over the world map, there are going to be multiple paths you can follow to hop from event to event, scraping up all those juicy Murmuring Obols along the way. There are some areas later in the game that have much harder enemy types, and along with them come more interesting events. Since you will want to start collecting your Obols as soon as possible, we've chosen the best path in the early game.

Starting from Kyovashad, you'll want to head out of one of the western exits. On the road to the Dry Steppes, there are three events that are in close proximity to each other, making it easy to just run from one to the next, and double back to do it again if you so please. We've marked them for you on the map image above, and have ranked their difficulty from 1-3, with 1 being the hardest. Happy hunting!

HOW TO ENCHANT ITEMS

How To Unlock Item Enchantment

The term "Enchantment" is used extremely loosely in Diablo games and can often refer to multiple things. Diablo 4's Sorcerer class has a unique specialization method called Enchantment, and Elite enemies' special effects are often referred to as "Enchantments." Hopefully this confusion will be reduced in further updates.

Just like many other more advanced features in Diablo 4, you won't be able to Enchant your items right from the start. For this particular service, players must reach at least Level 25. After this, any Occultist will offer to Enchant items in addition to the other options they already provide.

Enchanting Requirements & Restrictions

In order to Enchant an item at an Occultist, it must be Rare or Legendary in quality. As with most other services available in Diablo 4, Enchanting items has a gold cost. This one is particularly heavy, with the price going up each and every time you Enchant an item.

Additionally, Enchanting your items requires rare materials. Veiled Crystals are easy enough to find, since you collect them whenever you salvage Rare items at the Blacksmith. Fiend Roses are a little more complicated, and can only be obtained during Helltide Events. These occur randomly but last a full hour in real time — be sure to take advantage of any that you see on the map!

There is one more limitation related to Enchanting Items. Items in Diablo 4 can only have specific Affixes depending on what slot the item goes into. This is true for Aspects as well. For example, Boots may have +% Movement Speed, while Gloves may not. Plan your preferred Affixes accordingly.

How To Beat Vhenard

Avoiding Damage

Stay out of the bad! The Vhenard boss fight at the end of "The Cost of Knowledge" quest will have players scrambling to stay out of the constant area-of-effect attacks from enemies while still trying to do some damage. Technically, there are three different types of enemy area attacks that players should be avoiding at all times throughout the fight: Hell Spawns', Vhenard's and the blood stream that connects Vhenard to her Hell Spawns. Coincidentally, all three types of attacks are also the color red. Also, each phase of the Vhenard fight will spawn increasingly more enemies.

Each new round will spawn more enemies than the past one, so the fight gets increasingly more difficult as time goes by. In each phase, Vhenard will summon Hell Spawns, which are medium-sized baddies. Hell Spawns shoot the electric-looking smaller flying red balls, Vhenard's attacks are red snaky, floating things and there is also a red blood tether between Vhenard and the Hell Spawns that will damage players when touched by it. Do your best to avoid all three of these attacks in the fight. Also make sure to stay off the stairs on the sides, as The Black Lake will instantly drain a character's health.

How To Beat Vhenard

Winning the Vhenard fight is going to be mainly based around two things: movement and ranged damage. During the fight, you cannot damage Vhenard directly and must focus on the multiple Hell Spawns that are tethered to Vhenard through various waves of enemy attacks. Due to the fact that Vhenard's Hell Spawns are constantly in rapid movement, players will need to rely on their ranged abilities most of all. That means that melee classes are going to have the toughest time with this boss fight. So, Barbarians and Druids are probably going to struggle with this one.

It is recommended to respec your class for ranged damage, mobility or survivability if you can't win the fight in a current build. The combined act of avoiding all the insanity on the screen while laying out damage to the rapidly moving Hell Spawns can test a gamers skills and patience. This gets increasingly chaotic as the amount of enemies increases and the type gets more deadly. Eventually, Vhenard will begin to spawn Spewers, which fire ranged puss at you, and gigantic Pit Lords who have horns and swords the size of buildings. Make sure your fingers are warmed up for this boss.

HOW TO DEFEAT ASHAVA THE PESTILENT WORLD BOSS

Preparing To Fight Ashava

Before farming a World Boss, you'll need to gear up for the fight, locate a spawning World Boss, and gather a group of players. Each World Boss has different builds that work best for them, so knowing who you will be fighting is important.

❖ *Damage Type*

When fighting a World Boss, it is heavily suggested to up your resistance to their primary damage type. This can be easily done with Elixirs, and you can also use gear with relevant resistance if it is available.

Ashava does physical damage and poison damage. Gear with poison resistance, and an Elixir of Poison Resistance or Iron Barb will serve you best in this fight. If you have a build heavily reliant on poison damage currently equipped, you may also want to consider a respec to an alternative.

❖ *Spawn Time & Location*

Ashava spawns on a hidden world boss schedule and can spawn in any one of the five World Boss arenas found in Sanctuary. When seeking her out, players should keep an eye out for a marker on the map over a World Boss Arena. This indicates a World Boss will soon spawn and tells you which one will appear if hovered over. You can also look at the animation of the boss portal to tell if Ashava is the one spawning - her portal is greenish in hue and has bony spines around the outside.

If you are not seeing markers for World Bosses, this could be because you haven't yet beaten the main campaign. Players who haven't beaten the campaign can still take part in the fight if they arrive in time, but will not be motivated on the world map of any World Boss spawns.

❖ *Number Of Suggested Players*

World Bosses are intended to be a multiplayer experience similar to a Raid in an MMO. Ashava, like most World Bosses, is nigh impossible to beat in the time limit with fewer than five players. Conversely, her health and damage will scale with more players in the fight, so there is also a point where too many participants can make things more difficult. The sweet spot appears to be between 10 and 15 players.

How To Beat Ashava The Pestilent

Ashava is a World Boss, which means that she has powerful attacks and more health than your average boss. In order to successfully defeat her, you will need to keep an eye on certain special mechanics.

❖ *Health Bar*

Ashava is a World Boss with a middling amount of Health but lots and lots of armor. The result is that your attacks won't do as much damage to her as you might expect. In addition, there are three phases in this fight, marked with arrows. As Ashava's health gets lower, she will enter new phases and become more aggressive.

❖ Stagger Bar

Ashava has a Stagger bar directly below her health bar. Hitting her with crowd control effects such as a Sorcerer's Ice abilities will slowly fill this bar. Once the bar is full, she will fall down and stop attacking for about 12 seconds. Staggering is particularly important when fighting Ashava because her unique mechanic involves disabling some of her most powerful attacks.

❖ Unique Mechanics

Ashava The Pestilent has a unique mechanic tied to her stagger bar. When she is staggered, she will lose one of her arm blades and a sizable chunk of armor. Stagger her twice during the fight to severely hinder her ability to damage you and make her more vulnerable to attacks.

❖ Time Limit

World Bosses such as Ashava are only above ground for a limited time. From the moment the boss spawns, a timer for fifteen minutes will begin. If the timer expires before players successfully kill Ashava, then she will retreat below ground. This is considered an event failure and results in no rewards.

Abilities Of Ashava The Pestilent

During the fight against Ashava, she will use an impressive arsenal to scatter and damage players. Here are each of her abilities ranked from most to least dangerous.

❖ Poison Breath

Ashava's Poison Breath is one of her most threatening abilities. Not only will it melt through your health bar, but its area of effect is quite large. This can make it difficult to dodge if you find yourself in her path. To stay clear of this ability, it is best to be behind or underneath Ashava.

❖ Swipes

The other main threat of the fight will be Ashava's swipes with her massive claws. These are mid-range attacks that can one-shot players. To limit the effectiveness of this attack, you need to be either very close to her or very far away. Watch for her to raise her arms to know when this one is coming.

Ashava will only do partial damage with this attack if the arm being used no longer has a claw, so staggering her can nerf this attack drastically.

❖ *Ground Pound*

Sometimes, there will be an orange circular outline that appears on the ground. This indicates that Ashava is going to pound the ground with her fists. If the hand she uses still has its' claw, then the damage to this attack is massive. However, the ability to knock off her claws and the relatively small area of the attack means it is not usually a major threat.

❖ *Bite*

Occasionally Ashava will target a player with a bite. This is telegraphed by her rearing back a little to dash forward. The bite's hitbox is a rectangle going outwards from Ashava, so make sure to dodge sideways rather than backward.

❖ *Jump*

If none of the players are easily targetable in Ashava's current position, she will bend down and launch herself into the air to reposition. The direction she will go is telegraphed by whether her right, left, or both legs bend. Try not to be in the location where she will land, as this will deal sizable damage and CC your character.

Rewards For Beating Ashava

Beating Ashava will result in a number of rewards, including a Legendary Item, gems, a Scattered Prism, and a rotating weekly reward called Ashava's Spoils. In addition to these items and crafting materials drops, players will receive a large amount of gold and experience scaled to their current level.

HOW TO DEFEAT AVARICE THE GOLD CURSED WORLD BOSS

Fight Avarice The Gold Cursed

Preparing for a World Boss is a delicate balancing act - you don't want to go in unprepared, but you also don't want to miss the start of the event (as you can't join late). The best way to ensure you're there on time and ready is to know in advance exactly what you need.

❖ *Damage Type*

Knowing the damage type of a World Boss allows you to drink the appropriate Elixir and wear the best gear to sustain through this fight. Unfortunately, however, Avarice doesn't have a readily apparent damage theme like other World Bosses. He places mines that explode for fire damage, does physical damage with his mace, and lays down poisonous pools of gold.

One of the best pieces of gear to wear into this fight, therefore, is a ring with a high amount of resistance to All Element Types. You can also chug an Elixir of Acrobatics to make dodging his attacks easier.

❖ *Spawn Time & Location*

Avarice can spawn in any of the several Boss Arenas in Sanctuary. This happens on a hidden World Boss schedule and appears on the map for players to see only if they have completed the main campaign. This map icon appears 30 minutes before the boss spawns.

Once you have determined that a World Boss is spawning, you can tell which one it is by hovering over the map icon or viewing the animation in the boss arena. Avarice emits golden lightning from his portal while forming

❖ *Number of Players*

While the event will begin regardless of how many players are in the Arena, it is nigh impossible to complete this fight solo. This is because Avarice has a minimum health value that is too high for a single player to deal sufficient damage before the timer runs out.

Fighting Avarice is meant to be done in a large group, ideally between 10 and 15 players. There is no benefit from doing a World Boss Event in a smaller group, as each person receives unique loot. However, the event can get too difficult to complete in groups larger than 20, as the boss' health and damage increase with the number of players.

| Fight Avarice The Gold Cursed

There are several mechanics to keep in mind while fighting Avarice the Gold Cursed. Like all World Bosses, he has a multiphase health bar, a stagger bar, and a unique stagger mechanic. Additionally, the World Boss events are timed. You will only have 15 minutes to beat Avarice before he despawns, resulting in an event failure.

❖ Health Bar

Avarice has a large hit point pool broken up into three sections. Each section denotes a new phase that will cause Avarice to become more aggressive (by speeding up his attack rotation).

❖ Stagger Bar

World Bosses are immune to regular Crowd Control Effects. Instead, they have a stagger bar that slowly fills when CC is applied. Once the Stagger bar is full, they will pause their attack pattern for 12 seconds to recover, giving players a chance to deal maximum damage.

❖ Unique Mechanics

Each World Boss also has a unique effect when staggered. Avarice spawns two extra tanky Treasure Goblins when staggered. True to the boss' name, there is no effect of these Treasure Goblins on the fight other than the resulting temptation. Players must fight their greed to decide whether to chase after the goblins while the boss is staggered or deal damage to increase their odds of successfully completing the event.

Abilities Of Avarice The Gold Cursed

Avarice, the Gold Cursed, has a number of attacks that he cycles through. Most of them involve his mace and a giant treasure chest on a chain, although some spawn environmental hazards. Here are tips on what each attack does and how to avoid it ranked from the most dangerous attack to the least.

❖ Spin Attack

This is the most basic ability of Avarice, but it is no less deadly for it. He will wind up before spinning the Treasure Chest he carries around 360 degrees. Anyone in the path of the chest is liable to get one shot - making this ability your number one concern.

To dodge the attack, you can go inwards to where the chain is or outward past its range. Either location will result in no damage taken.

❖ Portal Charge

In addition to the spin attack, Avarice will also regularly teleport through golden portals. When a portal spawns, he will charge toward it, dealing moderate damage. Then, he will charge out of a second portal. The second charge is where his damage is, and getting hit by this ability is an instant death.

To avoid this ability, watch where the second portal spawns. Avarice will always charge in a straight line from where the portal is pointing, showing you where to dodge.

❖ Pillars of Gold

Beginning in the second phase of the fight, Avarice can summon pillars of gold on the ground. These pillars do very little damage when they appear, however, they are obstacles that cannot be run through. It's very easy to get stuck and then knocked out by his mace during this time. Additionally, he will pulverize the pillars, resulting in an explosion of molten gold which does quite a lot of damage. The detonation of the pillars occurs about five seconds after the markers appear on the ground. To avoid this, leave the area of the pillars as soon as they spawn, only returning once they've exploded.

❖ Mallet Thrust

Avarice will occasionally lash out with his mallet, dealing great damage in a cone. This attack is fast but has a wind-up period during which you can move behind him to avoid it.

❖ Golden Vomit

As the boss enters the third phase, he will begin to vomit pools of gold onto the ground. These do damage over time and can easily kill you if you stand in them. This, combined with the pillars, quickly turns the arena into a game of Minesweeper. However, these puddles are static and not instantly deadly. Simply move out of them as soon as you can.

❖ Ground Stomp

This attack does minimal damage but pulls you in toward him. It is often used just before the summon pillars or golden vomit actions. It is not easy to avoid being hit by this; luckily, most properly leveled characters will be able to tank the damage and move away again fairly quickly.

Rewards

As is fitting, Avarice the Gold Cursed has by far the most loot of any World Boss. Not only will he himself drop loot upon death, but you can attack his giant Treasure Chest he carries for additional rewards. This doesn't even count any Treasure Goblins you might have killed while fighting him. Types of loot you can expect include:

- Legendary Items
- Common to Rare Items
- Gold scaled to your level + additional gold drops
- Experience scaled to your level
- Scattered Prisms
- Gems
- Crafting Materials

If your group chose to kill all the Treasure Goblins that spawned (on average, four - two per stagger) and then had reasonably good luck with drops, you can walk away with 5-6 Legendary Items from this fight.

ALTARS OF LILITH LOCATIONS

ALTARS OF LILITH LOCATIONS IN FRACTURED PEAKS

What Are the Altars Of Lilith?

As previously mentioned, the numerous Altars of Lilith are scattered about the world of Sanctuary. These stone statues of the antagonist Lilith are generally somewhat-hidden, well off the main roads in the game. Fractured Peaks has 28 Altars of Lilith, each offering a one-time boon to the player's character. These benefits, all pre-determined and chosen from a list, include:

- +2 Strength
- +2 Dexterity
- +2 Intelligence
- +2 Willpower
- +5 Maximum Obol Capacity

Along with the above benefits, every Altar of Lilith the player discovers will also boost experience and Renown in the region.

❖ *Altars Of Lilith & Renown*

For every Altar of Lilith the player discovers, they'll receive a +10 Renown bonus to that corresponding region. For example, if an adventurer finds an Altar in Fractured Peaks, their renown increases in Fractured Peaks.

That said, players do not need to locate and activate every Altar of Lilith in a zone to complete that area's Renown. Still, with the permanent stat bonuses and Obol capacity increase, it's wise to track down each Altar early on for a quick power boost.

Fractured Peaks: Altars Of Lilith Locations

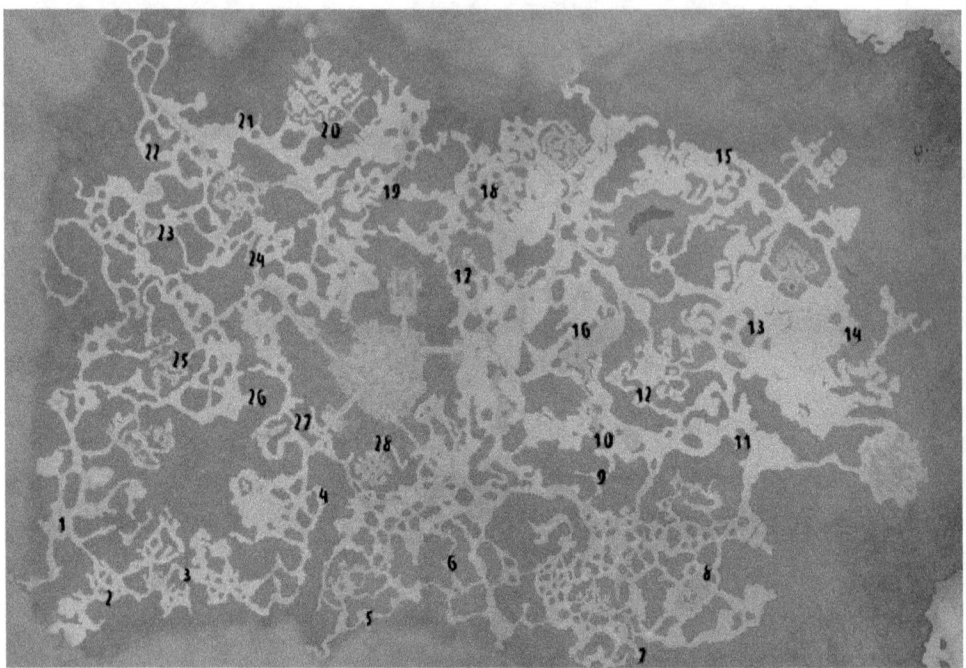

Locating each Altar of Lilith in a given zone may prove difficult for those without a keen eye. Every Altar is off the beaten path, and players aren't likely to stumble upon one by following a main route from quest to quest. Instead, it's essential to wander the woods, peek behind rocks, and look where no one else might. Or, you could easily use the map provided and track down each one.

Furthermore, each Altar is located outside any zone of interest in the game. There will never be one located directly outside the entrance to a Dungeon, for instance, or by a world event.

Altars Of Lilith Boons

Altar Location Number	Altar Reward
1	Max Obols +5
2	+2 Strength
3	Max Obols +5

Altar Location Number	Altar Reward
4	+2 Dexterity
5	+2 Willpower
6	+2 Strength
7	+2 Intelligence
8	+2 Willpower
9	+2 Dexterity
10	+2 Willpower
11	Max Obols +5
12	+2 Strength
13	+2 Intelligence
14	+2 Strength
15	+2 Dexterity
16	+2 Strength
17	+2 Intelligence
18	+2 Dexterity
19	+2 Intelligence
20	+2 Willpower
21	+2 Strength
22	Max Obols +5
23	+2 Willpower

Altar Location Number	Altar Reward
24	+2 Willpower
25	+2 Intelligence
26	+2 Dexterity
27	+2 Intelligence
28	+2 Dexterity

ALL WAYPOINT LOCATIONS

ALL WAYPOINT LOCATIONS IN FRACTURED PEAKS

Kyovashed

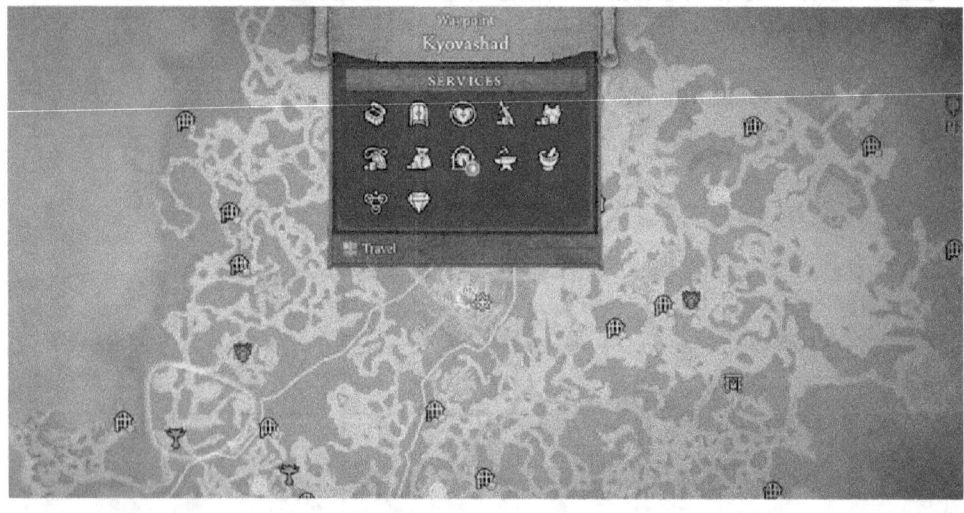

The first Waypoint you should pick up is located at the heart of Kyovashed, the capital city of the Fractured Peaks which you can find in the center of the region. You'll be led past this Waypoint as you start your first quests in the region, but the game won't explicitly tell you to activate it.

Make sure you grab this one early so that you don't have to backtrack later. There are also a ton of advanced services available in this city including accessing your stash, changing the world tier, imprinting aspects, and upgrading gems. You might not use these services every time you come back from a dungeon, but you'll definitely need them a few times before heading into the second act.

Yelesna

Yelesna is likely the second Waypoint you'll unlock in the Fractured Peaks. Located to the bottom right of the region, just below The Darkened Way, a dungeon where most of the main quests in the first act take place, Yelesna is a must-grab Waypoint that will help you jump out and into the main quest line whenever you want. Follow the road from Kyovashad to reach it.

While Yelesna only has the basics you'd need in between quests, it can still serve as a decent home base for a significant part of the first act. More important than its services is its location, which lets you explore the bottom of the map easily.

Bear Tribe Refuge

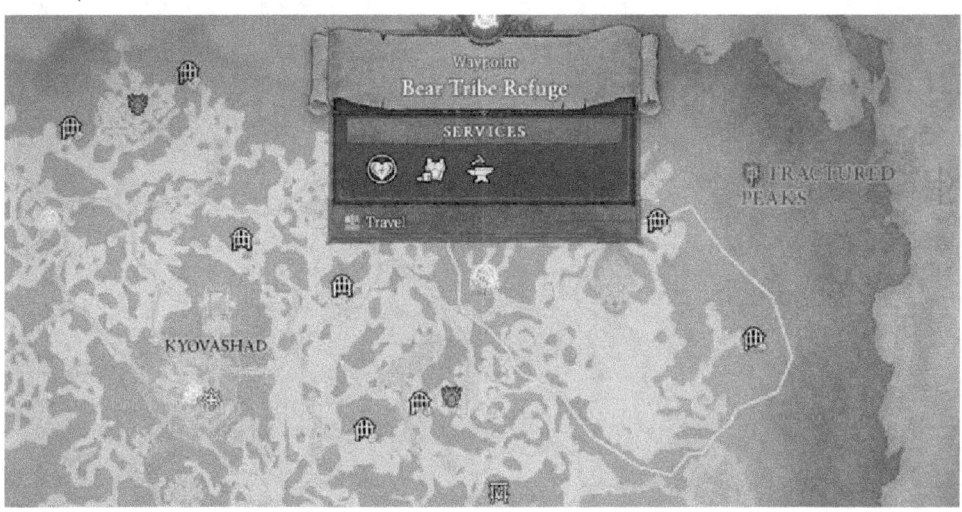

Bear Tribe Refuge is an easy-to-miss Waypoint in the top right of the Fractured peaks that, like Yelesna, will help you jump between points in the main quest line with ease and explore the expansive right side of the region. However, it can be very easy to miss since there are no roads leading to the Waypoint.

If you want to find Bear Tribe Refuge, deviate from the road towards the middle-left of the Seat of The Heavens area. You'll find two mountain paths that lead you to the hidden Waypoint. There isn't much in the way of services in this secluded town, only a blacksmith, armor vendor, and healer, but its location makes up for what it lacks as this Waypoint can easily save you from running through the same stretch of map three or four times.

Menestad

Menestad is the second-biggest village in the Fractured Peaks, located in the top left of the Fractured Peaks region. While there's not much in the way of quests around this Waypoint, it's close to tons of dungeons and is easy to grab at the end of the first act. On top of that, it's the only Waypoint in the top left, making it a must-grab if you plan on exploing the Fractured Peaks.

As far as services go, Menestrad boasts an impressive array of vendors. While it doesn't offer many advanced services, this town has weapons, armor, and rings for sale at its three vendors. It also has a handy stable that can help you explore Scosglen or the Dry Steppes.

Margrave

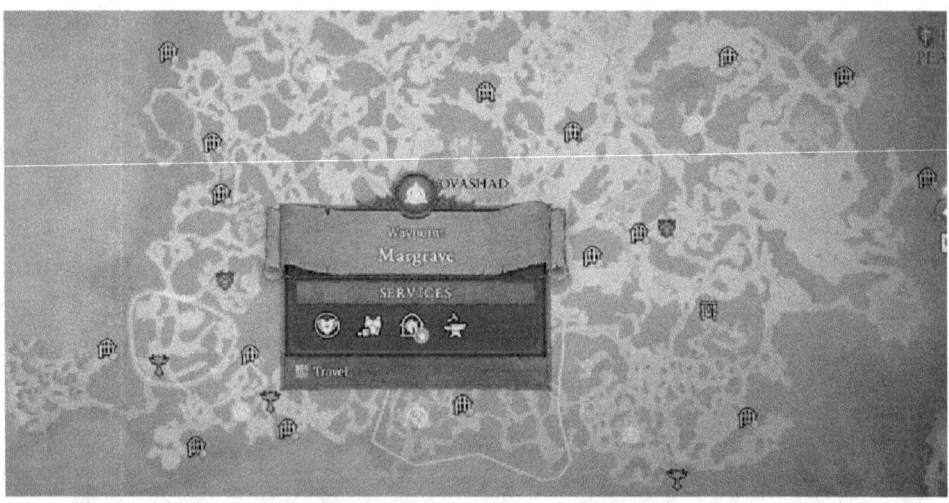

Margrave is an odd Waypoint that, while important, likely won't help you much in the early game. Margrave is located directly below Kyovashad, uncomfortably close to Yelesna. On top of this, there aren't many dungeons nearby, making Margrave ultimately an unimportant Waypoint.

Even in terms of services, Margrave doesn't have much to offer except one silver lining: It is the closest stable to the Hawezar region. When it comes time to explore this late-game region in full, Margrave will likely be where you set out from.

Nevesk

Nevesk is the corrupted village featured in the tutorial, and wouldn't you know it, there is a Waypoint here, but you'll have to revisit the town after making it to Kyovashad before activating it. Located in the bottom left of the map, Nevesk suffers the same fate as Margrave in terms of usefulness: too many Waypoints nearby, not enough to do.

On top of that, Nevesk has a depressing array of services, only hosting a blacksmith to scrap your loot and a healer to top off your health. Still, activating this Waypoint will give you a decent chunk of renown in the region, which can come with all sorts of bonuses.

Nostrava

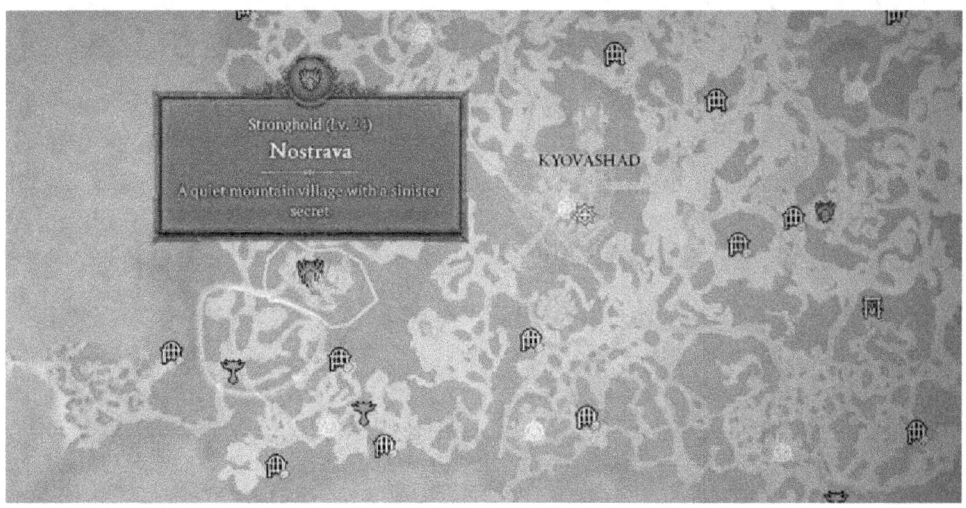

Nostrava is the elusive seventh Waypoint in the Fractured Peaks, as, unlike other Waypoints, you can't just stroll in and activate it without a hassle. Instead, if you want to unlock the Nostrava Waypoint, you'll first have to defeat the Stronghold that is located there. After doing so, you'll revitalize the town and be able to fast travel back all you want.

Located in the bottom left of the Fractured Peaks, however, it's hard to argue that the Nostrava Waypoint is all that important. There isn't much nearby, and the only notable services offered are a weapons vendor and a stable.

Firebreak Manor

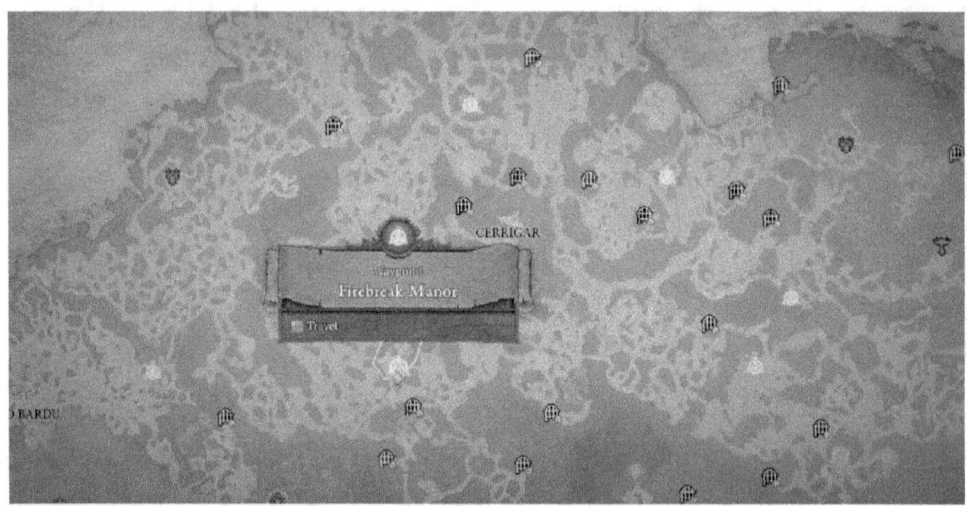

Firebreak Manor will likely be your first Waypoint in Scosglen. Located in the bottom middle of the region along the path from the Fractured Peaks, this Waypoint is different from most in that it can't be activated right away. Instead, you'll have to complete the first quest of act two, which will have you investigate Firebreak Manor before defending it from goat men.

Sadly, this Waypoint doesn't do much for you even after you've activated it. It offers no services and is quite close to other, more useful Waypoints. Instead, the real advantage of grabbing this fast travel location is that it'll let you complete the act two quest line quicker, as you'll be asked to visit Firebreak Manor a few times.

Cerrigar

Cerrigar is the capital city of Scosglen and the eventual arena for the boss of act two. This Waypoint can be found near the center of the region, just above and to the left of Firebreak Manor. Take the time to grab this Waypoint after starting act two as you'll need to travel back here later.

As far as services go, Cerrigar is your one-stop shop in Scosglen, offering a wide array of services like access to your stash, a handy occultist for equipping aspects, a jeweler, and more. On top of that, its relatively central location makes it a great place to unlock if you want to explore the region a bit more.

Tirmair

The Tirmair Waypoint is set in a small town located in the middle right of the Scosglen region. This otherwise unassuming town ends up hosting one of the main quests of act two. It's also a good Waypoint to unlock if only to complete those quests a bit faster.

As far as services go, Tirmair has all the basics and not much more. At this Waypoint, you can visit a blacksmith, take a horse out of the stables, grab some healing, and sell various junk to an armor vendor. On a brighter note, its relatively central location makes it a valuable fast travel point for the right side of the map.

Braestaig

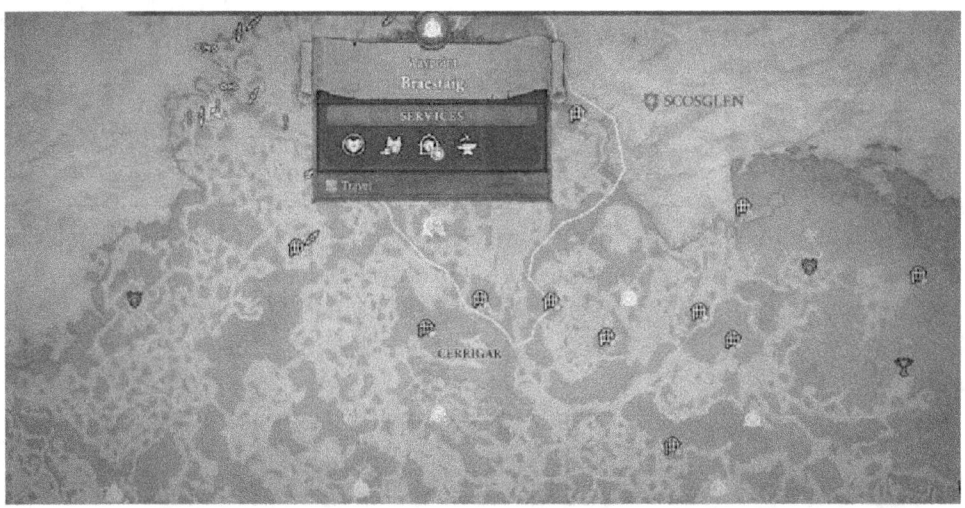

Braestaig, a town haunted by the rising dead, is also home to one of the most convenient Waypoints in Scosglen. Located in the top middle of the region, it is not only near a main quest that will have you exploring the surrounding area, but it also sits close to tons of dungeons and side quests.

Braestaig offers most of the same services that you'd find at Tirmair, making it a decent stopping point between adventures. The main draw of Braestaig is its proximity to much of the region. It allows you to trek across much of the upper portion of Scosglen from a central spot.

Under The Fat Goose Inn

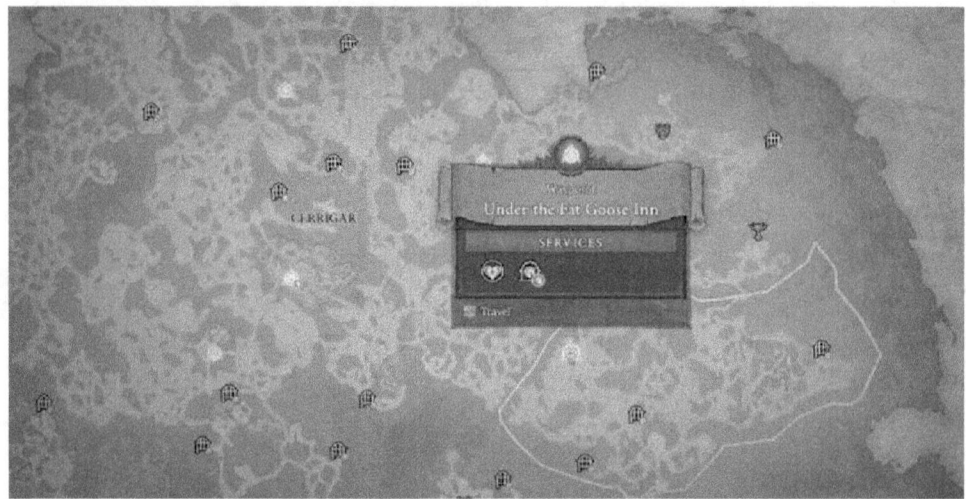

Under The Fat Goose Inn is an aptly named Waypoint that sits just below the aforementioned Fat Goose Inn in the bottom left of the Scosglen region. While this Waypoint may look uncomfortably close to Tirmair, it's just slightly closer to quite a few dungeons. This makes it a worthwhile travel point in its own right.

However, it leaves something to be desired in the way of services. Unlike most Waypoints, Under The Fat Goose Inn doesn't offer any sort of vendor or blacksmith. It does, however, have a healer and stable.

Corbach

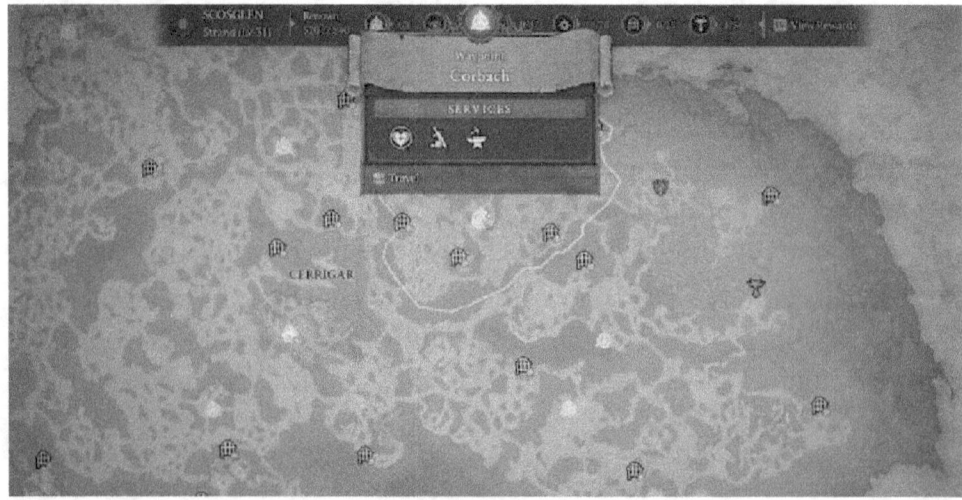

Located between Tirmair and Braestaig in the top right of Scosglen, Corbach is a small town with a surprisingly convenient location. Despite being sandwiched between two useful Waypoints, there are still plenty of reasons to visit Corbach. For instance, the surrounding countryside is littered with events and dungeons.

As far as services go, Corbach has a few to go around. With a blacksmith, weapon vendor, and healer in town, it can easily serve as a quick home base. It might even become a decent spot to shop for some weapons.

Marowen

This port town in the top left of the Scosglen region hosts a Waypoint of the same name. While the location leaves a bit to be desired, it does let you quickly get to nearby strongholds or dungeons.

As far as services go, Marowen has quite a few for its size. It has most of the basics that you could want, and importantly, it also has the only jewelry vendor outside of Cerrigar.

Tur Dulra

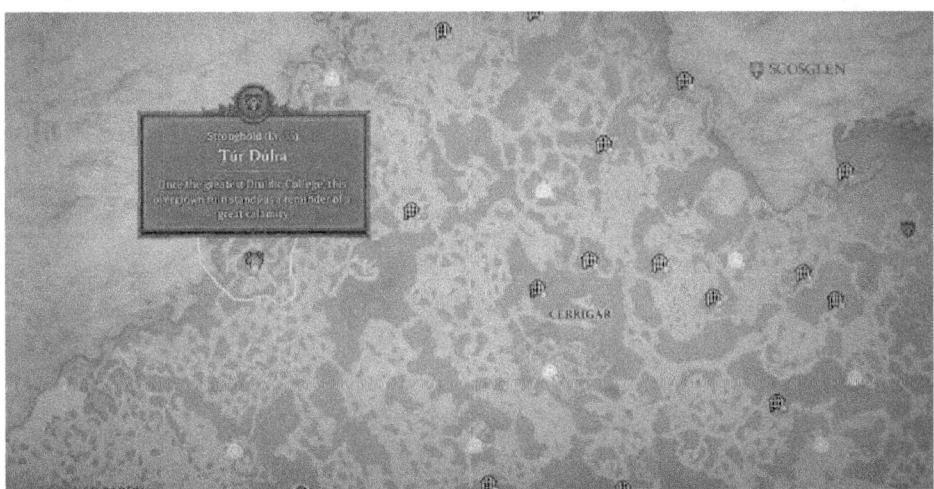

Tur Dulra is the last and hardest-to-get Waypoint in Scosglen. Located in the middle left of the region, this former college is a stronghold that you must defeat in order for it to become a Waypoint.

The location of the Waypoint makes it an extremely useful travel point to grab as, with it, you'll be able to easily reach the entire left side of Scosglen. However, there is one big catch. The services offered at Tur Dulra once it's cleared are meager at best, making it a terrible home base location.

ALL WAYPOINT LOCATIONS IN DRY STEPPES

Farobru

The first and likely least used Waypoint in the Dry Steppes is the small border town of Farobru located in the top middle of the region. This Waypoint is along the natural path from Scosglen into the Dry Steppes, making it easy to grab as you move from the second to the third act. However, it offers little in the way of usefulness.

The services at Farobru are decent as both a weapon and jewelry vendor make it their home, but its location is downright awful. There are no nearby dungeons that aren't closer to another Waypoint, and the main quest stays far away from this town.

Ked Bardu

Ked Bardu is the sprawling desert trade city that marks the Dry Steppes capital. Located in the top middle of the region, it is the closest Waypoint to a surprising chunk of the map, and you'll also spend a lot of the main quest in and around this city.

In terms of services, Ked Bardu has it all. Access to your stash, an occultist, a jeweler, plenty of vendors, and more. This will be a must-grab Waypoint as you work your way through the third act.

Hidden Overlook

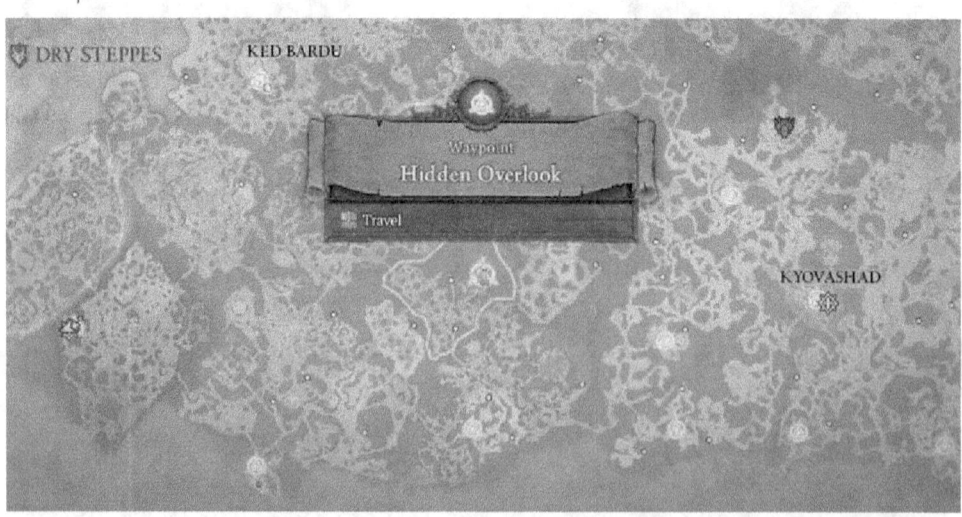

The Hidden Overlook is a bit of an odd Waypoint. Located in the middle right of the Dry Steppes, it serves as a decent travel point, but more importantly, it is right next to a few dungeons that also get used in the main quest line.

There are no services to speak of, but you can't get much closer to a dungeon This makes Hidden Overlook a good place to farm experience, as you can clear the dungeon, step outside, and reset it — all without ever having to deal with enemies outside the dungeon.

Fate's Retreat

Fate's Retreat is another minimalist Waypoint. Located in the middle right of the region, just above the Hidden Overlook, Fate's Retreat is the closest Waypoint to a handful of quests near the end of act three.

As with Hidden Overlook, there are no services to speak of; however, Fate's Retreat does offer a decent location on the map, allowing you to get much closer to a handful of dungeons and events.

The Onyx Watchtower

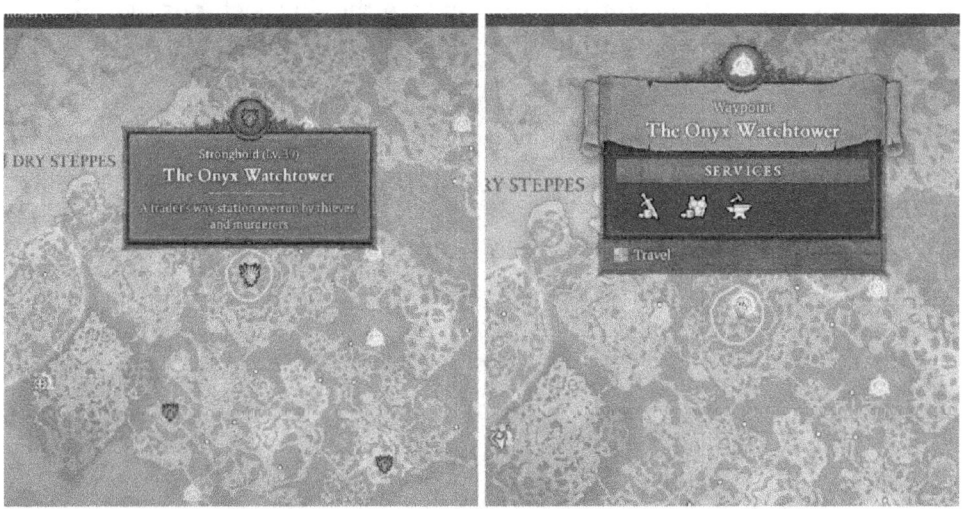

The Onyx Watchtower is one of the hidden Waypoints in the region, as you'll have to clear out the Onyx Watchtower Stronghold before it appears. Located in the center of the Dry Steppes, this Waypoint offers a very convenient fast-travel location and a modest array of services.

Clearing out the Onyx Watchtower will have you go head-to-head with a bandit group, sabotaging their supplies and killing their leaders before ultimately dueling with the captain, a stealthy rogue with a taste for firebombs. Once the Waypoint is unlocked, you'll have access to a weapon vendor, an armor vendor, and a blacksmith.

Ruins Of Qara-Yisu

In a slight departure from earlier regions, the Ruins of Qara-Yisu is another stronghold that you'll have to complete in order to unlock the Waypoint. Located in the bottom right of the map, this Waypoint serves as an exceptional fast travel location, letting you quickly access a huge swath of the map that has very little access otherwise.

Clearing out the stronghold will have you battling a host of demons erecting huge spires before duking it out with the head demon — a spindly spell caster for a change. Once unlocked, the settlement will offer a decent array of services, including stables, some vendors, and a blacksmith.

Jirandai

Jirandai is a border town Waypoint with the southern region of Kehjistan, located in the bottom middle of Dry Steppes. Like Farobru, you'll likely pass through this town as you continue further into the third act, but there are no quests located directly next to it.

Despite its modest location, the services in Jirandai are actually quite good. With a curiosities vendor, armor vendor, weapons vendor, and jewelry vendor, this Waypoint is a great place to stop and shop every once in a while.

Alzuuda

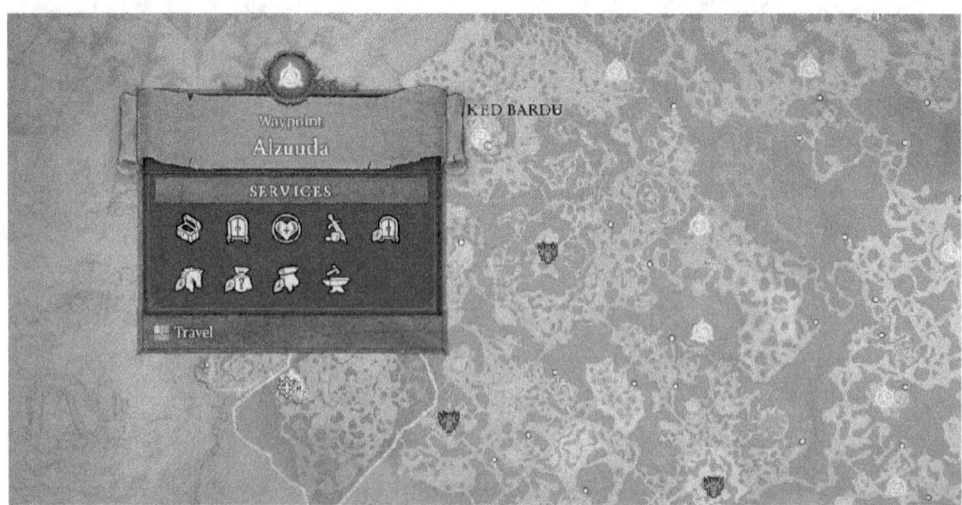

Alzuuda is the final and perhaps most important Waypoint in the Dry

Steppes. Located in the middle right of the region, this large town sits next to the earliest PvP area in the game, the Plains of Hatred. This means it has all types of services, will be a great place to travel to whenever you feel like fighting it out, and even with all of that aside, it still gives you access to a huge swath of the Dry Steppes.

As a PvP Waypoint, it comes packed to the brim with all types of services, and some of those services can only be found here. There are four shops where you can spend your Red Dust, the PvP currency of Diablo 4, to buy better gear, exclusive cosmetics, and powerful PvP items. This Waypoint is an absolute must-grab.

ALL WAYPOINT LOCATIONS IN KEHJISTAN

Tarsarak

Tarsarak is the first and undeniably most important Waypoint in Kehjistan. Located in the middle right of the region, this bustling desert town will serve as the closest Waypoint to nearly every main quest that happens in Kehjistan. You don't need to do anything special to unlock it, however, so run over to activate it as soon as you can.

The services in Tarsarak are decent. Containing multiple vendors, a blacksmith, and a healer, this town can serve as a decent base in between missions, which is convenient since you'll have to stop back here often throughout the fourth act. Even outside the main quests, Tarsarak is well situated on the map, offering you access to a handful of nearby dungeons.

Denshar

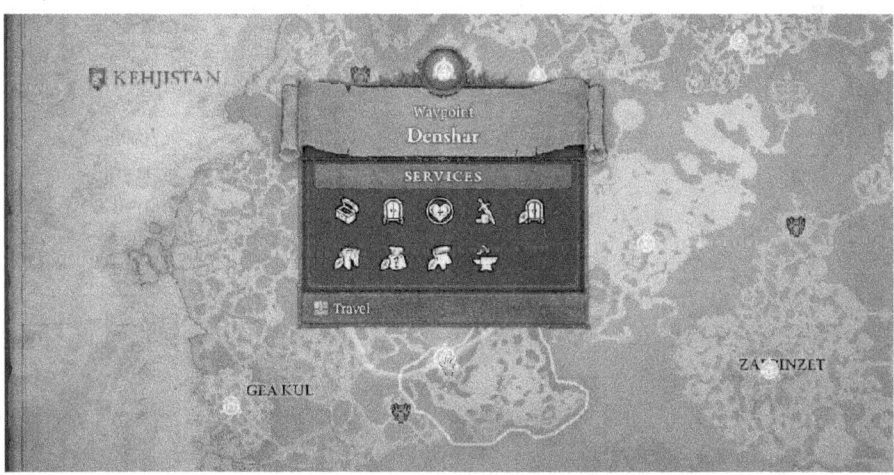

Denshar is one of the biggest towns in Kehjistan and only the second PvP town in the game aside from Alzuuda in the Dry Steppes. Located in the bottom middle of the map, the main draw of this town is its proximity to a PvP zone and the special services offered here.

Speaking of those services, you'll be able to upgrade, repair, and sell weapons as well as access your stash, but the main draw is of course the PvP-specific services. These special vendors will let you buy limited cosmetics and high-level gear with your Red Dust, the PvP currency of Diablo 4. Outside its appeal for PvP players, Denshar is also located quite conveniently, standing a stone's throw from a few nearby dungeons.

Gea Kul

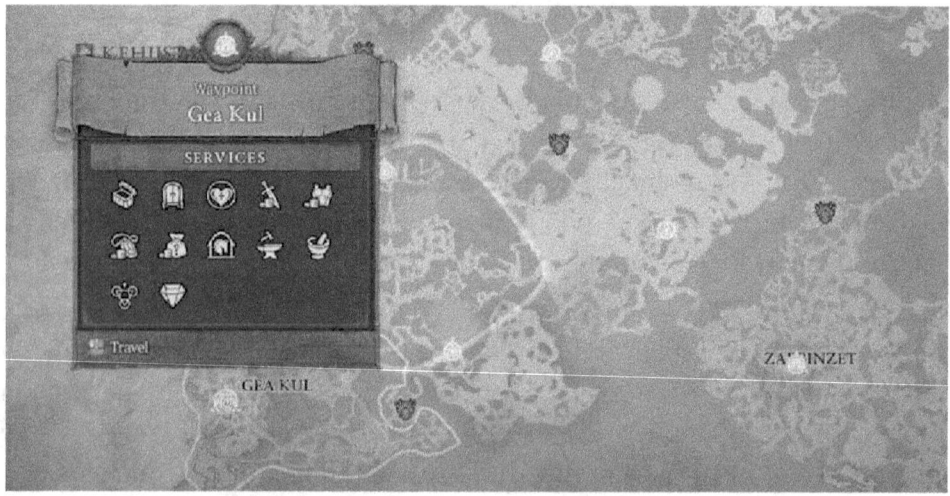

Gea Kul is the unlikely capital city of Kehjistan located in the bottom left of the region. This gigantic port city is quite stunning, but not everyone gets to see it. It's quite easy to miss being tucked into the bottom corner, and there are no main quests that will lead you to this city. What makes it worse is that you can unlock this city at any time, but you'll never be pointed in its direction.

Gea Kul shares the same benefits that most capital cities do in Diablo 4; it has an unparalleled amount of services. You can access your stash, visit a jeweler, change aspects at an occultist, check out the curiosity vendor, and do everything else you could do in a normal town. However, it pays for this abundance by lacking in terms of location. Gea Kul is awkwardly too far from most of the nearby dungeons, often making it faster to visit other Waypoints instead.

Iron Wolves Encampment

The Iron Wolves Encampment is located in the middle left of the region, and it is the last Waypoint in the Kehjistan that you can unlock at any time. This military outpost is bristling with soldiers, but aside from aesthetics, it offers very little.

Its services are limited to a single vendor and a blacksmith, and while it is close enough to dungeons to be worth traveling to, there aren't a whole lot of reasons to choose this Waypoint in particular to reach them. This problem only gets worse as the game goes on and you unlock some of the other, nearby Waypoints.

Imperial Library

The Imperial Library is an odd Waypoint. Located in the center of Kehjistan the entire area containing it is blocked off until you approach the end of the sixth act. You'll have to battle through the streets surrounding it to finally make it to the Waypoint located at the very back of the city.

Even once you unlock it, the only reason to travel here is to run through the nearby dungeons of which there are quite a few. There are no services to speak of, and due to to the previously locked nature of this area, it is hard to move from this Waypoint out into the rest of the map despite its central location.

Altar Of Ruin

The Altar Of Ruin is the sixth and final Waypoint in Kehjistan, and in keeping with the trend set by other regions, you'll have to clear a stronghold by the same name before unlocking this fast travel location. It's definitely worth the effort, however, as this Waypoint occupies a coveted position in the top left of the region.

To unlock this Waypoint, you'll have to storm the altar and collect keystones guarded by various cult members before entering the ritual chamber and facing a demon-summoning bishop head to head. Once unlocked, it won't offer any services, but it'll serve as a crucial fast-travel location since it sits so close to so many dungeons.

Zarbinzet

Zarbinzet is the shining capital of the swamps, hosting all sorts of services and acting as the leaping point for quite a few quests. Located in the bottom left of Hawezar, this Waypoint also lets you access a decent portion of the region with relative ease, and you can activate it at any time just by strolling up to it and clicking.

As for services, Zarbinzet has everything you could ask for and more. Like the other capital cities in the game, it is the only Waypoint in the region to offer specialty services like combining or unsocketing gems at a jeweler, equipping aspects with an occultist, upgrading your health potion, and much more.

Wejinhani

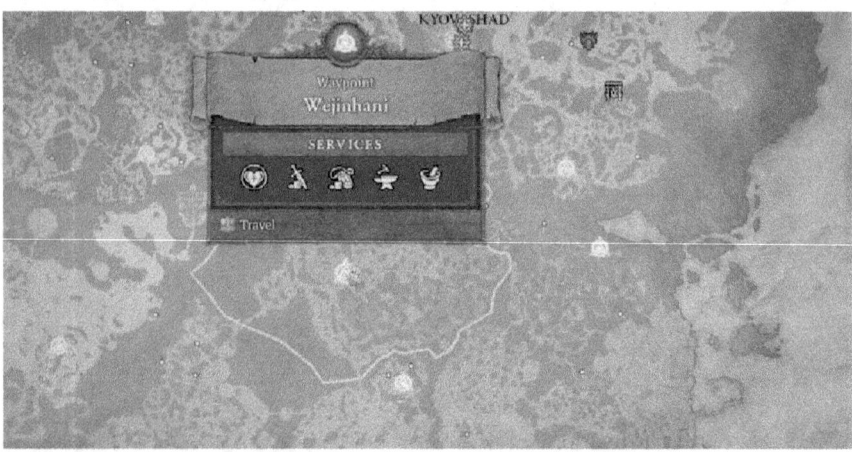

Located in the top middle of the region, Wejinhani is a relatively small swamp town with a well-placed Waypoint. While you can access this Waypoint at any time, the main quest line of act five will have to visit the area, providing the perfect excuse to activate fast travel in this town. You'll have to revisit this town a handful of times throughout act five, so it's a great Waypoint to pick up early.

As for services, this town offers the basics of a few vendors and a blacksmith along with the surprising inclusion of an alchemist. These services make it a great place to stop in between dungeons, and its location in the top middle of the region is perfect for reaching a handful of otherwise isolated dungeons.

Backwater

Backwater is the port town of this lowland region, sitting along the coast in the bottom left of Hawezar. You can activate this Waypoint at any time, and while it is quite far away from all the other Waypoints, its location leaves a little to be desired. While it's the closest fast travel point to quite a few dungeons, it's not particularly close to many of them, meaning you'll still have to walk a fair distance if you're forced to travel to Backwater.

What it lacks in location, however, it seems to make up for in terms of services. The town hosts all sorts of vendors that sell weapons, armor, and even jewelry as well as a blacksmith to upgrade or salvage your gear. On top of that, you can find an additional curiosities vendor in this town

Ruins Of Rakhat Keep: Inner Court

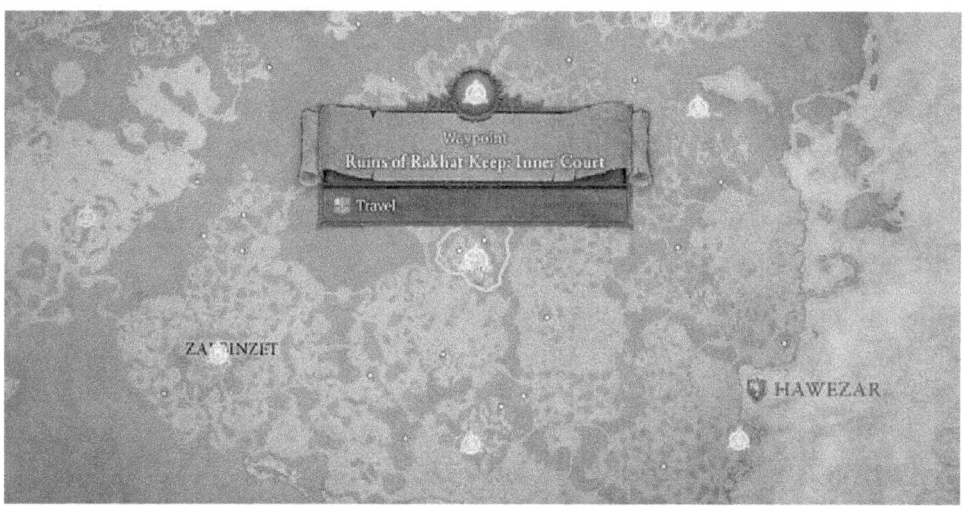

The Ruins Of Rakhat Waypoint, located in the center of the region, is the first one that you'll have to progress in the main quest line to unlock. Donan will ask you to find a way into the keep, and there you'll be able to activate the Waypoint which will let you travel back here to complete a handful of quests.

There are no services whatsoever at the Ruins Of Rakhat, but the Waypoint will still be quite useful as it's directly used in a handful of quests in the area drastically cutting down on your travel time. Even outside of the quests, the central location of the Waypoint makes it an easy favorite, and on top of that there are two dungeons inside the ruins that are within spitting distance of the fast-travel location.

The Tree Of Whispers

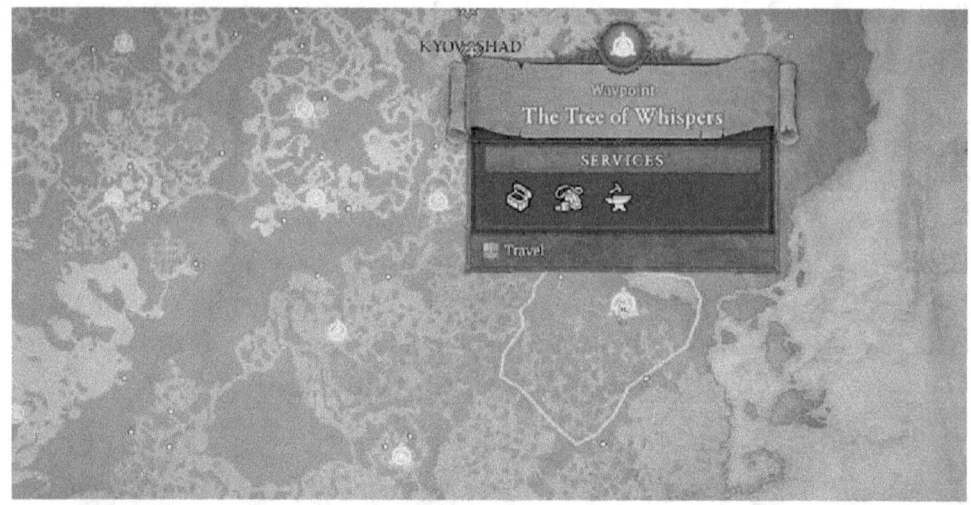

The Tree Of Whispers is the second main quest-related Waypoint, dominating the top right of the region. This Waypoint is used quite a few times throughout the campaign, and once the campaign is complete, you'll use this Waypoint to turn in Whispers of the Dead that you collect around the map. On top of that, it still serves as a convenient fast-travel location, letting you reach a handful of nearby dungeons.

Interestingly enough, this Waypoint offers a balanced array of services. There's a jewelry vendor that you can sell gear to, a blacksmith to salvage items, and access to your stash, so you can put away anything you'd like to keep. Altogether, this makes this Waypoint one of the most convenient places to access these basic services in the game.

Vyeresz

The sixth and final Waypoint in Hawezar sits in the bottom middle of the map. This old swamp town turned snake cult haven is originally a stronghold, and to turn it into a Waypoint, you'll have to storm in, open the path behind a ritual door, and slay the oversized naga at the end.

In terms of services, this Waypoint offers the basics and nothing more. It serves as a decent base in between dungeons, but its main draw is its location. Sitting next to seven dungeons, Vyeresz is a must-grab Waypoint if you plan on running these dungeons in the late-game.

ALL STRONGHOLD LOCATIONS

ALL STRONGHOLD LOCATIONS IN SCOSGLEN

Moordaine Lodge

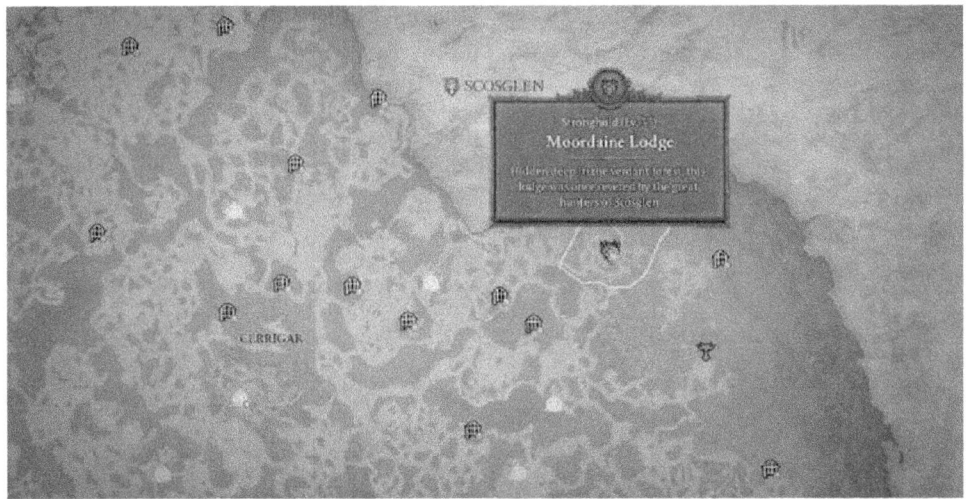

Located in the top right of the map, Moordaine Lodge is a former hunting ground turned savage refuge for all sorts of twisted beasts. Clearing out this stronghold will pit you against all sorts of animals that love to spring elaborate ambushes at a moment's notice.

To clean out Moordaine Lodge, you'll have to find the bodies of three slain hunters scattered around the area, defeating the enraged beasts guarding each one. Eventually, you'll be attacked by what seems like a werewolf during your investigation which will retreat back to its lair for the final fight.

Clearing out Moordaine Lodge unlocks two new dungeons: Ferals' Den and Twisted Hollow, which offer a few new aspects for druids and rogues. Of course, you'll also get a decent chunk of renown that can over time give you extra skill points and potion charges.

Hope's Light

Hope's Light is a zombie-pirate-infested lighthouse located in the top left of Scosglen. In this Stronghold, you'll have to fight your way across drenched shipwrecks and find a way to make it to the lighthouse in one piece.

Amidst the rocks and broken hulls, you'll find winches that when activated, will summon an elite and their small crew of enemies. Defeating them will let you progress to the next area. Repeat this until you make it all the way to the lighthouse, and you'll have to face a witch with complete mastery over the tides.

Clearing out this coastal stronghold will reward you with a decent chunk of region renown, and it will also allow you access to one new dungeon, The Flooded Depths, which contains one new necromancer aspect.

Tur Dulra

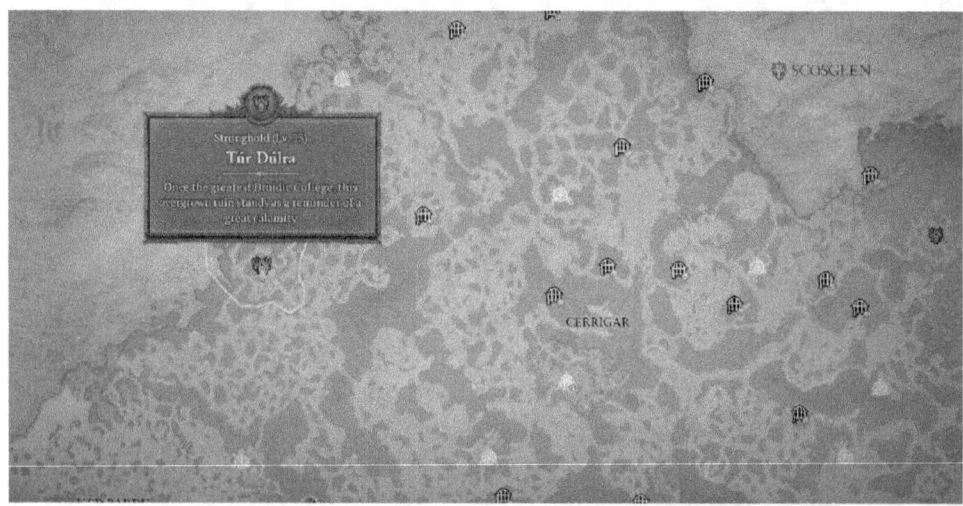

Tur Dulra is a former druidic college in the bottom left of Scosglen, mysteriously abandoned and overgrown with moss. Inside you'll find a strange memory of when the college first fell, and you'll have to run through its stone corridors as it burns around you.

Within the memory, you'll have to find the spirits of three powerful druids, trapped by their anger and harvested by a great demon. After freeing and talking to each one, you'll have to fight them in their corrupted form, and once all three are free, you'll have to face the demon itself before returning to the real world.

Once you complete the stronghold, you'll have access to the final Waypoint in Smcosglen, and the college will be revitalized, offering all sorts of goods and services. Of course, you'll also get a fair chunk of renown and unlock two new dungeons, Underroot and Wretched Delve, that offer a few new aspects.

How Many Strongholds Are There In Fractured Peaks?

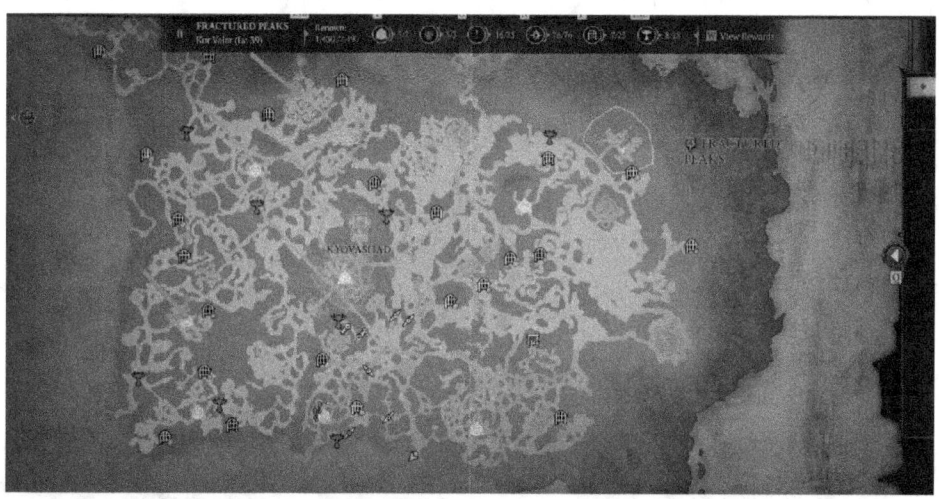

Each region in Diablo 4 has three Strongholds, and Fractured Peaks is no different. Strongholds are home to the Overworlds' most difficult enemies and can be completed once per character. If you'd like to complete a stronghold a second time, you'll need to start a new game or party up with a friend who hasn't done the stronghold.

While most of Diablo 4's enemies are level synced to your level, a Stronghold's enemies appear to have a level floor. This means that fighting them before you reach a zones' minimum intended level is very ill-advised.

Kor Dragan (Level 25)

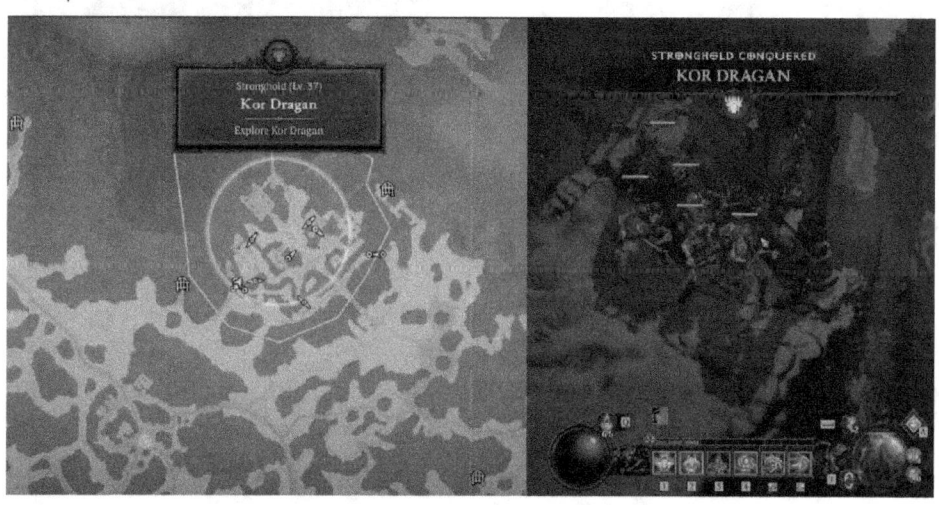

Kor Dragan is a corrupted fortress on the Northern edge of the Fractured Peaks region. This Stronghold is filled with Vampiric enemies, which can only be banished if players destroy three Vampire Incubators. Each Vampiric Incubator is shielded by three small patches of corruption, which can be located by following the fleshy tendrils coming out of each incubator.

Once all three Vampiric Incubators have been destroyed, you can smash your way past a wall of corruption into the chapel. Inside this room is where you'll find Nilcar, the Forgotten Bishop. Nilcar isn't a particularly hard-hitting boss, but he's very mobile and summons powerful friends.

Upon defeating Nilcar, relight the Wanderer's Shrine to conquer the Stronghold and get 100 Renown.

Malnok (Level 23)

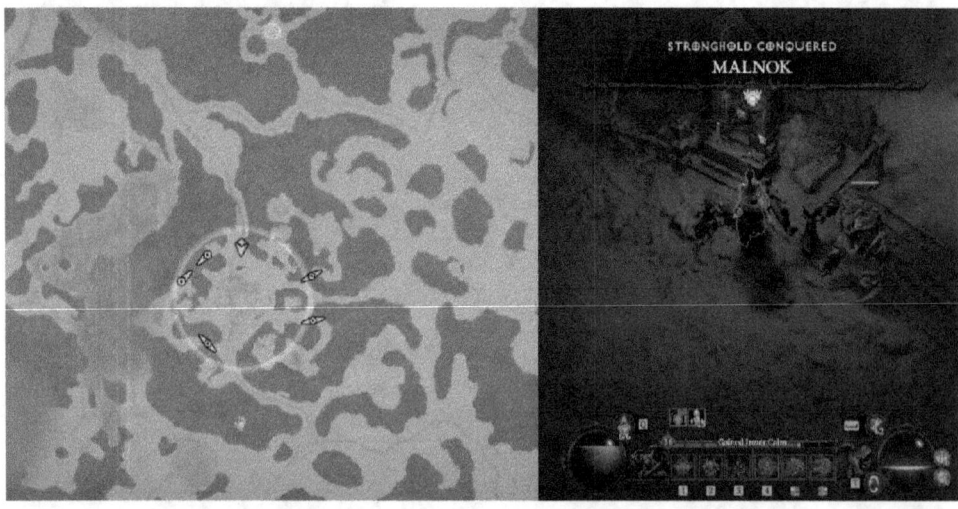

Malnok is a small town just South of the Bear Tribe refuge Waypoint. This Stronghold has been beset by an unnatural ice storm of epic proportions. The area has been overrun by the Ice Clan, and you will occasionally see an undead enemy spawn from the various townspeople that have been frozen solid.

To clear the Stronghold, you'll need to kill a daisy chain of connected enemies. The first challenge you'll see is actually the Stronghold's boss - a giant goat-man near the center of town with three icy wind tendrils extending from him to the nearby cliffs. He is immune (and thankfully non-aggressive) until you kill the Ice Clan Stormcallers on those cliffs. However, before you can kill those guys you need to kill their protectors the Ritual

Guardians. So, expect to run up to each Stormcaller, attack them once, then fight a guardian, rinse, and repeat until all three are dead. Then fight the boss while dodging him and all the elites he summons.

After expelling those icy goats, relight the Wanderer's Shrine to clear the Stronghold, get your Renown, and gain access to an Altar of Lilith on the Southwest side of town.

Nostrava (Level 22)

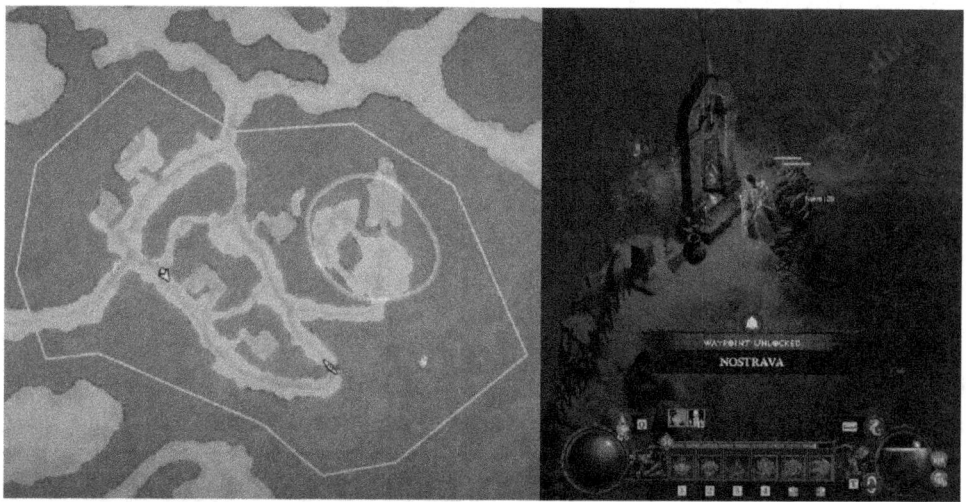

The final Stronghold of The Fractured Peaks is immediately north of Nevesk (the town from the Prologue). This Stronghold initially appears like a random settlement until you enter the Church. Here, a group of NPCs is worshiping Lilith's demonic power and attempts to sacrifice you.

After dispatching all the cultists in the church, you'll need to search the houses in town for five Demonic Effiges. These look like altars and have trash mobs and elites guarding them. In some cases, the house will also have a survivor for you to rescue. Destroying the final construct will cause the church bell to start ringing - head there next.

Inside the church will be a succubus named Negala, Lilith's Chosen. She will spawn two more Succubi: Korzira and Torvala to assist with killing you. Each is a powerful, tanky magic user who attacks with a unique element. As an added challenge, they attack faster the lower the total health pool between them goes.

Because each of these boss monsters deals with a different element, you may find it helpful to initially focus on the one your struggle to dodge the most or have the fewest resistances against. This advice may not be necessary at normal game difficulties but is worth keeping in mind if you are playing at a high world tier.

After defeating Negala and her friends, relight the Wanderer's Shrine to conquer the Stronghold. Upon doing so, you'll receive 100 Renown, a new Waypoint, and access to an Altar of Lilith inside one of the houses.

ALL STRONGHOLD LOCATIONS IN DRY STEPPES

Ruins Of Qara-Yisu

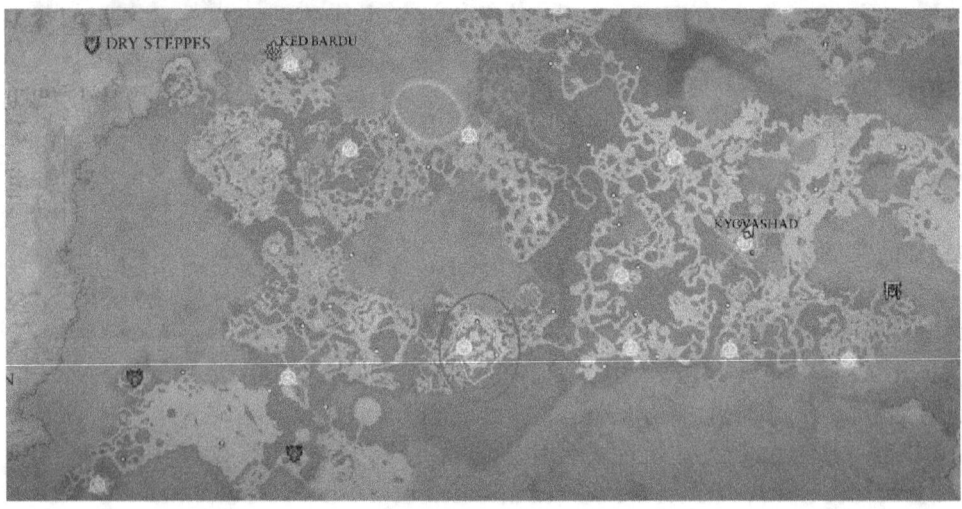

This is likely to be the first Stronghold you come across in the Dry Steppes region. The Ruins of Qara-Yisu are just a brief journey west of Nevesk and Nostrava. Both of these towns are southwest of Kyovashad, the main city when you first start Diablo 4. Be prepared to fight Demons who cast Lightning magic and have powerful melee attacks.

You'll get access to a new Waypoint as well as two new dungeons once you conquer Qara-Yisu. That makes it one of the most rewarding Strongholds to beat early in the game. One of the dungeons gives a Sorcerer aspect for bonus critical strike chance, while the other dungeon provides a Rogue aspect for bonus energy regeneration.

The Onyx Watchtower

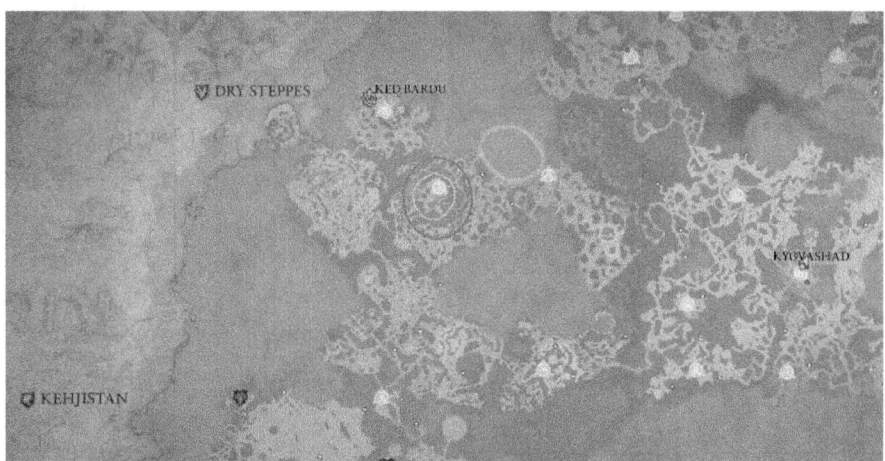

Bandits have taken over this Stronghold in the northern part of the Dry Steppes. It's a bit far from Kyovashad, but it's remarkably close to the town of Ked Bardu. You can easily find it on your way to start Act 3, by walking directly west from the Fate's Retreat Waypoint. Or simply Fast Travel to Ked Bardu itself if you've been there to begin Act 3 already.

Once you conquer this Stronghold, you'll have access to The Onyx Watchtower Waypoint as well as the Onyx Hold dungeon. The Waypoint here is extremely useful as a launching point for several other dungeons in the region as well. Clearing the Onyx Hold dungeon gives a Sorcerer aspect that can greatly increase damage to Vulnerable enemies. Just be ready to fight through narrow canyons filled with bandit clans.

Temple Of Rot

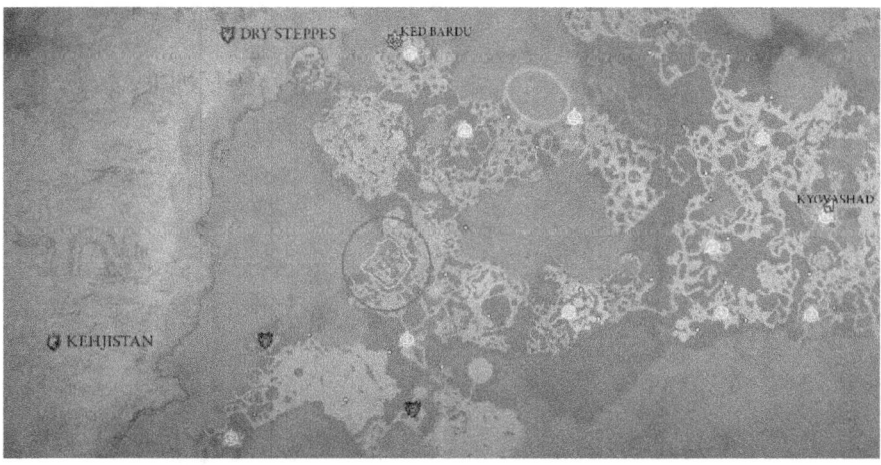

The Temple of Rot Stronghold is the most remote of all three found in the Dry Steppes. However, Jirandai is a town in the canyons to the south with a Waypoint that's super close. Jirandai is situated on the border with the Kehjistan region, and is also just a short walk away from a couple Strongholds down there. The journey out to this distant place could definitely be made easier with a mount.

Unfortunately, there are no dungeons unlocked by conquering the Temple of Rot. And with the Waypoint in Jirandai already so close, there was no need to add another one here. But there are several dungeons in the areas surrounding Jirandai and the Temple, making this a good zone for dungeon farming in general. There's also a large PVP area just a short run to the west. And you'll definitely need to clear all the Strongholds in Sanctuary in order to max out your Renown.

All Stronghold Locations In Kehjistan

Alcarnus

The first and most obvious of Kehjistan's Strongholds, Alcarnus can be found directly south of Jirandai and north-west of Tarsarak. Traveling south from Alcarnus and hugging the western cliff until you find a narrow canyon is the easiest way to get there.

Once a peaceful town, Alcarnus is now under the curse of a powerful witch. You'll have to defeat her many minions and deal with her extremely powerful magic attacks to conquer this Stronghold. Unfortunately, doing so doesn't unlock any new dungeons or Waypoints. But there is an Altar of Lilith within Alcarnus, and another to the west.

Altar Of Ruin

Getting to this Stronghold from the Iron Wolves Encampment takes you through some winding canyons to the northeast. If traveling from Alcarnus, continue through the canyon to the west and then traverse the desert northwest to reach the Altar of Ruin.

Like other dark places of worship in Diablo 4, the Altar of Ruin is full of evil cultists. But, this is easily the most rewarding Stronghold in Kehjistan. There's an Altar of Lilith here, as well as a Waypoint and a new dungeon. Necromancers can find the Hulking Aspect there. The Baal statue is also at the Altar of Ruin, which is required for The Way of the Three side quest.

Omath's Redoubt

This Stronghold can actually be pretty difficult to find unless you know where to look — although if you enjoy PVP, it may be easier, since it's just southwest of Kehjistan's Fields of Hatred. You can also get there very quickly from Gea Kul by the southernmost canyon.

Be prepared to face many undead hordes at Omath's Redoubt, along with a necromancer for their Boss. You can find an Altar of Lilith in Omath's Redoubt, and two more on the way if you travel from Gea Kul. Clearing this Stronghold will give you access to a new dungeon with the Sorcerer's Aspect of Splintering Energy. Although there's no new Waypoint to unlock, the one northeast in the Fields of Hate is already very close.

ALL STRONGHOLD LOCATIONS IN HAWEZAR

Crusaders' Monument

Located in the top left of the Hawezar region, this abandoned monument is home to all sorts of skeletons and other restless dead that you'll have to deal with in order to lift the curse laid by mistakes made long in the past.

To put the dead to rest in the Crusaders' Monument, you'll have to find the bodies of four grave robbers and burn their skulls in a ritual pyre at the center of the monument. While there are plenty of these corpses lying around, look towards the outer ring of the structure as those are the only bodies that will drop skulls when looted. After you burn all these bones, you'll have to face three heroes of old fighting in tandem.

Unfortunately, the stronghold won't give you any additional bonuses when defeated except for the 100 renown points you get for completing any stronghold in the region.

Eirman's Pyre

Deep in the Cinder Wastes in the top portion of Hawezar stands the stronghold of Eirman's Pyre. This ever-burning town is home to Eirman, a possessed body atop a large pyre that you'll have to put out in order to free the trapped spirits of the villagers.

To do this, you'll have to run around the area, looking for the remains of the villagers which you can use to put out the focal points feeding the flames of the pyre. Doing so will unlock a new area that will have another set of remains hidden within it. Extinguish all the focals, and you'll have to fight the spirit inhabiting Eirman's body to vanquish it once and for all.

Once you complete this stronghold, you'll gain access to the Oblivion dungeon. Running through this dungeon at least once will reward you with the Aspect of Shared Misery, which has a neat crowd control-based effect that any class can use.

Vyeresz

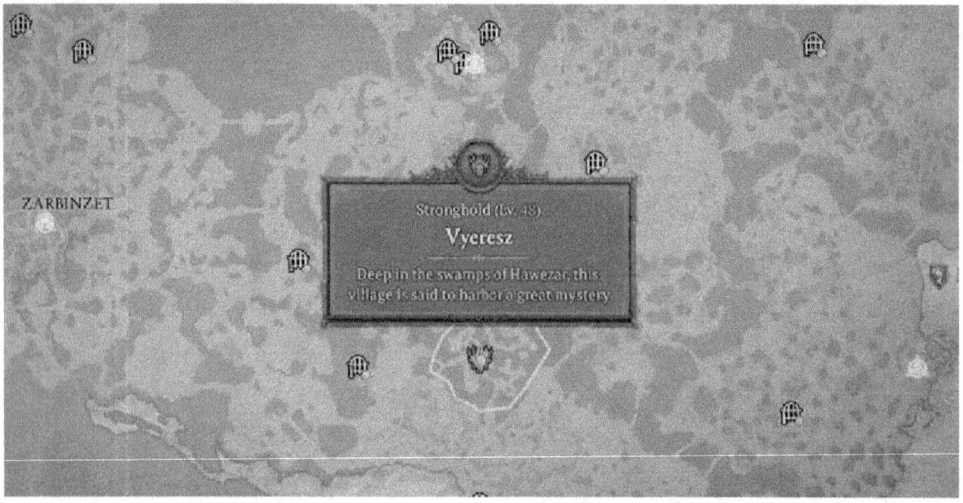

The third and final stronghold in Hawezar is the swamp town of Vyeresz in the bottom middle of the region. You'll quickly find that this town has been taken over by serpent cultists and their reptilian friends.

Around this snake-infested village, you'll find Serpent's Eyes, gems that dot the town in small snake-themed altars. You'll have to collect all three of these eyes, defeating the cultists that guard them, to open the door in the center of the village. Behind that door, you'll face an oversized naga.

The trouble is worth it, however, as clearing out this stronghold will unlock the Vyeresz Waypoint and the Shadowed plunge dungeon. The dungeon offers a decent aspect for rogues. While the services in the newly revitalized town aren't anything to write home about, Vyeresz sits in a great place on the map, letting you travel easily to anywhere in the bottom portion of Hawezar.

ALL SIDE DUNGEON LOCATIONS

ALL SCOSGLEN DUNGEON LOCATIONS IN SCOSGLEN

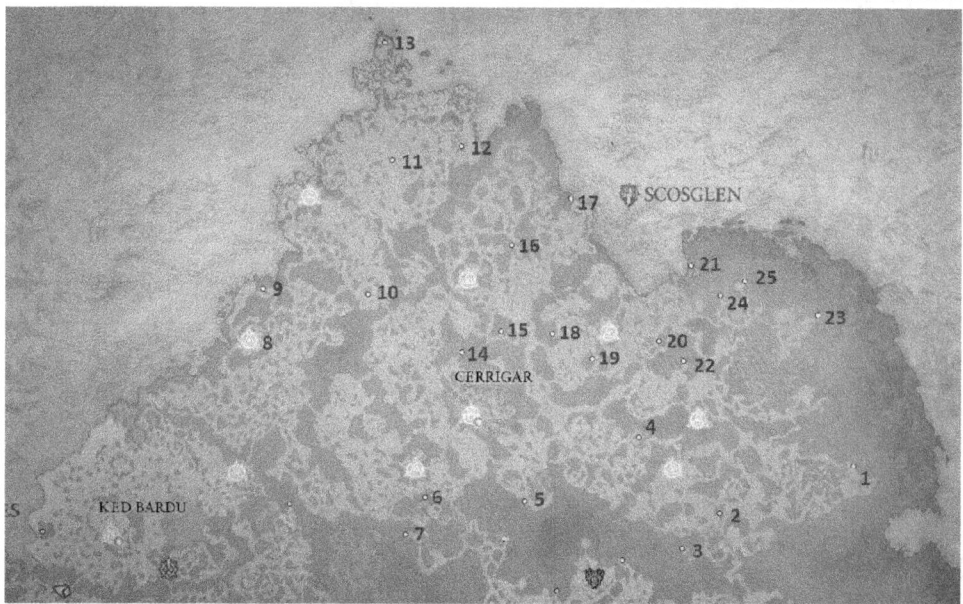

Scosglen has 25 different side dungeons scattered throughout the region, and for the most part, they're easy to find if you know where to look. The game automatically fills in your map in large chunks, meaning you'll only have to get near the dungeon you want to clear for it to be marked on your map. If you don't see it after getting close, it will either be locked behind a quest or a stronghold. Here's a list of where you can find each dungeon:

Number	Name	Aspect	Classes
1	Whispering Pines	Ballistic Aspect, Druid	Druid
2	Hive	Aspect Of Swelling Curse, Necromancer	Necromancer
3	Maddux Watch	Charged Aspect, Sorcerer	Sorcerer
4	Oldstones	Edgemaster's Aspect, All Classes	All
5	Sarat's Lair	Snowveiled Aspect, Sorcerer	Sorcerer

Number	Name	Aspect	Classes
6	Demon's Wake	Aspect Of uncanny Treachery, Rogue	Rogue
7	Broken Bulwark	Ghostwalker Aspect	All
8	Underroot	Aspect Of The Expectant	All
9	Wretched Delve	Aspect Of Static Cling	Sorcerer
10	Howling Warren	Aspect Of Arrow Storms	Rogue
11	Calibel's Mine	Aspect Of Relentless Armsmaster	Barbarian
12	Sunken Ruins	Aspect Of Ancestral Force	Barbarian
13	Flooded Depths	Aspect Of Empowering Reaper	Necromancer
14	Stockades	Crashstone Aspect	Druid
15	Raethwind Wilds	Aspect of inner Calm	All
16	Penitent Cairns	Death Wish Aspect	Barbarian
17	Vault Of The Forsaken	Requiem Aspect	Necromancer
18	Domhainne Tunnels	Aspect Of Efficiency	Sorcerer
19	Luban's Rest	Cheat's Aspect	Rogue
20	Garan Hold	Aspect Of The Dire Whirlwind	Barbarian
21	Mariner's Refuge	Overcharged Aspect	Druid
22	Aldurwood	Aspect Of Reanimation	Necromancer
23	Jala's Vigil	Bladedancer's Aspect	Rogue
24	Twisted Hollow	Shadowslicer Aspect	Rogue

Number	Name	Aspect	Classes
25	Ferals' Den	Aspect Of Quicksand	Druid

Locked Dungeons In Scosglen

While you'll be able to see 12 of the dungeons in Scosglen just by exploring every corner of the map, while 13 of those dungeons will be locked behind various strongholds and quests in the region.

There are five total dungeons unlocked by strongholds. The Moordaine Lodge stronghold unlocks the Twisted Hollow and Ferals' Den, Hope's Light unlocks the Flooded Depths, and Tur Dulra unlocks Underroot and Wretched Dive.

Eight dungeons total are unlocked by completing quests in act two. Two dungeons just below the Firebreak Manor Waypoint, Demon's Wake and Broken Bulwark, are both locked behind parts of the main quest. The Stockades will only become available once you have beaten all of act two. Jala's Vigil and the Aldurwood will both unlock after completing the same quest, and Raethwind Wilds, Penitent Cairns, and the Vault of The forsaken will all unlock after completing another quest

ALL SIDE DUNGEON LOCATIONS IN DRY STEPPES

All Dry Steppes Dungeon Locations

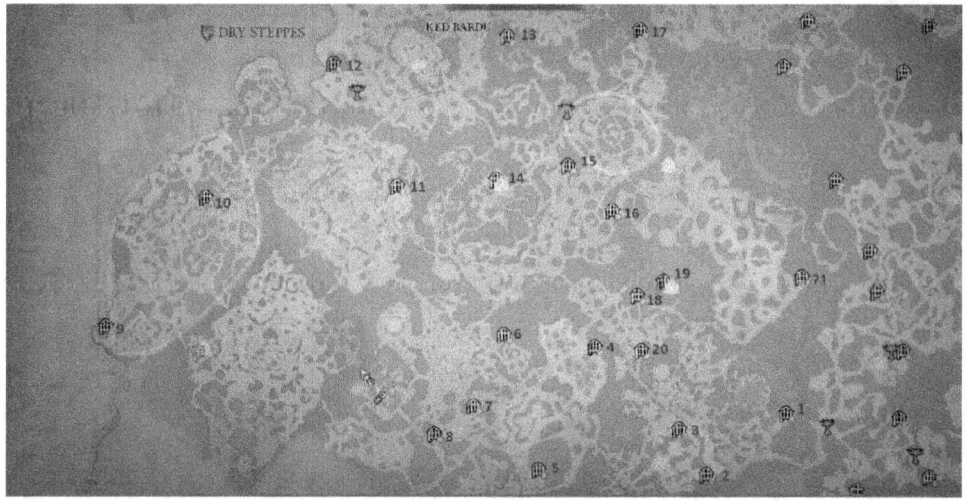

There are 21 dungeons for you to discover spread around the Dry Steppes, and most of them aren't that hard to find. The map will automatically fill out for you in large chunks, so if you even get close to a dungeon you're trying to find, your map should update, and it'll be added as a marker.

If this doesn't happen, that likely means the dungeon you're trying to enter is locked behind a quest or stronghold. You'll have to complete that content first before the dungeon will appear on your map.

Each Dungeon offers an Aspect reward related to a specific class, so make sure to hunt down any dungeons that contain an Aspect of interest!

Number	Dungeon Name	Aspect	Class
1	Betrayer's Row	Aspect Of Potent Blood	Necromancer
2	Pallid Delve	Elementalist's Aspect	Sorcerer
3	Shifting City	Ravenous Aspect	Rogue
4	Ancient's Lament	Aspect Of Volatile Shadows	Rogue
5	Champion's Demise	Aspect Of The Umbral	All
6	Bloodsoaked Crag	Aspect Of The Shepherd	Druid
7	Sealed Archives	Aspect Of Mending Stone	Druid
8	Charnel House	Aspect Of Perpetual Stomping	Barbarian
9	Komdor's Temple	Aspect Of The Bounding Conduit	Sorcerer
10	Carrion Fields	Aspect Of The Iron Warrior	Barbarian
11	Forgotten Depths	Aspect Of Bitting Cold	Sorcerer
12	Seaside Descent	Aspect Of Retaliation	Druid
13	Dark Ravine	Aspect Of Might	All
14	Onyx Hold	Storm Swell Aspect	Sorcerer

Number	Dungeon Name	Aspect	Class
15	Mournfield	Aspect Of Beserk Ripping	Barbarian
16	Grinning Labyrinth	Aspect Of Calm Breeze	Druid
17	Path Of The Blind	Aspect Of Bursting Bones	Necromancer
18	Guulrahn Canals	Trickster's Aspect	Rogue
19	Guulrahn Slums	Splintering Aspect	Necromancer
20	Buried Halls	Rapid Aspect	All
21	Whispering Vault	Aspect Of Unstable Imbuements	Rogue

Locked Dungeons In The Dry Steppes

Of the 21 dungeons in the Dry Steppes, only 13 can be discovered simply by stumbling across them. The other eight dungeons are locked behind either main quests or strongholds.

Five dungeons are locked behind a few quests in act three. Namely, the Dark Ravine, Forgotten Depths, Guulrahn Slums, Guulrahn Canals, and Whispering Vault all must be moved through as part of a quest before they become available to complete in the open world.

As for stronghold dungeons, there are only three in this region. Two dungeons, the Shifting City and Pallid Delve, are locked behind the Ruins of Qara-Yisu stronghold, while the other dungeon is uncovered after you beat the Onyx Watchtower stronghold. Believe it or not, the Temple Of Rot Stronghold does not unlock any additional dungeons.

All Kehjistan Dungeon Locations

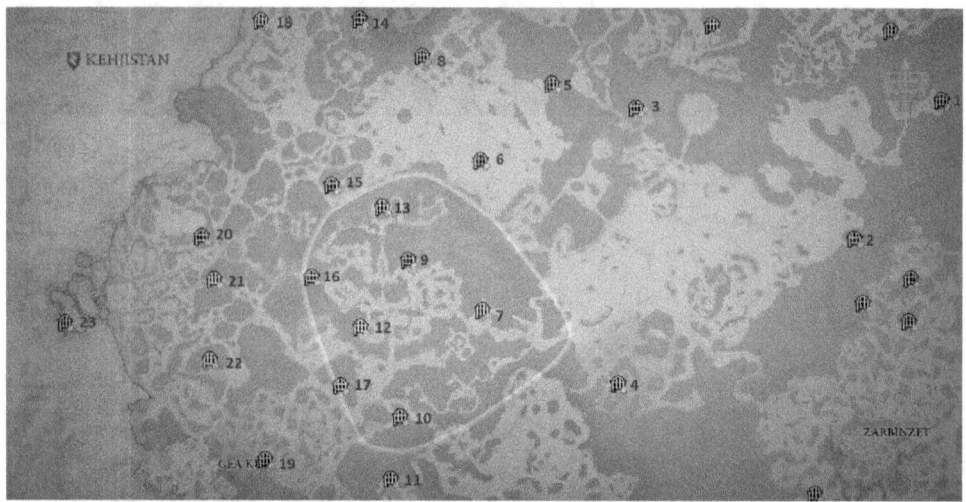

There are 23 dungeons scattered across the dunes of Kehjistan, but you will only be to discover 16 of them before completing certain parts of the main quest. To find a dungeon on your map, all you'll have to do is move near where it's located. The map should fill in large pieces of the region as you step into them, and once you enter the piece with the dungeon you're looking for, you'll be able to see exactly where it is.

Locked Dungeons In Kehjistan

Seven of the 23 dungeons in Kehjistan are locked behind various quests, and in a departure from the earlier regions in the game, very few of those locked dungeons are unlocked by completing strongholds.

Only two dungeons are unlocked by clearing out the strongholds they're located in. Sepulchur Of The Forsworn is unlocked by defeating the Altar Of Ruin Stronghold, and Crumbling Hekma is uncovered by clearing the Omath's Redoubt stronghold. The third stronghold in Kehjistan, Alcarnus, doesn't unlock anything once cleared.

The other five locked dungeons are Fading Echo, Prison Of Caldeum, Renegade's Retreat, Crusader's Cathedral, and Yshari Sanctum. All of these are locked behind the main quest progression, and unfortunately, you'll have to nearly complete act six before these dungeons become available to you.

All Hawezar Dungeon Locations

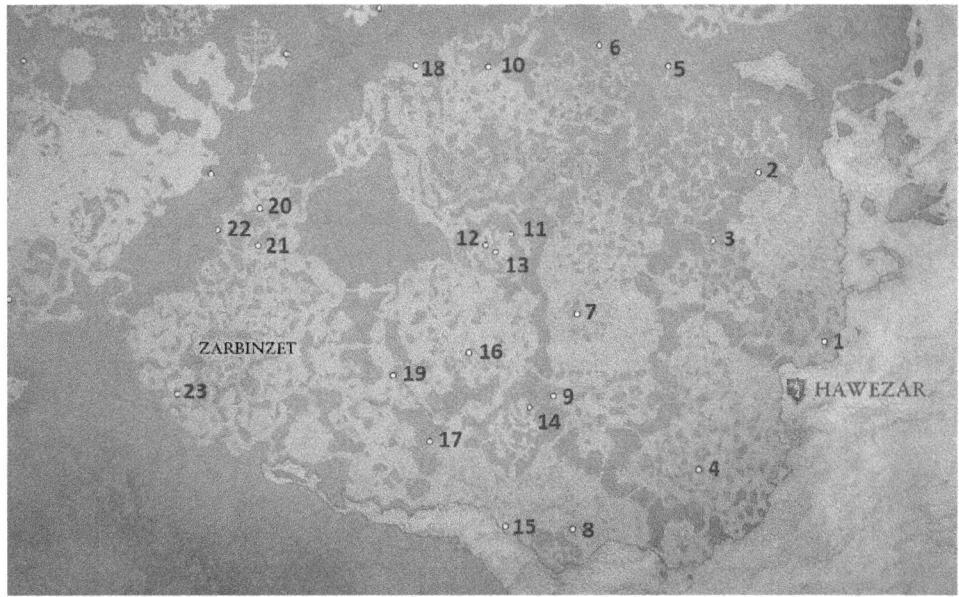

Hawezar has 23 dungeons scattered throughout the tangled undergrowth of the swamp, but you won't be able to unlock all of them at the start of the game. Of those 23 dungeons, only 16 can be discovered at any point in the game. For the others, you'll have to unlock them in various ways.

If you're trying to discover a dungeon, simply approach its location, and the game should fill in the area for you automatically. If you can't reach the location or if the dungeon doesn't pop up on the map when you get close, that means it's locked behind other content.

Number	Name	Aspect	Classes
1	Belfry Zakara	Aspect Of Ursine Horror	Druid
2	Anceint Resevoir	Aspect Of Ancestral Echoes	Barbarian
3	Haunted Refuge	Braweler's Aspect	Barbarian
4	Faceless Shrine	Unyielding Commander's Aspect	Necromancer
5	Fetid Mausoleum	Snowguard's Aspect	Sorcerer

Number	Name	Aspect	Classes
6	Oblivion	Shared Misery	All
7	Serpent's Lair	Aspect Of Three Curses	Sorcerer
8	Ghoa Ruins	Enshrouding Apsect	Rogue
9	Witchwater	Prodigy's Aspect	Sorcerer
10	Heathen's Keep	Aspect Of Numbing Wrath	Barbarian
11	Iron Hold	Fastblood Aspect	Necromancer
12	Akkhan's Grasp	Blighted Aspect	Necromancer
13	Steadfast Barracks	Vigorous Aspect	Druid
14	Shadowed Plunge	Aspect Of Branching Volleys	Rogue
15	Leviathan's Maw	Aspect Of Siphoned Victuals	Rogue
16	Maugan's Works	Earthstriker's Aspect	Barbarian
17	Ruins Of Eridu	Sacrificial Aspect	Necromancer
18	Light's Refuge	Aspect Of Bul-Kathos	Barbarian
19	Blind Burrows	Aspect Of The Tempest	Druid
20	Bastion Of Faith	Trickshot Aspect	Rogue
21	Endless Gates	Aspect Of The Rampaging Werebeast	Druid
22	Lost Keep	Deflecting Barrier	All
23	Earthen Wound	Aspect Of Singed Extremities	Sorcerer

Locked Dungeons In Hawezar

You can discover 16 of the 23 dungeons in Hawezar since the start of the game, but those last seven dungeons will have to be unlocked either by continuing through the main quest or by completing strongholds in the region first.

Five of the seven locked dungeons are hidden behind various quests. You'll have to progress most of the way through act five before you get access to the Iron Hold, Steadfast Barracks, Akkhan's Grasp, the Serpent's Lair, and the Fetid Mausoleum. These dungeons either don't appear until you've completed a similar story-related dungeon or are kept in locked locations that you need the main quest to get into.

Only two of the locked dungeons in Hawezar are uncovered by clearing strongholds. Beating Eirman's Pyre will unlock the aptly named Oblivion dungeon, and cleaning up Vyeresz will give you access to Shadowed Plunge. You won't unlock any additional dungeons for completing the Crusader's Monument Stronghold.

EXPLAINED

Which World Tier Should You Play On?

World Tiers directly affect the monsters of the world while you play; the higher the tier, the stronger everything is in the world. For those looking to get the most challenge out of Diablo 4, playing on the highest World Tier available to you will offer the biggest challenge.

As you increase the World Tiers, you'll get more money, XP, and better item drops to make up for the additional challenge. Playing on a higher World Tier will make your character much stronger, faster and is recommended for those wanting to level up quickly.

How To Change Your World Tier

When logging into the game, on the screen where you select your character, the menu to the right side of the screen will allow you to choose which World Tier you'll be playing. Once in the game, the World Tier can still be switched, but it can't be done just anywhere. To change your World Tier in-game, head to any of the major cities and look for the large statue of the angel called the World Tier Statue. Interacting with this statue will allow you to change the World Tier without having to log out of your character and back in again.

How To Unlock Every World Tier

The first two World Tiers are automatically unlocked when you first start up the game. Adventurer is the basic World Tier, offering basic difficulty with no bonuses to loot, gold, or XP. Veteran is also available and offers a decent boost to difficulty with moderate increases to XP and gold.

Nightmare is the third World Tier and is recommended for players levels 50-70. This is aimed at players beginning to focus on endgame content. This World Tier offers a bonus of 100% to XP, Sacred and Unique item drops, along with Nightmare sigils. This World Tier does also decrease your overall resistance to incoming damage while greatly increasing the strength of enemies. To unlock this World Tier, you'll need to complete the Cathedral of Light Capstone Dungeon in Kyovashad, which is unlocked after finishing the main campaign.

Torment is the fourth and final World Tier and is designed for players level 70+. This World Tier offers a 200% bonus to XP earned but further decreases your resistances and greatly strengthens monsters in your world. Enemies on this World Tier do drop Ancestral items, which are some of the best in the game. To unlock this World Tier, you'll need to complete the Fallen Temple Capstone dungeon. This is found toward the end of the endgame content and is only meant for very powerful characters.

DRUIDIC SPIRIT OFFERINGS & BOONS, EXPLAINED

Druidic Spirit Offerings

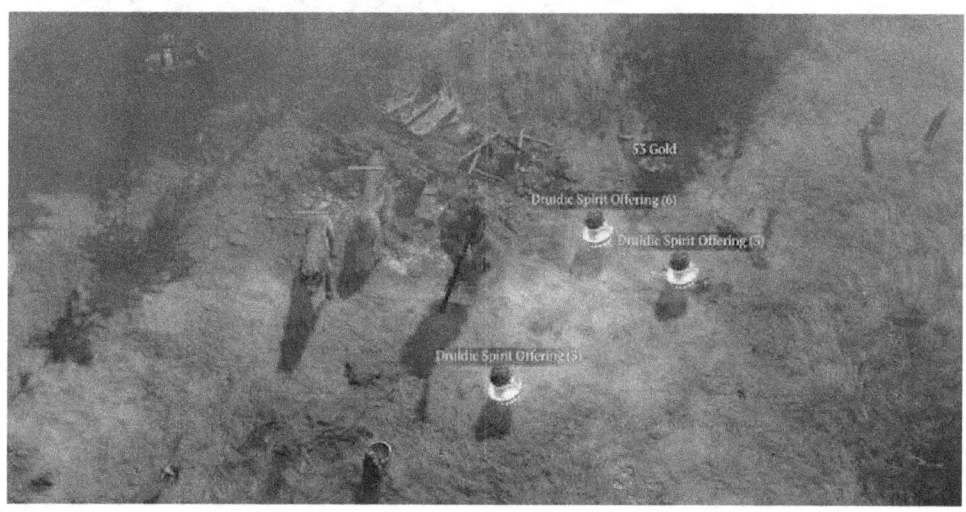

These little curios will start dropping right after you hit Level 15. Don't worry about farming specific enemy types or locations looking for them. They're totally random and can be found anywhere at any time. Just be sure to pick up any that you might see, because you're going to need 400 of them altogether to make the best use of the Spirit Boons. Unfortunately, they aren't subject to the auto-pickup effect that applies to things like gold or potions. So, be sure to pick them up manually until you hit 400. Since Diablo 4 is quite a long game with tons of content, that won't take too long at all.

Spirit Animal Boons

Once you reach Level 15 your Journal will automatically update with the Spirits of the Lost Grove quest. Follow through with that Druids-only quest, and that will unlock access to Spirit Animals and their Boons. There are four different Spirit Animals for Druids to embody in Diablo 4: Snake, Eagle, Wolf, and Deer. Each Spirit Animal offers 4 potential Boons to choose from. Some of these are general buffs that benefit all builds, whereas others are specific to certain builds like Nature casters or Werewolves. All of them can be extraordinarily useful when starting a Druid.

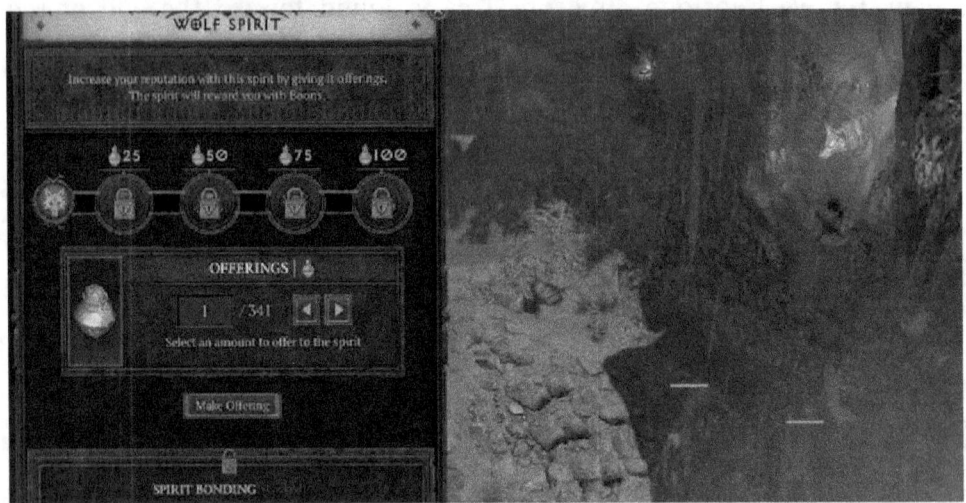

You can unlock Boons for 25 Druidic Spirit Offerings each for the Eagle, Wolf, and Deer Spirits, for a total of 100 Offerings per Spirit Animal. The Snake Spirit requires you to pay the full 100 all at once even just to see what its Boons' effects are. Coincidentally, this Spirit's Boons are also the most specialized for particular builds.

Spirit Animal	Boon	Effect
Snake	Obsidian Slam	Every 10th kill will cause your next Earth Skill to Overpower
Snake	Overload	Dealing Lightning damage has up to a 20% chance to cause the target to emit a static discharge, dealing 96 Lightning damage to surrounding enemies
Snake	Masochistic	Critical Strikes with Shapeshifting Skills heal you for 3% maximum Life

Spirit Animal	Boon	Effect
Snake	Calm Before The Storm	Nature Magic Skills have up to a 15% chance to reduce the Cooldown of your Ultimate Skill by 2 seconds
Eagle	Scythe Talons	Gain 5% increased Critical Strike Chance
Eagle	Iron Feather	Gain 10% maximum Life
Eagle	Swooping Attacks	Gain 10% attack speed
Eagle	Avian Wrath	Gain 30% Critical strike damage
Wolf	Packleader	Critical strikes have up to a 20% chance to reset the Cooldowns of your Companion skills
Wolf	Energize	Dealing damage has up to a 15% chance to restore 10 Spirit
Wolf	Bolster	Fortify for 10% of your maximum Life when you use a Defensive skill
Wolf	Calamity	Extend the duration of Ultimate Skills by 25%
Deer	Prickleskin	Gain 44 Thorns
Deer	Gift Of The Stag	Gain 10 maximum Spirit
Deer	Wariness	Take 10% reduced damage from Elites
Deer	Advantageous Beast	Reduce the duration of Control Impairing Effects by 15%

Renown Explained

What Is Renown?

Renown is the statistic that lets a player know how close they are to completing an area. A total of 2000 points are required to complete stages 1-5, with each area having at least that much up for grabs. Most regions have a bit more maximum renown for you to claim (Fractured Peaks for example has 2,495 total Renown points).

Reaching stages of renown in an area will unlock account-wide rewards such as:

- Potion charge increases
- Ability points
- Increased Obol capacity
- Paragon points

Your renown is character locked, allowing you to start all over with each playthrough, however, you will only receive the above rewards for completing a tier once. The bonus gold and experience can be received multiple times.

How To Get More Renown

Because of the impressive boost Renown tier rewards give you, many players want to know how to get more. There are many ways to earn renown including:

- Discovering new areas of the map
- Activating Waypoints
- Clearing Strongholds
- Finishing side quests
- Completing side dungeons
- Activating Altars of Lilith

You can see your progress on these objectives in an area by opening the map and hovering over the region with your cursor.

Where To See Your Renown

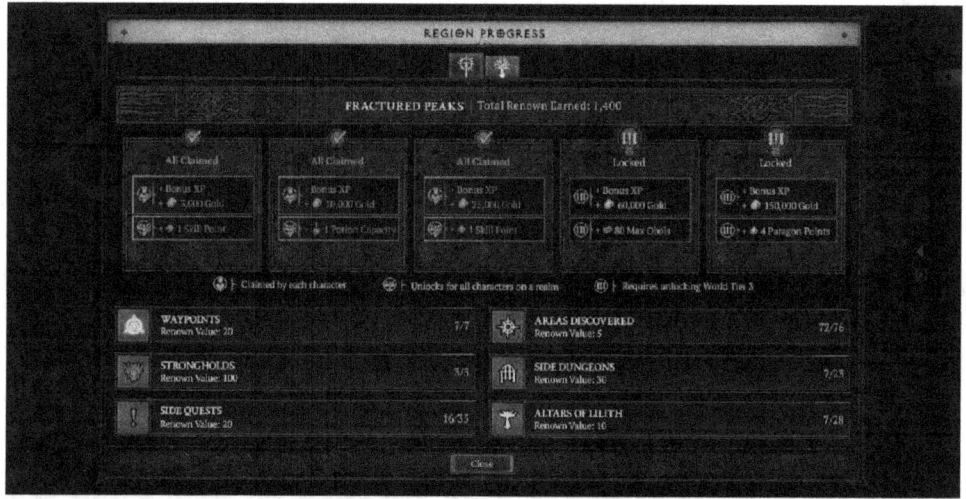

Renown can be viewed by opening the region progress menu. To open this page:

1. Open your map, and hover your cursor above the region you'd like to check.

2. Look on the far right-hand side of the top banner which shows your progress on collectibles.

3. Press the button prompt next to "View Rewards." This will vary based on the system and key bindings you're using.

This screen is also where you'll be able to collect your rewards, so check back periodically.

How To Unlock World Tier 4 & 5

The last two tiers of Renown for each region, you'll notice, are locked on your initial playthrough of the game. This is because they are only available on higher world tiers. The minimum world tier to unlock the rest of your Renown progression is Nightmare (world tier 3).

Unlock Nightmare by meeting the following requirements:

1. Be at least level 50

2. Finish the campaign

3. Complete the Cathedral of Light Capstone Dungeon

These achievements are no joke, especially for players new to the Diablo franchise, but they are the gateway to unlocking end-game content. Once you've unlocked Nightmare mode, change your world difficulty at the central statue of each town.

LUCKY HIT EXPLAINED

How Lucky Hit Works

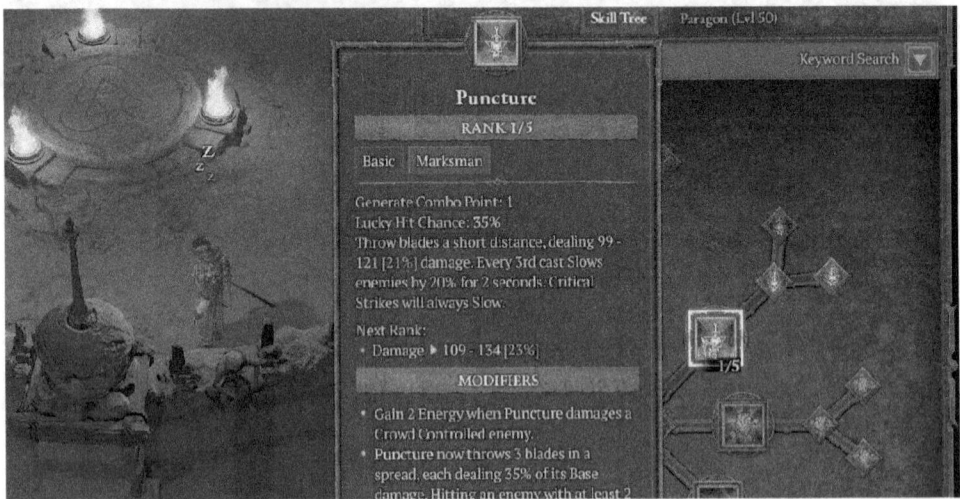

At its core, Lucky Hit is a bit similar to critical strikes except that the effects that can happen on a Lucky Hit are determined by your skills and equipment. Instead of dealing extra damage like a critical hit or overpower would, Lucky Hits acts as a way to allow other effects to happen on a hit. However, there are a few issues with this comparison, and they all come down to the difference between Lucky Hit Chance and Lucky Hit Effects.

Most skills have a base Lucky Hit Chance which you can see by turning on advanced tooltips in the game settings. This Lucky Hit Chance is an estimate of how likely a skill is to cause a Lucky Hit. If your basic attack has a 50% chance to Lucky Hit, roughly every other attack should be a lucky one but that doesn't mean you'll be triggering effects left and right.

Again, Lucky Hit does nothing on its own. Instead, it needs at least one effect that happens on a Lucky Hit as well to actually do anything. You can get this from a wide variety of skills and equipment, but you'll likely notice one constant between all of these. They all say that the effect has a chance to happen on a Lucky Hit, not that it happens automatically.

This is the biggest departure from critical hits: Lucky Hit effects all have a chance of happening on a Lucky Hit; they're not guaranteed. So if you have a 50% chance to deal a Lucky Hit, and an effect has a 30% chance of happening on a Lucky Hit, it only has a 15% chance of occurring on any given hit.

If you have multiple effects that could happen on a Lucky Hit, they are all calculated separately from one another whenever a Lucky Hit happens, and Lucky Hits can happen on damage over time ticks, but the tooltips for damage over time skills average the chance of a Lucky Hit happening at all during the entire damage over time effect.

How To Build Around Lucky Hits

The separation between Lucky Hit Chance and Lucky Hit Effect Chance can make it challenging to build around Lucky Hits in a meaningful way. You can boost your Lucky Hit Chance, but there isn't an easy way to increase the chance of an effect occurring, so if that chance is already very low, you'll never be able to make it happen consistently.

Gear can come with an additional Lucky Hit Chance Bonus, but this only increases the chance of a Lucky Hit happening, not of an effect activating. If you want to run the numbers, the formula for a Lucky Hit Effect to go off looks a bit like this:

Lucky Hit Chance x (1 + Lucky Hit Chance Bonus) x Lucky Hit Effect Chance

Using the numbers from above and assuming a Lucky Hit Chance Bonus of 50%, it would look something like this:

0.5 x 1.5 x .3

For a total of a 22.5% chance of the effect happening on any given attack, and this shows why it can be hard to build around Lucky Hits. Lucky Hit Chance Bonus applies multiplicatively to Lucky Hit Chance, so you need a significant bonus to see any sort of meaningful results, and you'll never be able to hit 100% if the skill isn't already at that point.

On top of this, the Lucky Hit Effect Chance will almost always be the limiting factor in this equation, meaning you'll have to find an effect with a decent chance to activate it simply won't become consistent no matter how much you try to make it work. With most of the powerful Lucky Hit Effects having a low chance to activate, it can be tough to find a good effect to focus a build around.

Level Scaling Explained

Is There Level Scaling In Diablo 4?

Yes! Diablo 4 has level scaling in both single and multiplayer settings. In single-player, all the monsters of the world will scale to your current level, allowing you to travel around and properly fight the monsters in any area. After completing the main campaign, later characters may explore the world without any boundaries, as all the monsters you face will scale to your level.

In multiplayer situations, all the monsters in the world will scale equally between all party members, no matter the gap in level. It's easier to think of each monster not having a specific level. Instead, they're dealing and taking damage scaled properly to whichever player is attacking them. Both a level 10 and level 30 player can fight the same boss in the same party. They'll both find it to be equally challenging while also earning gear and items that scale to their character's level. Higher-level characters will have more abilities and tricks to use that will make them seem stronger, but even the flashiest of gear will be appropriately scaled so as not to dominate a lower-level friend's world.

What Are World Tiers?

World Tiers are one-way players can scale the game's difficulty to their liking. In single-player or in a party, the World Tier will determine the overall strength of the monsters you'll be facing and the rewards they will drop upon being defeated. The World Tier is scaled equally for any party member, making higher world tiers equally challenging no matter the gap in party level. New World Tiers are unlocked by reaching and completing certain dungeons. World Tiers also have recommended levels to achieve for the higher challenge provided with each tier. Should players want to challenge these tiers with lower-level characters, it is possible. The rewards will be great, but it'll be a fight through hell.

Capstone Dungeons, Helltides, and Strongholds

While much of the game offers the usual level scaling, Corrine areas or events will be more challenging and scale to be sure of this. When participating in either Helltide events or Strongholds, the enemies within will scale to slightly higher than your current level, usually about two levels. Capstone Dungeons are also unique in that they have set levels. The

Cathedral Of Light Capstone dungeon, unlocked right after beating the main campaign, has all enemies within at level 50. These Capstone dungeons may be nearly impossible for those under-leveled, but they are one of the few places where higher-level players can truly feel powerful while clearing.

BARRIER GENERATION EXPLAINED

Barriers in Diablo 4

Barriers are a form of shielding that your character can use outside of physical shields. It forms a small aura around your character that can absorb a certain amount of damage before your character's health takes the brunt of it. Barriers can be a life-saver for any weak characters you may be building to help negate minimal health.

Each class in the game comes with its own version of Barriers, and the ability to use a Barrier can come from various items and equipment you find scattered around the world. Keep an eye out for the item description when you pick something up to see if it will give you a certain amount of Barrier.

You can also unlock Passive abilities to help with Barrier.

Barrier Generation

This is the rate at which your Barrier will generate as you play and take damage. It will regenerate faster once it has been hit, along with being stronger in general.

Equipment will come with their own base stat for Barrier Generation. You can also find items like Diamond Gems to slot into sockets to further boost their Barrier Generation. It is a great way to passively keep your defenses up and make sure that your character can withstand enough damage in a fight.

GUIDE

COMPLETE BLACKSMITH GUIDE

How To Upgrade Gear

One of the functions of the blacksmith is to allow you to upgrade your weapons and armor. You may do this a limited number of times to help items become stronger. These upgrades will increase its base damage, along with any bonus attributes that come with the item. The amount of times you can upgrade an item is limited, but will help keep an item relevant just a bit longer.

Go to the nearby blacksmith in town and go to their third menu. Here you'll be able to pick the gear piece you'd like to upgrade and see what the total cost will be. Upgrading a piece of gear will take both gold and resources that match the rarity of the item you're trying to upgrade. Depending on the rarity, you will need multiple consumable materials of the same rarity to upgrade the weapon.

Obtaining Crafting Materials

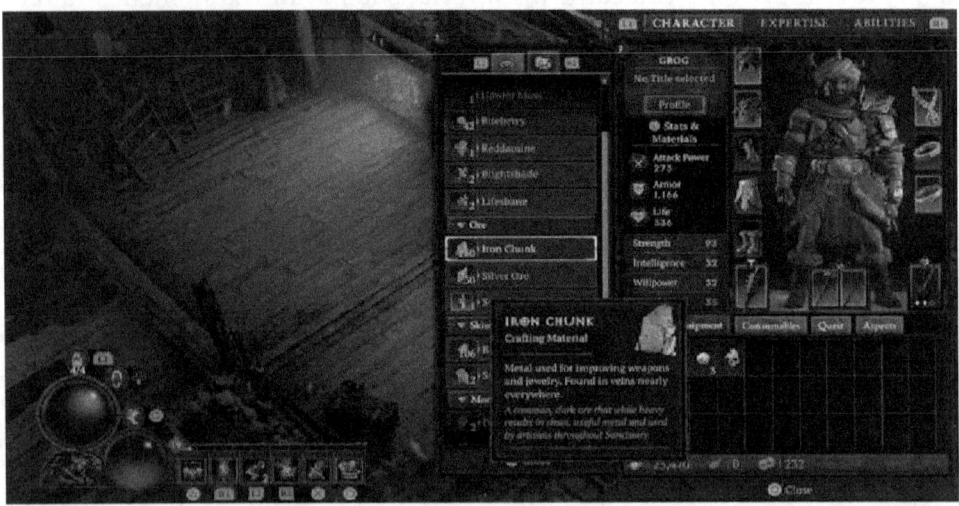

To obtain the right crafting materials to upgrade your gear at the blacksmith you'll need to break down older pieces of gear in the blacksmith's first menu You'll be able to break items down through junk or by rarity. Breaking down an item will give you crafting materials that match the rarity of the item. This requires you to break down yellow items to upgrade other yellow items.

Early into the game, it makes sense to break down all older gear. You'll constantly find better gear, and yellow rarity crafting materials will be very useful later on.

To see which crafting materials you have, go to your inventory and look along the left side of the menu. Below your character's name will be "Stats And Materials." Press the corresponding button for your platform that appears next to these words. From here, switch to the Materials menu and scroll down to see your total material menu. Blacksmithing materials are near the bottom.

How To Repair Gear

The blacksmith is also where you can go to repair your damaged armor. The second menu in the blacksmith will allow you to repair equipped or damaged items in your inventory for gold. While the cost will get higher as more armor pieces start to wear down, switching them out constantly or repairing them will often stop the price from becoming too steep.

KEEPING THE OLD TRADITIONS QUEST GUIDE

Starting The Quest And Finding The Statue

This quest is found in the Untamed Scarps area of the Dry Steppes and begins after reading a book with a note that tells the player to "Keep The Old Traditions." After reading this note, the quest will begin, and the location of the statue will be marked on your map. The statue is just to the north, on the other side of the nearby mountains and is easily found when checking your map. Now at the statue, you'll need to make your character keep the old traditions.

How To Complete The Quest

To complete this quest, players will need to use a specific emote, one that does not come already slotted in their emote wheel. To open your emote wheel, you'll need to press up on the d-pad for both PlayStation and Xbox or "E" if you're playing on PC. Following this, you'll need to equip and use the "Yes" emote.

Press the button to customize your emote wheel, "Y" on Xbox, triangle on PlayStation, or simply press customize on PC. Doing so will open up the full emote wheel and allow you to customize it with any of the other provided emotes. Now, using the emote wheel, use the "Yes" emote standing in front of the statue. Doing so will keep the old traditions, and a hidden chest will pop out of the ground near the statue. Looting this chest will complete the quest and reward you with whatever is found in the hidden chest.

Spirits Of The Lost Grove Quest Guide

Conquer Túr Dúlra

Strongholds are locations in Sanctuary that must be cleansed of terrible evil forces. Túr Dúlra is temporarily occupied by Baelgemoth, Infernal Tormenter, and he knows how to pack a punch. Before facing him, you'll first need to free the spirits of four Druids spread out around the Stronghold

Fighting Baelgemoth himself isn't too bad, as long as you can avoid getting hit a lot. Shapeshifters may struggle with this fight if they're specialized purely for dealing damage. This boss doesn't have a lot of health, so as long as you keep hitting him with well-timed heavy attacks, you'll be fine.

Find Gathlen, The Spirit Lord

Once relative calm has returned to Túr Dúlra, you can truly begin the Spirits of the Lost Grove quest. Druid Ardreth can be found at the bottom tier of the Stronghold, in the grove of the Spirit Animals. This is where you'll spend Druidic Spirit Offerings on powerful Boons that can change your game.

Ardreth will direct you to the southeast in order to commune with the Spirit Lord. It's a fairly short run from Firebreak Manor. You can save time with Fast Travel. Once you fight through the poachers to reach the Spirit Lord's Altar, Gathlen will give you another task. You'll need to travel to Fainne, the Abandoned Grove, in order to free a physical aspect of the Spirit Lord himself.

Fainne is only a short run to the north from the Spirit Lord's Altar. Once you arrive, you'll need to deal with a Goatmen ambush led by Gorefeast. This Elite has two powerful special effects, so take him down first. After all the Goatmen are defeated, you can free the Spirit Lord from the effigy and return to Túr Dúlra.

Return To Túr Dúlra

Getting back is simple enough with Fast Travel, or you can just walk since Fainne is close. Once back, you'll have to go through the rigamarole of climbing back down to the lowest tier to see Ardreth. He'll direct you to place Gathlen's skull on Túr Dúlra's Altar, completing the quest.

Now that you've done the hard work, it's time to reap the outstanding rewards! Spirit Boons are powerful passive effects with a wide range of benefits. You can mix and match up to 5 altogether eventually, making these essential for Druids of any level or build. This is just one of the many ways you can take your Druid game to the next level in Diablo 4.

TREASURE GOBLIN GUIDE

What Are Treasure Goblins?

Treasure Goblins are random spawns that will drop some pretty great treasure when you kill them. Once you see one, you can get some great items (including legendary items) and money from them. They will run pretty quickly, so don't let them get away. These enemies will not fight with you. Instead, their main goal is to escape from you. They will only flee from you.

If there is a Treasure Goblin around, you will see it on your mini-map. The icon for these enemies looks like a small goblin with a sack. If you're close enough to it, it will even show up on your regular map.

What Happens If A Treasure Goblin Gets Away?

As soon as they are spotted, Treasure Goblins will run away. This is why keeping an eye on your mini-map is a great idea. Once far enough away, they will begin to open a yellow portal to escape.

If you attack them while they are doing this, they will stop summoning the portal and run again. If the portal opens all the way, the Treasure Goblin will be lost, and you cannot get it back.

How Do You Find Treasure Goblins?

As mentioned previously, Treasure Goblins are random spawns. You are able to find them anywhere in the game. They can spawn in cellars, out in the open, or in dungeons. Anywhere you can fight enemies, they have a chance of spawning into the game. Interestingly, YouTuber DM: Diablo 4 found out that cellars have a chance of spawning either a Treasure Goblin or a whole cellar full of Treasure Goblins. Without any real way of knowing what may be in the surrounding cellars, you'll definitely want to check them all out, just in case.

MAUGAN'S WORKS GUIDE

Where To Find Maugan's Works

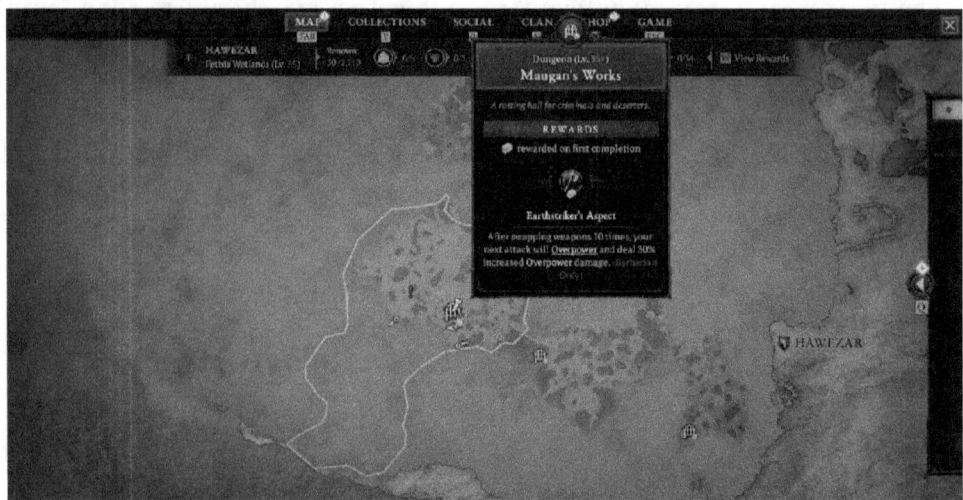

It's recommended that before you approach Maugan's Works, you should be around Level 35 to avoid biting off more than you can chew. The dungeon will be in the region of Hawezar, south of Fractured Peaks.

Maugan's Works will be in the third section towards the western part of Hawezar, shown in the first image above. You'll find the entrance to the dungeon in an area of ruins, following down a staircase into a cellar. You'll then arrive in Maugan's Works, and you'll receive the following the Earthstriker's Aspect for the Barbarian class, which will do the following: After swapping weapons 10 times, your next attack will Overpower and deal 30 percent increased Overpower damage.

How To Complete Maugan's Works

The overall objective of Maugan's Works is to save 6 prisoners in total. As you first enter into the Interrogation Rooms, you'll want to defeat the knights and then make your way down the path to the west. As you follow down this path up ahead, you'll find the first prisoner to your right at the end of the hallway. As you free them, keep heading forward and defeat the enemies up ahead. Eventually, you'll arrive at a shrine on the right which you can use to gain an advantage in battle.

As you continue down the hallway, you'll find a locked door that will require a key to open. First, free the prisoner nearby to the door. Then, continue forward down the hallway to the next shrine to find the third prisoner.

You can find them right of the shrine, however, all that will be left of them is some remains. You'll want to lay them to rest, and then make your way down the western path past the shrine you just activated.

Make your way quickly through the enemies, and follow the path south to find the next two prisoners. One will be off to the left, while the other will be in the middle of the room. Then, continue south to find the last prisoner and lay their remains to rest.

You will now have an elite enemy appear, The Warmaster. Depending on your World Tier level, this could be an incredibly easy battle or relatively tough. The Warmaster has incredibly slow attacks, so you should have no issues avoiding him if you time your dodges well. He can also attach a chain to you, so whenever you see the Hellbinder being deployed, you'll want to get away as quickly as possible.

After the battle, follow the path on the right going back towards the eastern section of the dungeon. Then, head north towards the locked door you passed by earlier. You'll now be able to access this area.

Through here, you'll just want to follow the path ahead until you head down a staircase into the Deserter's Den. Go down the path to the west, and then head towards the south. In the very last room, you'll want to defeat all the enemies in the room while attempting to keep at least one of the hostages alive. The best way to defeat all of them while saving the hostages is to use an Ultimate Skill to take out a large amount of enemies at once.

Now, head back north towards the top of the map. You'll have a couple more elite enemies to run through, which will help you raise your level quickly. Now, follow the eastern path and take the hallway heading north. This will take you into the Council of Thieves room, where you'll take on the three final bosses: Sacred Physician, Grand Inquisitor, and Lord Commander.

Image of the boss battle with Sacred Physician, Grand Inquisitor, and Lord Commander in Diablo 4.

For this section, we suggest using Skills that can hit multiple enemies at once, as well as Ultimate Skills to deal maximum damage. When you've successfully finished them off, you'll now have access to the Earthstriker's Aspect, available to the Barbarian class.

How To Start Menestad Coffers

You can start this quest as soon as you have finished the prologue to the game which brings you to Kyovastad with Lorath, and it is recommended to be at least Level 5 before starting this quest.

You can find the NPC who gives you the quest, Kudomyla the Tithe Collector, just to the left of the town's fast travel point, near the center.

Kudomyla will explain to you that a monk named Bozan left the town to make a delivery to the nearby settlement of Menestad, but has not been heard from since. She fears for the monk and asks you to help find Bozan out in the wilderness to check on him and see if he is okay.

How To Complete Menestad Coffers

If you look at your map, you will notice a large, blue area on the map to the north/northwest of Kyovashad. This area is where you will need to explore in order to track down Bozan, so head out of the town's northwest exit and begin making your way to the blue section of the map.

Be ready to fight, as there will be plenty of enemies to fight along your path to Bozan, mostly consisting of Ice Clan Marauders. They aren't too powerful of enemies, but there are enough that you can easily get overwhelmed if you're not careful and mindful of your health. Just be sure to take them out as you go, and you will be fine.

As you explore the blue section, you will eventually come to a cliff where you can find Bozan slumped against the rock, not looking too good. Luckily, he is still alive and you can speak with him. He will explain that his guards turned on him and left him for dead out here, and because of his condition, he cannot finish his delivery of tithes to Menestad.

He will ask you to finish it for him, and he will head back to Kyovastad. Pick up the Strongbox next to Bozan and start heading to the left to take the tithes to where they need to go.

You can find Menestad real close to where you find Bozan. Again, there will be some Ice Clan Marauders that will make your journey a little tougher, but they aren't anything that you can't handle.

Once you get to Menestad, you can find Telgun the Merchant Lord in the middle of the settlement, who is the person you need to hand off the

Strongbox to in order to complete the quest.

RAISING SPIRITS QUEST GUIDE

How To Start Raising Spirits

You can start this quest pretty much as soon as you reach Kyovashad after completing the game's prologue. You will come to the city with Lorath, and once he has gone on his way and the world opens up, you can find the quest-giver near the center of the town.

The quest-giver is a guard named Boza, who explains to you that she is concerned about the morale of the soldiers and guards in the city. She is wanting to cheer them up and raise their morale, but she is scared of coming across as soft to the ranks. Instead, she wants you to help her out and cheer them up for her.

How To Complete Raising Spirits

In order to cheer up the guards, you will need to go to the training area and barracks for the city guards. On your map, a blue section will appear just northeast of where you can talk to Boza to get the quest.

There is a direct route to the barracks from Boza, and the entrance to the room will be on the western side of the building. You will see guards practicing combat on the other side of the wall to clue you in that you are in the right place.

All you need to do is walk into the room among the guards that are training and pull up your emote wheel. You can do this by pressing E on your keyboard if you're on mouse and keyboard, or by pressing up on the D-Pad if you're using a controller.

With the wheel pulled up, go to the left tab and select the Cheer option there Your character will do the Cheer emote, and then you will be tasked with returning to Boza. Speak with her again, and she will thank you for your help and give you your rewards for completing the quest: 1,596 XP, 440 Gold, and an Herb Cache.

CHAMPION'S DEMISE DUNGEON WALKTHROUGH

Where To Find Champion's Demise

To locate the Champion's Demise Dungeon, you'll want to head over to the western region of Dry Steppes. This area is incredibly big, however, so we will help you locate exactly where on the map you can find Champion's Demise.

In the city of Kyovashad, you'll want to head to the very southern tip of the Desolate Highlands area. Continue west, making your way into the Pallid Glade, and then further into The Accursed Wastes. You'll now be in the Dry Steppes region, and all you will need to do is continue west into the Untamed Scarps area. Here, you'll head down into a cave, The Barren Steeps, which will eventually lead you to Champion's Demise. You can use the images above as reference to better locate the dungeon, located deep within the caves.

How To Complete Champion's Demise

Champion's Demise has a relatively easy set of tasks to complete. You will need to:

- Return 3 Stone Carvings to the Pedestal
- Defeat 2 Cairn Defilers
- Defeat the Khazra Abomination

The first Stone Carving can be found directly south of the Pedestals in the center of the Dungeon. The second can be found north of the Pedestals at the very end of the hallway. Finally, the third and final Stone Carving will be in the area west of the Pedestals. The images above show the exact location of each Stone Carving, so you can easily acquire them.

Once you return them all to their spots, you'll then need to defeat 2 Cairn Defilers. It's best to use abilities that will cause damage over time. You'll also want to make sure to have a few defensive skills available to protect you from their powerful attacks.

Finally, you'll want to head into the last area to take on the boss, the Khazra Abomination. This enemy can be a bit fast and will use poison attacks on you, so you'll want to make sure to use skills that will allow you to dodge his attacks and have a shield to protect you. Once you finish him off, you'll successfully get the Aspect of the Umbral.

PARAGON BOARD GUIDE

What Is The Paragon Board?

The Paragon Board opens up for you as soon as you hit Level 50 and will differ based on which class you are playing as. Prior to Level 50, you are essentially choosing the core facets of your build that will then carry over once you hit this level. From here on out, your XP will be going towards the Paragon Board and choosing the options here to further your build how you want.

Your XP bar will change at Level 50, as well, changing to a bar with four segments. Every time you fill out one of these segments, you will be given one Paragon Point to spend. This means that every level you gain will give you four Paragon Points to use.

Each of the nodes that you select in the Paragon Board are tied to your Attributes, rather than unlocking abilities like it was during Levels 1 to 49. There are four kinds of Attributes that you can build on:

- Strength - boosts your armor
- Intelligence - boosts your skill damage and resistance to all elements
- Willpower - boosts your resource generation, healing, and overpower
- Dexterity - boosts your dodge chance and critical hit change

You will need to also pay attention to the equipment you are using to help further bump up these Attributes to really bring the best out of your build. Be sure to choose the right armor and weapons that increase the Attributes you want to focus on, while also making up for any drawbacks in the other areas, and then use your Paragon Board to further help with these Attributes.

You will be progressing your Paragon Board to Level 100, at which point you reach the 200 Paragon Point cap. This is different from Diablo 3's system that allowed you to infinitely level your character up. No longer, though, and you will need to be strategic on how you spend your points as you have a finite amount.

Paragon Board Node Types

As you progress through the Paragon Board, you will come across six different types of nodes that will bring different effects to your character.

Each one comes with it own color to help you know what kind of change you are investing in if you spend your points on it.

- Normal Node (Gray) - these basic Nodes will give you a +5 boost to any Attribute
- Magic Node (Blue) - while these will give some boosts to your Attributes they will also give you a bump in armor, cooldown reduction, and more
- Rare Node (Yellow) - these nodes will give you the previous boosts, while also giving you another bump should you meet a certain criterion
- Legendary Nodes (Orange) - these nodes will be integral to your build as they grant specific boons that will help your character
- Glyph Sockets (Red) - these nodes let you socket a Paragon Glyph in this spot
- Board Attachment Gate (Silver and Blue) - as you finish a board, you can use these nodes to boost all Attributes by +5 and open a new board

Paragon Board Attachment Gates

While you are given an initial Paragon Board at Level 50, you will be unlocking more as you progress your character and gain more XP. Eventually, you will reach the Board Attachment Gates, which will unlock another board for you to add on to the one you have already filled out.

This new board will come with its own new batch of nodes to unlock and add to your character, and you can choose which path you take to build it out. You will want to pay attention to how the new board will interact with what you have done so far and decide if you want to focus on stats, abilities, or whatever you want.

Paragon Glyphs

The final part of the Paragon Board system is the Paragon Glyphs, which offer another unique effect to your board and nodes.

When you reach one of these sockets on the Board, you can choose to insert a Glyph into them, and their purpose is to enhance the effects of the Nodes that are surrounding them. Each one comes with its own radius of influence, which means that any Node within that radius will receive the effect of that Glyph.

This adds a whole new aspect of strategy where you need to pay attention to where the Glyph socket is and if the radius will cover enough of the Nodes that makes it worthwhile. A misplaced Glyph can completely throw off your Build and really mess things up for you. Glyphs are absolutely an integral part to building your character, and you need to be intentional about how you use them. It may be worth it to wait on socketing one until you have a point where it makes more sense.

Once you have reached this point in leveling your character, you will begin unlocking Paragon Glyphs in a variety of ways:

- Looted from enemies that you defeat
- Rewarded to you as part of finishing a quest
- Purchased from certain vendors

Glyphs come with their own rarity, as well, and the higher the rarity, the more difficult it will be to unlock them. However, the higher rarity ones also offer the biggest benefits and effects. Keep an eye out for the best of the best and be sure to utilize them to the best of your ability.

REJECT THE MOTHER GUIDE

Where To Find The Tablet

If you have not yet explored the Dry Steppes, we recommend making a trip to one of the largest towns in this region, Ked Bardu. Found in the northwestern section of the map, Ked Bardu is positioned not far from where you will find the tablet that gives you the Reject The Mother quest. There are some challenging enemies in this area, so make sure you have completed Act 1 before venturing into these lands.

From Ked Bardu, head southeast into the area in the map image above, Here, you'll have to face dozens of enemies as you make your way down the path to the tablet. Most likely, you'll first discover this area while on a campaign quest with Lorath. However, it is possible to just go directly to the tablet and start the side quest. You will, however, have to face many more enemies and a boss if you do this side quest during the mission with Lorath.

Reject The Mother Solution

After reading the tablet, you will have learned that you need to "Shout your rejection, 'no Mother of mine' at her towering statue in rift's hidden shrine." To find the statue of Lilith it is referring to, you'll need to continue exploring this area until you reach the keep at the end of the trail.

Once you arrive, you will need to stand in front of the large statue and use the "No" emote. This emote isn't initially equipped by default, so you'll need to customize your emotes first. After using the emote, a chest will appear next to the statue and the quest will be complete.

CAIRN DOWNFALL GUIDE

How To Find Cairn Downfall

In order to get to Cairn Downfall, you will need to find the Champion's Demise dungeon which can be found in the Dry Steppes area of the game.

The dungeon lies near the beginning of the game, to the west of Kyovashad. It's going to be a long walk so if you are able to warp to a waypoint - specifically the Jirandai Waypoint - do so to make the journey a little easier. The dungeon will be in the Untamed Scarps area of the map.

How To Complete Cairn Downfall

Near the beginning of Champion's Demise, you will come to a section with three pedestals in the center, and multiple paths branching off into different directions. A wall is blocking your path to the dungeon's boss fight and your goal is to bring the wall down. This is the Cairn Downfall section, and the goal is to run out and grab three Stone Carvings to then bring back to this pedestal. The only issue: there are swarms of enemies that will start attacking you as you try to get to the Stone Carvings. There are enough that it can be easy to get swarmed, causing you to slow down and open yourself up to being hit from all angles.

The three statues are to the south, southwest, and northwest, and using these directions, you can easily find the right hallway to get to them. This is when the enemies will attack, and the best strategy here is to clear out all the enemies as you go. You may be able to run past, grab the carving, and then run back, all while avoiding the enemies, but it's just so much easier to wipe them out as you go. Use any area of effect abilities you have to easily take the enemies out at the same time and give yourself some breathing room. And carry some health-replenishing items and abilities with you as well to keep it topped off; you will take quite a few hits from various enemies so it's important to keep your health as high up as possible.

This means that once you get to the Stone Carvings, you can pick it up and carry it back to the pedestal without worrying about anything attacking you. Then you just repeat this process for the other two carvings, still taking the time to fight off all the enemies on your way to them, until you have all three Stone Carvings on the pedestal. With these three in place, you can now move on to the dungeon's boss: the Khazra Abomination.

THE WOODSMAN OF NEVESK QUEST GUIDE

Starting The Quest

You can find this quest in Nevesk, which is southwest of Kyovashad. When you enter the area, you will need to find Magdalena, who is scrounging for something near the middle of town, outside the chapel. You can look for the exclamation mark on your map to find her exact location.

Approach her and start the conversation. She will tell you that she is looking for a mythical axe, but she is both lazy and unable to figure out its location. So naturally, she asks you to find the axe for her and bring it back to her. She mentions that the axe is in the woods near the settlement and marks the general area on your map.

Completing The Quest

Now, this part is a little tricky, because when you look at your map, you will notice that the area you need to search is pretty big. It covers about four different paths you can take, and even worse, there are a lot of enemies in the area that will be swarming you when you go in. But that's made easier when you know where it is: the axe is at the very top of the area that is highlighted at a little ledge that overlooks a small clearing. You will find the large axe sticking out of a tree stump near a couple of torches; it's very hard to miss given its size. You can approach the axe and interact with it to pick it up. But when you do, be ready for a fight.

As soon as you pick the axe up, The Woodsman himself will spawn and attack you. This large demonic mini-boss is slow and powerful, utilizing skills similar to that of the Butcher. The fight itself isn't too difficult as long as you do your best to avoid as many of his powerful hits as possible. Eventually, The Woodsman will fall, and the battle will be over. Time to take the axe back to Magdalena, who can be found in the same location she was in before. She will not be a fan of the story you tell her about getting it. As a result, she will forego keeping the axe and leave it with you instead to use.

She will also give you a Cache, Gold, and some XP.

TRAVELER'S PRAYER QUEST GUIDE

Where To Find The Shrine

Though the highlighted area on the map isn't too big, you may be lost as to what exactly is the shrine you're meant to pray to, given that it honestly looks more like a notice board than a shrine. Regardless, the image above will show you the exact spot on the map, while the featured image shows the player character standing right next to the shrine in question.

However, if you moved to a different zone and aren't even sure what section of the map that is, this other image should help out with that. It's in the bottom right of Kyovashad, the main city hub in Fractured Peak, and it's directly north of Yelesna, the town where you accept the quest. It's located in the Gale Valley area, which itself is part of the larger Fractured Peaks zone, the game's starting zone located on the eastern side of the overall world map.

How To Give Thanks

The quest doesn't directly specify, but when it states "give thanks," it means that it wants you to perform the 'Thanks' emote. Don't be upset if you were running circles around the shrine figuring out how to activate it; it happens to the best of us.

To pull up the emote wheel, press Up on the d-pad of your controller — or press 'E' if you're playing on PC. Scroll one page to the left, and you should be able to see the 'Thanks' emote on the top right. As soon as you activate it, the quest will be completed, and you'll be handed your rewards.

THE PILGRIM'S FOOTSTEPS QUEST GUIDE

Where To Find The Pilgrim's Footsteps Quest

The Pilgrim's Footsteps Quest is located in the Amber Sands zone of the Kehjistan region. To begin the quest, players will need to locate and read a Blood Spattered Scroll on the ground in a courtyard.

How To Complete The Pilgrim's Footsteps Quest

Once you've interacted with the note to begin the quest, the first step is to read this note carefully. It is the only clue you receive for how to complete the quest. It reads:

After closing the note, you'll notice that a location to the North has been marked on your map. If you do not see this, make sure the Pilgrim's Footsteps quest is currently tracked.

1. Once at the chapel, go to the small courtyard on the right side of the building. There should be a statue of Akarat here.

2. Stand in front of the statue.

3. Perform the Follow emote to complete the quest. This should be bound by default to your action wheel unless you've removed it.

You'll need to open a chest that spawns nearby (between the benches on the right of the courtyard) to claim your reward.

Rewards For Completing The Pilgrim's Footsteps Quest

Once the game has registered that you've done the proper emote, a chest will spawn nearby. Inside you will find two Elixirs of blue quality. Additionally, players will receive +10 Renown, level-synced gold, and level-synced experience.

BROUGHT TO HEEL QUEST GUIDE

Where To Find Brought To Heel

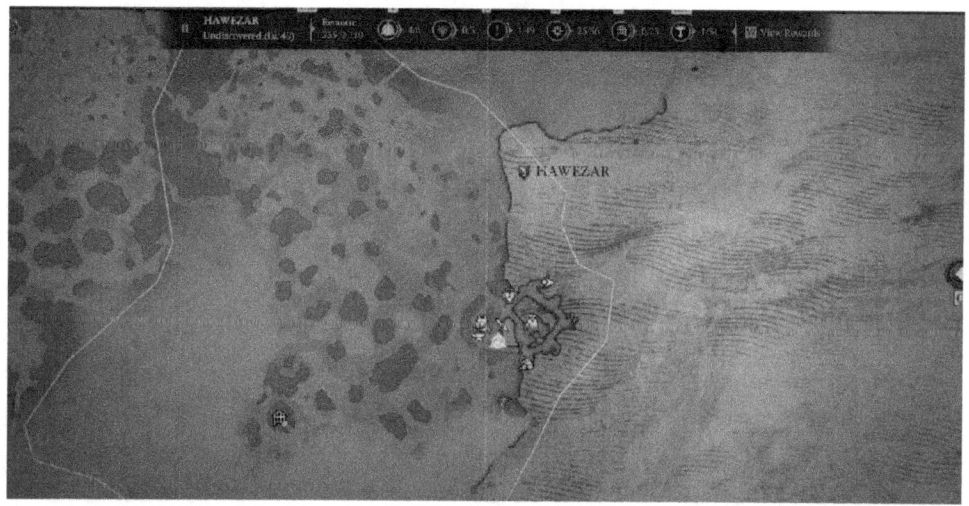

To pick up the Brought to Heelside quest, players will need to journey to the

Eastern Coast of the Hawezar region. If you have the Backwater Waypoint unlocked, teleporting here is an easy way to get where you need to be.

Once in Backwater, speak with a man named Lumina on the Northeastern side of town. He will complain about being beaten up and ask you for your help to get back at his bully.

How To Complete Brought To Heel

After picking up the quest, you'll have the task of retrieving some red mushrooms for Lumina. He intends to trick his bully into eating them and throwing them up as a method of revenge.

1. Begin by tracking the quest. This will be a useful reference point on where you need to go.

2. To find the mushrooms, you will need to head North and slightly inland. They are located on the edge of the highlighted zone.

3. The red mushrooms grow on the edge of a brackish water puddle and can be interacted with to collect them.

4. Once you've collected the mushrooms, they will disappear, and you will have them in your quest inventory. Take them back to Lumina, and talk to him again to finish the quest.

Rewards For Completing Brought To Heel

Upon bringing back the mushrooms, Lumina expresses his pleasure with your help, and you receive a reward for the quest. This consists of:

- +10 Renown
- Level-scaled gold and experience
- A piece of Rare gear (example above)